Celebrity Capital

Celebrity Capital

Assessing the Value of Fame

Barrie Gunter

B L O O M S B U R Y

NEW YORK • LONDON • NEW DELHI • SYDNEY

Bloomsbury Academic
An imprint of Bloomsbury Publishing Inc

1385 Broadway	50 Bedford Square
New York	London
NY 10018	WC1B 3DP
USA	UK

www.bloomsbury.com

Bloomsbury is a registered trade mark of Bloomsbury Publishing Plc

First published 2014

Library of Congress Cataloging-in-Publication Data
Gunter, Barrie.
Celebrity capital : assessing the value of fame / Barrie Gunter.
pages cm
Includes bibliographical references and index.
ISBN 978-1-62892-773-3 (paperback) – ISBN 978-1-62892-396-4 (hardback) 1. Celebrities in mass media. 2. Fame–Economic aspects. 3. Fame–Social aspects. 4. Branding (Marketing) 5. Mass media and business. 6. Consumer behavior. I. Title.
P96.C35G86 2014
306.4–dc23
2014014698

ISBN: HB: 978-1-6289-2396-4
      PB: 978-1-6289-2773-3
      epub: 978-1-6289-2737-5
      ePDF: 978-1-6289-2332-2

Typeset by Newgen Knowledge Works (P) Ltd., Chennai, India
Printed and bound in the United States of America

Contents

Preface

What is celebrity?

The concepts of celebrity and fame have been traced back through history and defined as integral aspects of developing societies (Braudy, 1986). 'Celebrity' can be considered as a state of being that follows from 'fame' which is, in turn, a process that embraces the communication of information about individuals to a wider population that shapes a specific reputation or image of the person being talked about. Celebrity carries a type of social status that sets the recipient of the accolade apart from others in their community. Indeed, historically, celebrity status has meant that the holder has been imbued with special qualities that can render them 'immortal' (Giles, 2000). This should not be taken literally to mean that they will live forever, but there is a strong chance that their name and their reputation or achievements will survive in a wider public consciousness long after they have died.

In the modern era of mass media, celebrity has become closely tied to the outputs of media productions. At the same time, the size of the population of 'celebrities' has grown along with their diversity in terms of the reasons why they became famous. Celebrities have also come to be redefined as 'commodities' whose value is determined not so much by the degree to which they bring cultural enrichment on the back of their talents or achievements but by the level of fame they achieve and how this can be converted into added value for themselves and for others, where value is often measured in economic terms or other lifestyle benefits.

People who attain fame provide exemplars of individual identity role models and benchmarks or points of comparison that enable other (non-famous) people to determine the type of person they are or would like to be. 'Celebrity', as its ontological origins would suggest, derives from the idea of a celebration. In this context, early celebrities were celebrated for their achievements. In Braudy's analysis, these included historically important military, political and religious figures such as Alexander the Great, Julius Caesar, Jesus Christ, and later Charlemagne, Dante, Napoleon, Lincoln and Washington. These public figures were later joined by artists, poets, writers and theatrical impresarios (Braudy, 1986; see also Inglis, 2010).

This criterion of celebrity has survived through until the present day, but in contemporary society, individuals can attain a high public profile or 'fame' and enjoy a 'celebrity' status simply by getting a lot of media attention and without really having achieved anything else. For Braudy, 'celebrity' revealed much about the cultural characteristics and changes that occurred in specific periods of history. For some historical celebrities, their personal profiles were reflections of the greater glory of the communities they led. For others, it was merely a platform through which spiritual enlightenment could be spread. Such public figures were at once real people who led extraordinary lives and were therefore also exceptional and a class apart from the 'ordinary' who held them in special regard. In more contemporary times, celebrities of this type have still emerged but have been swamped by the creations of the mass media who cannot be considered as 'real people' (Dyer, 1998).

In more modern times, specific celebrities have been held to stand for social value changes and their followers or 'fans' identify with them and adopt favourite celebrities as role models for specific cultural changes. The rise of female stars such as Madonna, for instance, has been explained not only in terms of the popularity of the artist for her musical talent, but also because of the social image she projects of the self-made, financially and emotionally independent woman who has acquired not only fame but also considerable economic and political influence and an example to women in a male-dominated world (Fiske, 1989).

This proliferation of 'celebrities' that had been created simply through media publicity rather than as an outcome of genuine achievement was referred to by one writer as 'the demotic turn'. This phenomenon was manifest in the conversion of ordinary people into celebrities when they had no special talents (Turner, 2004). The phenomenon of instant celebrity became particularly commonplace with the rise in prevalence and popularity of so-called reality television shows. While some such shows were simply voyeuristic fly-on-the-wall productions of 'contestants' who had volunteered to place themselves into an often contained environment and have their every movement filmed (e.g. Big Brother), others at least conveyed an ethos of seeking to discover genuine new talent – usually for some part of the entertainment industry (e.g. the *Got Talent*, *Pop Idol* and *X-Factor* franchises).

This mass mediated factory farming for 'talent' however often achieved little more than giving ordinary individuals a fleeting moment of fame (Gunter, 2014).

There is nothing intrinsically unethical and wrong about giving 'ordinary' people a chance to be discovered. The history of the modern entertainment industries is littered with examples of talent scouts finding 'unknowns' that have attributes or qualities that fit the needs of these industries and the markets they serve. The difference between the process then and now is that it was traditionally conducted in private with the public eventually finding out only about the success stories. In contemporary mediated reality talent scouting settings however the whole process is made public. This means that even the failures get a high profile and attract a degree of celebrity that could even have spin-off benefits for them despite their lack of progress in a televised competition – something that in this book is called 'celebrity capital'.

This celebrity outcome for people who have done little more than turn up in front of the cameras might be seen as undeserved. Certainly, it can create an expectation of fame as being within anyone's grasp and as being deserved if the participants believes they are worthy of public accolades – perhaps for trying. Participants that fail to impress experts in reality competition shows, nonetheless often possess a somewhat deluded view that their attempts at, for example, singing pop songs make them worthy of further consideration even when they are clearly tone deaf simply because they are untrained and therefore cannot be expected to be any good . . . yet (see Turner, 2006). While, the reality of achieving celebrity and fame is that they take effort over time, media formats that thrust fame upon ordinary people without special talents can give the misleading impression that it is easy and that anyone can achieve it (Giles, 2000).

Even the seasoned campaigners that enter television talent contests acknowledge that such temporary high-profile publicity is no guarantee of continued career success. Ultimately, to scale the heights of fame and achieve lasting celebrity status, even talent may not be sufficient. In addition, a celebrity must also become a 'brand'. This means that their talent, public persona and reputation must aggregate into an image that is at once part of them and also apart from them in terms of an 'added value' that underpins lasting fan appeal (Lawrence, 2009).

Perhaps what is significant in all this, however, is that the concept of 'fame' itself has become emergent as an end-goal. Fame that is bestowed upon public figures through slow-moving word-of-mouth such that it reaches its zenith only after the 'celebrity' has died or through the much faster-moving mediated world of electronic media might be seen as acceptable when deserved. It is then the worthy spin-off recognition of notable achievements. In an increasingly consumer-oriented world, celebrity is a commodity and fame is the fuel that promotes its prominence and ultimately its value (Gamson, 1994).

The historical lessons show that celebrities before the era of modern mass media were usually people who attracted public attention and won public esteem because they had achieved something extraordinary, whether in art, literature, science, politics, religion or military encounters (Braudy, 1986; Inglis, 2010). In a similar vein, Daniel Boorstin wrote about the increasingly illusionary character of celebrity as the modern mass media took hold in the twentieth century. The media had a hunger for celebrity matters knowing that these would always hold the public's attention. Although coverage might be given still to individuals whose genuine achievements earned them public plaudits, when these were in short supply, the media would create new celebrity figures who were famous simply for being well known (Boorstin, 1962).

For some scholarly commentators, the phenomenon of celebrity and fame form part of a wider deterioration of society and of the preoccupations of people within it to take refuge in secondary experiences, which today take the form of mediated activities such as watching television or reading popular magazines, and placing value less on personal development and fulfilment and more on commodities and consumerism. People make judgements of others not on the basis of who they are but more in terms of how they appear (DeBord, 1967/1995). The notion of preoccupation with appearance resonates closely with the status now attached to 'celebrity' whether or not it is deserved on the grounds of significant achievement. This shifting of emphasis in the criteria that determine 'celebrity' status from the need to have accumulated real achievements through political or military leadership or other worthwhile profession to the need to be a desired object by the masses on the basis of the entertainment or distraction value delivered was certainly a theme echoed by a number of authors who wrote about the evolution of celebrity in the mid-twentieth century (see Lowenthal, 1961; Stacey, 1994).

Celebrity has been conceived as an outcome of a 'culture industry' which positions 'culture' as a form of entertainment to be bought and sold rather than a high art form built upon an ethos of performance excellence and wider enrichment of society. This new form of celebrity was driven by the rise of capitalism in the twentieth century in which producers of cultural outputs such as popular music, movies and television programmes were driven by economic motives to deliver entertainment on a large scale to the masses. At this time, the primary motive was the construction of the mass audiences through entertainment outputs that pitched their narratives at levels designed to appeal to widely distributed tastes. Audiences were treated as consumers of mediated commodities. Those commodities, in turn, acquired value of their own that became manifest mainly in their ability to deliver large numbers of consumers to advertisers. At the same time, they cultivated a common consumption-oriented ideology with celebrities positioned centrally as commoditized vehicles for the promotion of other commercial commodity products and services (Horkheimer & Adorno, 1944). Hence, through this analysis of the middle of the twentieth century we witness the crystallization of the idea of celebrities having 'capital' value.

These observations about the creation of commodities out of cultural forms, of which celebrity is one, also drew attention to a division between 'high-brow' and 'low-brow' notions of culture. Modern celebrity culture – promoted through and primarily associated with the newer (at the time) mass media such as cinema, popular magazines, radio and television – was positioned at the lower end of the spectrum, while art forms such as painting, poetry and literature were regarded as high in cultural status. Different sets of values were devised to define where along the high-brow to low-brow spectrum a cultural output should be placed. Yet, even the high-brow cultural producers such as the creators of literature began, during this period, to adopt the practices of modern celebrity-driven culture to find bigger and more diverse markets for their outputs. Arbiters of high art-form literature utilized the concept of 'fame' as developed through modern cultural forms to exploit markets for their works and, in the process, captured some celebrity status for themselves along the way (Jaffe, 2005).

Some observers of the evolution of contemporary celebrity forms have argued that if it is 'celebrity' that is being sought, regardless of the original occupation or professional or social status of the celebrity seeker, it is essential to adopt the practices that have grown out of the ethos of commoditized culture. The successful achievement of celebrity status today must embrace the notion of 'celebrity as commodity' and utilize appropriate marketing methods to get to the end-goal (Rein, Kotler & Stoller, 1997).

Celebrity status can generate added value (or 'capital') in different ways. There can be economic benefits for the holders of celebrity as well as for others who associate themselves with a specific high-profile public figure. There might also be other kinds of value that flow from celebrity where it is used to benefit others in non-financial ways. Celebrities both benefit from and can benefit the media that helped to create them. They can shape fashions in terms of people's appearance and mode of dress. They can also encourage consumers to purchase specific brands across all kinds of commodity sectors (Pringle, 2004). They can even promote political and health issues, cultural values and patterns of social behaviour (Lawrence, 2009).

Impact of celebrity on people's lives

Celebrities are at once real people and other worldly. They are in fact real people who have displayed specific abilities or achievements or in today's extensively mediated world ordinary individuals who have simple attracted widespread publicity. For many fans, they are real but exceptional and as such they become highly desired. This emotional response to celebrities can lead fans to look upon them as 'friends' or even to adopt more extreme attachments that have romantic or even religious overtones. This can lead fans to forge a vicarious psychological bond with or to engage in a form of worship of their celebrity 'idol' (Rojek, 2001).

Fans often engage in a kind of pretend relationship – sometimes referred to as a 'parasocial' relationship – with their favourite celebrities. From this, they may then adopt some of their idol's values or behaviour patterns. Some fans carry this behaviour to extremes and become obsessed with their idols, constantly seeking to find out the latest news about their lives. Fans can vary in the exact way they go about this, with some seeking constructive avenues of celebrity attachment such as belonging to or running fan clubs, collecting memorabilia and through writing letters to them (Leets, de Becker & Giles, 1995). Others take to trying to locate where their idols work, live or hang out so that they can try to see them in person through impromptu meetings.

American girls aged 8 to 12 years who were fans of the boy band 'New Kids on the Block' identified with them not just because of their music but also because of the way they behaved, or were reported to behave, more generally. Celebrities can provide their fans – and especially young ones – with a moral compass. Equally, if celebrities fail to live up to the standards they originally set for themselves fans will notice and may turn away from them (Einerson, 1998).

There is an inherent tension created at this point between the urgency of fans to know more about their idols so that they can feel closer to them and the needs of celebrities to retain a distance between themselves and their worshippers, in part to preserve their own needs for privacy and in part to maintain an air of mystique that underpins their status as public icons and as such as a class apart from everybody else (Marshall, 1997).

The chances of fans forming a revised and possibly less flattering opinion of a celebrity might be enhanced if they are allowed to get too close to celebrities. There are times when celebrities must step down from whichever stage they perform on to allow tantalizing glimpses of the real person behind the image. The outcomes of these contacts can be affected by the nature of any encounters between celebrities and their followers.

Very often, fans get opportunities to meet their idols at events that are organized by celebrities themselves or by their advisors and managers. These pre-planned events can function as public relations exercises for which the attendant celebrities are well prepared, the contact with their fans is carefully staged, and the distance between stars and their followers is maintained, even though fans get to see celebrities in the flesh. There are other occasions when chance meetings occur and for the celebrities, control is relinquished to the public and how they behave in these circumstances can significantly affect their social standing. Problems can arise for celebrities when determined fans take even further control by stalking them and seeking to create apparently spontaneous meetings (Ferris, 2001).

Celebrities can find themselves in a double bind however when it comes to opening up their 'real lives' and their 'real selves' to their fans. There are risks that by doing so, the reality will be a disappointment for fans if they perceive that the celebrity in person does not live up to their mediated image, whether this is judged in terms of their appearance or their behaviour. At the same time, there are risks attached to being too aloof or distant, especially when fans have proactively attempted to make direct contact and their idol's response is judged as inappropriate or insufficient. Sometimes fans can be rendered so frustrated and angry at celebrities because of a perceived slight, that they are driven to extreme measures to attract the celebrity's attention as in the case of John Hinkley whose unrequited worship of film actress Jodie Foster led him to shoot US President Ronald Reagan (Schickel, 1985).

As we will see in this book, the value of celebrity can be gauged in different ways. Celebrities can enrich people's lives at one extreme by providing a focal point to their existence and at another by representing mild distractions to the drudgery of their ordinary lives. In between these extremes, there is a spectrum of influence whereby celebrities can provide valuable sources of information about commodities, services, and issues, sources of influence over public opinion, and even sources of influence over public behaviour patterns. Such influences may not extend as far as determining entire codes or values by which people live their lives, but tend to be more concentrated on specific areas of their existence (Lawrence, 2009).

Hence, celebrities have been found to have value as commodity endorsers. Marketers recruit celebrities onto advertising campaigns in the hope that any positive sentiments consumers hold about a celebrity will transfer across to advertised brands. There is scientific evidence, which will be reviewed in this book, to support this expectation. Equally, there are risks attached to the use of celebrities in this context if a celebrity is perceived to lack relevant experience or expertise to be a reliable source of endorsement for a particular product or service. In addition, the popularity of a celebrity is not always a constant and if events take such a turn in the celebrity's own life such that the public begin to question their integrity, negative sentiments can rub off on endorsed brands as readily as positive ones (Till & Shimp, 1998).

Celebrities can be used to draw people's attention to important issues. For example, Basil (1996) investigated the influence of celebrity endorsers. In this specific instance, he studied the effects of star American basketball player, Magic Johnson's endorsement of safe sexual practices. Basil found that the celebrity's pronouncement in this case did strike a chord with those who heard his message and especially among his fans.

The fans of celebrities may derive some psychological benefit through illusionary relationships they imagine they have with their idols. Celebrities can determine to some extent how much largesse of this kind they distribute through choosing to get involved in activities that generate public good or in terms of how visible they make themselves to their fans. In the end of course it is the public who determine whether fame and celebrity are to be bestowed on someone. No amount of media publicity can change this if the public ignore it. Hence, the value of stardom can be ephemeral and often beyond the control of the celebrity (Cowen, 2000).

This book will examine the capital or value of celebrities across a range of contexts – business, commodity promotion, social, political and even health. As we will see, if a celebrity has established an intrinsic value through achievement or public exposure, this gives them 'capital' that can be spread elsewhere. The trick for those who would apply celebrity capital is making the right choices about which celebrities to use and where, while for the celebrities, the question is how long can they hang on to their capital.

1

What is Celebrity Capital?

We live in a world fascinated and in many ways increasingly preoccupied with celebrity. For many young people today, when asked what they want to be when they grow up, they reply saying they want to be famous. Intriguingly, they do not qualify this remark by stating something – a special skill or talent perhaps that they wish to acquire and cultivate – that they seek to be known for. Instead, they seek fame and the public admiration or celebration that it often attracts for its own sake in the belief that it carries with it some special status from which they can and will benefit. Advantages of 'being famous' are imagined to be manifold. Perhaps with it you will get a better table at restaurants, get upgraded at airline check-ins, and if you are a guy have attractive girls offering you sex free or if you are a girl get your own branded clothing or cosmetics range without needing to go to design school. Thus, celebrity has value in its own right. Or as this book will question, it has 'capital' – or does it?

The *Oxford English Dictionary* definition of celebrity states simply that it is a famous person. The word derives from the Old French *celebrite* or Latin *celebritas* meaning frequented or honoured. Celebrity is therefore linked to the idea of celebration, but in this case, the celebration is not of an event but of a person who has attained a degree of 'fame'. In early uses of the term, it was generally used to refer to someone who was being much talked about by others. For a person to be talked about in the days before the modern mass media, of course, fame was established on a different scale. Word of mouth was the principal form of communication.

Although cultural icons could be celebrated through works of art in the form of drawings, sculptures and writing throughout the classical civilizations of the Egyptians, Greeks, Persians and Romans and beyond, the 'audiences' for these communications were limited in size and geographical distribution. If celebrities did exist they tended to be locally known public figures – mainly the rulers and leading thinkers of the day. As technological developments produced print communications that were more portable during the Renaissance and Reformation periods across the fifteenth to seventeenth centuries and the works of philosophers, scientists, and writers spread across wider geographical boundaries, new forms of celebrated public figure emerged linked to the arts and sciences (see Leslie, 2011).

We might still not recognize these public figures in the way we do the 'celebrities' of today. Academics such as Professors Niall Ferguson, Richard Feynman and Brian Cox might be classed as celebrated experts in their fields, but their celebrity profiles take on a different hue from those of Rene Descartes or Isaac Newton in their heyday. One reason for this is that celebrity today is bound up tightly with the mass media that endow public figures with a status that places them apart from the masses. To qualify as members of the celebrity club, celebrities must be ubiquitous on a large scale and possess rare qualities that give them a certain degree of exclusivity (Currid-Halkett, 2010). This combination of attributes requires a particular kind of media environment that only began to appear in the eighteenth century with the establishment of the earliest wide circulation newspapers. As we will see, their distinctive attribute profile in turn lends celebrities a premium value or 'capital' in the eyes of the general public that forms a currency that can be utilized elsewhere. It is this aspect of celebrity that we will examine more closely in this book.

Thus, we can say that in contemporary society, a 'celebrity' is a person who has a high public profile, usually promoted by appearances in the mass media and they are consequently readily recognized by others. We might all claim to be recognized by people we know, but celebrities are recognized by people who they do not know personally. Celebrities frequently are characterized by exceptional or extraordinary qualities in terms of their abilities, attractiveness, personalities and lifestyles. Today, however, becoming a 'celebrity' or a figure that is celebrated by the mass media is not contingent on having any special talent. Celebrities are also defined by the people they hang out with – usually other celebrities. As some astute observers have noted, celebrities are also distinguished by the places where they can often be found (Currid-Halkett, 2010). Sometimes, a celebrity can only be a 'celebrity' if they go to certain events or are seen in certain places. Celebrity status is not guaranteed for life, it can fluctuate and not all members of this exclusive community have the same status. Celebrities feed off other celebrities in terms of enhancing their celebrity status and they do this by keeping the company of each other, especially on occasions that will be witnessed by lots of people (Currid-Halkett, 2010).

Celebrities are often linked to specific types of occupation. These will tend to be occupations that propel them into the public spotlight. Traditionally, celebrities are the most successful within their field and they are therefore characterized not just by being recognizable but also by being successful or talented. Hence, leading actors, artists, entertainers, musicians, singers, sports stars and writers dominate in celebrity communities. In addition, highly successful entrepreneurs and business people, lawyers, politicians, medical practitioners and scientists can achieve celebrity status if they are regularly featured in media coverage (Leslie, 2011). Celebrities are also iconic aspects and outcomes of the cultures in which they are created. They represent role models that stand apart from the masses because of specific and often special qualities they possess or are believed to have (Rojek, 2001). In today's media-saturated world however the community of celebrities has expanded as more individuals are able to command mass attention courtesy of digital communications networks that remove the need for mediators in the shape of media gatekeepers who used to control access to mass audiences.

Celebrities are not just social role models whose actions or statements can influence the many, they are also cultural commodities and their value is increasingly calculated in terms of their ability to generate financial gain for others. As such, celebrities can have real and significant monetary value for others who use these iconic figures to promote their interests. The capability of celebrities to generate financial returns therefore in effect bestows upon them a 'capital' value in real monetary terms. As we will see, however, 'capital' as an indicator of value can be measured in many other ways.

Taking this point further, for some writers, 'celebrity' is a creation of capitalism. It was this analysis that led to the idea that celebrities can be conceived as commodities. This conception also differentiates 'celebrity' from 'fame' with the latter being an outcome of having achieved a sufficient level of public visibility to be widely known. Being well known is an aspect of celebrity but does not define it (Collins, 2008).

The earliest forms of the modern mass media – initially in the form of mass produced printed material – contributed to the creation of this concept of celebrity as commodity when highly visible people who were known for their creations – whether as artists, poets, writers or performers – received orchestrated publicity to cultivate a specific type of image. Although maintenance of a high level of public visibility was a key purpose of this activity, it was equally important that a specific type of reputation circulated about the individual with fame so that they not only knew about them but also held them in high regard. This in turn would serve to popularize their outputs and enhance the extent to which they could be monetized. This growth of the celebrity as commodity accompanied the emergence also of an increasingly 'commoditized' cultural environment that characterized capitalist societies (Ewen, 1988; Gabler, 1998).

Celebrities that emerged out of specific cultural products such as films or radio or television broadcasts had dual value and identity. They were ingredients of cultural outputs that had economic value and they were cultural commodities in their own right that also had economic worth (Dyer, 1986). In the Hollywood movie industry, 'stars' emerged and could attain enormous economic value for studios with the power to determine the box office success of a new movie release. They also stood apart from the movies in which they appeared with a value all of their own that rendered them attractive in other settings, such as magazines, public, private and corporate events, and advertising, where they were perceived to add value for others in terms of status, publicity, and sales and through which their own economic value was indicated (de Cordova, 1990; McDonald, 2000).

For producers, all this mix of celebrity performance indicators proves to be invaluable in determining the ongoing value of any one 'celebrity'. This assessment is essential when cultural commodities can require significant upfront investment and investors need to know they will get a good return. The job of producers is to ensure that the best interests of investors are catered to. This places them in the risk management business. They must therefore trust in the reputation of a celebrity to deliver audiences and the revenue they can generate (Miege, 1989).

The decisions that take place within the political economy of cultural production centre on risk management. Audience tastes can vary and they can change over time. Cultural producers engage in a form of risk management practice based on diversification of cultural outputs in the hope that some will resonate successfully and profitably with some sectors of their markets at least some of the time (Garnham, 1990; Hesmondhalgh, 2002).

Being successful in the marketing of celebrity therefore also means having a keen awareness of the shifting sands of audience tastes and more than this the diversity of tastes that exist across fragmented audiences or 'niches'. The value of celebrity derives from raising a performer's visibility in mass markets or relevant niche markets and following that up with successful and sustained delivery of satisfaction to audiences (Magder, 2004). This outcome can be achieved in part through the celebrity's own performance and also through the choice by producers of cultural commodities of effective publicity and commodity distribution strategies (Garnham, 1990).

Diverse celebrity capitals

As this book unfolds it will become apparent that the value of celebrity and fame can be determined in a multitude of ways. What really makes a celebrity potentially valuable is that they possess different kinds of 'capital'. Capital here can be measured in monetary terms, but also in other ways. This includes consumer capital, economic capital, political capital, and social and psychological capital. Celebrities have idiosyncratic value as brand endorsers who can be used to persuade consumers to make specific purchase decisions. In joining with sponsors, they can add value to a company's stock market valuation. Conversely, if a celebrity's reputation takes a tumble this can impact upon the corporate value of sponsors linked to them. Celebrities can promote politicians, political allegiances and political causes. Celebrities can also add value to the lives of members of the public, serving as social role models and sources of psychological companionship. In this book, we will examine and explore the nature of each of these types of celebrity 'capital' in assessing the value and importance of celebrity in the world today.

A brief history of celebrity

The presence of mediated coverage and publicity has always played a crucial part in the creation of celebrities. Celebrity has often grown out of major social events which even before the era of electronic mass communications attracted the attention of the many. The close links between sport and celebrity exemplify this phenomenon and date back to Greek and Roman times when the first major sports contests were held. Often the contestants were not volunteers but were slaves forced to compete. The best and most successful competitors – whether free men and women or not – often acquired significant fan bases. Their fame was enhanced by having their likeness or image represented in works of art.

Further, among the early celebrity figures were men of power – politicians and royalty – whose portraits appeared on coins, sculptures and paintings that were on public display. As societies evolved, even before the celebrity game-changing era of the modern mass media, new celebrity figures emerged in competition to nation states' leaders in the form of artists, poets and writers. While the twentieth century saw the emergence of Hollywood film actors, over a century earlier the acting profession that was situated in the theatre was a further source of societal icons who enjoyed wide public acclaim (Inglis, 2010).

Coins, engravings, paintings and statues were the early media. Once paper and presses were invented, images could be represented and circulated in books, pamphlets and eventually news sheets. Initially, these representations took the form of sketches and paintings and later as photographs. Subsequently celluloid, light screens and plastic tape saw not just still likenesses but also dynamic moving representations of famous people distributed and preserved on film, television and video (Leslie, 2011).

Historically, a primary criterion of 'celebrity' status was achievement. Hence celebrities were defined by events and how they performed in them. Their personal qualities as demonstrated through their deeds were the determinants of their social status and public profile (Rojek, 2000). In more recent times, with the emergence of capitalist societies in the twentieth century, accompanied by the spread of mass media, 'celebrity' became defined more in terms of structural societal changes and in particular with the rise of consumerism. Culture itself became commoditized and along with it so too did celebrity (Adorno & Horkheimer, 1944/1972; Gamson, 1994). Against this background, subjective qualities were superseded by structural changes to society – especially as these impacted upon the structure of the cultural and media industries – which underpinned the new metrics for determining the value of celebrity and fame.

With the rise of capitalism, societies evolved into hierarchical structures in which a few acquired enormous wealth and many remained poor, struggled to survive and became increasingly socially alienated. The rise of celebrity was conceived by some observers to provide both a distraction from the privations of everyday life and also a call to enjoin the consumer culture, taking the lead from the projected lifestyles of celebrities (Lowenthal, 1961; Stacey, 1994). Appearance became all-important and celebrities provided visual representations of what could be achieved by emulating aspects of their lives (DeBord, 1967/1995).

In time, mediated representations were sufficient to create celebrities regardless of their resonance with structural changes in society (Dyer, 1998).

In a post-structuralist phase, the cultural industries remain the agents of celebrity creation, reinforcing the structuralist thesis that culture had become commoditized in capitalist economies. In the much evolved mass media era, star status could be determined by media producers and the publicity machinery of the media fuelled not just by their appearances in whichever aspect of entertainment they worked but also by integrated, multi-faceted publicity campaigns (Dyer, 1998; Rojek, 2000).

Following the early sports performers and political figures, writers, poets and artists also joined the celebrity class. As theatrical performances spread, authors of plays such as Shakespeare attained celebrity status. As literacy became more widespread, poets such as Lord Byron attained a status not unlike that accorded to Hollywood film actors and pop music stars today. Writers such as Charles Dickens achieved a high public profile both through writing novels and being a journalist.

With the emergence of film, the phenomenon of the Hollywood film star surfaced in the early twentieth century. Radio was the other dominant medium of the time and while audio performers could not be seen, they could be heard by mass audiences simultaneously and attained vocal celebrity status. With the arrival of talking pictures in the years between the two great world wars of the twentieth century, film stars became pre-eminent among celebrities. Theatrical performers also built up fan bases via their live appearances, but their celebrity status was transformed if they migrated across to the movies (Dyer, 1998).

The 1950s and 1960s saw the emergence of musicians and singers as the most celebrated celebrities. Some of these moved between the worlds of recorded music, live performance and movies, but music's brightest stars no longer needed to be film stars to attain celebrity status. The rise of television as the primary medium during this period also saw the emergence of new breeds of celebrity in the form of former music hall entertainers who hosted their own comedy and music television shows, journalists who migrated from print media and attained a high level of mass public visibility, and a multitude of other 'presenters' who were not known for having any special talent other than talking to the audience via the camera.

On television programme genres also emerged that featured ordinary members of the public. These included factual general interest programmes, quiz and game shows, and broadcast talent contests. Later, the emergence of 'reality TV' accorded a multitude of other opportunities to ordinary people to attain celebrity status even without having to demonstrate any special knowledge or skills.

Television also promoted a diversity of celebrities from among a range of specialist occupations and professions. Doctors appeared on talk shows giving medical advice, chefs gave cooking demonstrations, craftsmen provided do-it-yourself home repair help, designers provided fashion tips, archaeologists and historians gave lessons in history and scientists talked about the latest scientific discoveries.

The arrival of the internet was another game changer. Previously, even though many different types of people could become celebrities, they needed the compliance and assistance of the mass media. The major media were controlled by elite gatekeepers who set their own standards in terms of who was deemed to be worthy of celebrity. The spread of online digital technologies empowered ordinary people to become media producers and publishers in their own right and offered them platforms from which they could reach large audiences under their own editorial control.

These developments led Andy Warhohl to say that anyone can be famous if they are in the right place at the right time. Celebrities can be created out of people who possess little or no specialist talent. Merely by saying or doing something unusual or idiotic, ordinary people could grab the attention of the mass media for a limited time and be thrust into the public limelight.

With these new media at their disposal, anyone with a minimal technology literacy could potentially obtain celebrity status for themselves by doing almost anything, provided whatever it is they do attracts enough attention. The motivations underlying this behaviour include wanting to make one's opinions known, belief that one has a special talent that needs to be discovered or quite simply because celebrity is sought for the lifestyle it is believed to bring.

Widespread public visibility can quickly be attained through YouTube. Anyone can post a video recording and attract viewers. Quirky videos of cats or dogs performing strange tricks can pull in mass audiences for a limited period, but sustaining a fan base usually requires refreshing the content regularly with material that holds people's interests. One example was 20-year-old Charlie McDonnell who became the first person in Great Britain to reach a regular audience of 1 million viewers on YouTube with his video channel called charlieissocoollike. He started making short videos which he posted online from the age of 16. One video he produced, called Duet with Myself, used camera special effects to give the appearance that he was singing with himself about his acne and attracted 5.87 million views. Another video short called Fun Science showed him plying a ukulele while singing a self-composed song about how sound works quickly attracted 1.7 million views. The site attracted a large female fan base and the attention of Hollywood film makers and global brand advertisers (Chittenden & McAviney, 2011). YouTube videos have also led to the discovery of new talent that subsequently attain worldwide fame and ubiquitous media coverage. Within four years of having an online video performance spotted by a talent manager, Justin Bieber had sold over 15 million albums worldwide and amassed a fortune of over $50 million.

Despite the diversity of types of celebrity, one factor that unites them all is that they bring fame and with fame, it is commonly believed, fortune will usually follow. A celebrity 'culture' has evolved that is linked to a certain standard of living that brings financial and social rewards that ordinary ways of life cannot deliver. Celebrity originated in the celebration of talent. It has evolved in a pursuit for fame for the sake of it and for specific types of rewards that are believed to follow close behind. Celebrities with genuine talents who achieve the greatest heights of success in their field are often portrayed in the mass media enjoying affluent lifestyles characterized by luxury and glamour. The effort that may have been invested in developing their talents and gaining their achievements is seldom articulated. Observers only see the end results.

Even when successful people talk about the amount of hard work they have had to invest in their careers to get to and maintain the highest level of performance, the message can be overlooked as the media are preoccupied with the way they live and the money they have made. At the same time, the media have opened up channels through which individuals with no special talents and no work ethic can still achieve a high level of fame and, in some case, also make a lot of money. One characteristic that many celebrities seem to share, regardless of the pathway to fame they followed, is a narcissistic sense of embracing attributes such as a need to be in control, to show off, a willingness to exploit opportunities that might benefit them and a feeling of entitlement in terms of being famous. In fairness to celebrities, these characteristics are more pronounced among some (e.g. reality TV show contestants and comedians) than others (e.g. actors and musicians) (Young & Pinsky, 2006).

Just as fame can be accessed more readily in a digital world, celebrity can be just as readily lost. In most cases, a lack of talent will expose celebrities known only for getting media attention. Furthermore, even deserving celebrities who have displayed genuine talents and hard work can fall from grace if they misbehave or miscalculate the standards that the public expect from them. Celebrity does not just bring potential fame and fortune it can also give great power to influence.

Celebrities are iconic figures that others are curious about, they are also role models with the power to create social trends or to trigger specific actions among members of the public. With great power also goes great responsibility. A failure to live up to public expectations on the part of celebrity figures can result in a dramatic fall from grace and even the loss of celebrity status.

It is important that celebrities behave themselves because they can acquire god-like status for some people who regard them as role models in terms of how they should behave themselves. Consistent with this idea some psychologists have coined the term 'celebrity worship' to describe the way some people can get emotionally involved with famous public figures (McCutcheon, Ashe, Houran & Maltby, 2003). Some celebrities attain fantastic heights of fame such that it becomes difficult to find anyone who has never heard of them. *The Sun* newspaper once conducted an unscientific enquiry to find someone who did not know who David Beckham was. It took a long search to find someone in the Saharan city of Timbuktu who did not know of him (Drake & Miah, 2010).

Or at the very least, their fans may feel compelled to defend their favourite stars when they are publicly or privately maligned. One story that appeared in the United Kingdom's *Sunday Times* reported on a 28-year-old female electricity engineer who had developed an attachment to a new celebrity called David Sneddon who had just won the BBC's TV talent show, *Fame Academy*. She had already gathered together 6 years' worth of newspaper clippings about the Irish boy band, *Boyzone* and had 70 videos of their performance. She also confessed to seeing another Irish boy band, *Westlife*, 17 times in concert. Now her attention had switched to Sneddon, she had already cornered him at two of his recent television appearances. She argued that she was not disturbed and was not a stalker, but was prone to develop strong fascinations with certain celebrities (Harlow, 2003).

The importance of celebrities in the lives of so many people is no doubt driven by the constant media attention given to these public figures. While they may be seen as their professional lives in movies, on television, in theatres and concert halls, or at sports venues, this exposure is backed by regular newspaper and magazine coverage. Glossy magazines such as *Hello* and *OK* specialize in celebrity coverage, often linked to major events in celebrities' lives such as getting married or moving into a new home.

According to some experts, celebrities provide important social and cultural functions. They are not simply role models, but act out social narratives that both entertain and educate us in terms of life courses for ourselves, and learning how to behave or not to behave in different settings (Cashmore, 2006; Drake & Miah, 2010). According to Francisco Gil-White, an evolutionary anthropologist at Pennsylvania University celebrities can point us in the direction of success. They are a source of fables or fairy tales we once sought through religious sermons and scripts (Harlow, 2003). Through the media coverage they receive, celebrities gain social status and prestige and this can bestow upon them powers to influence others. Such influences can be manifest in a multitude of ways. They might take the form of taking fashion tips, wearing specific types of clothing or make-up, changing a hair style, choosing which books to read, taking up a new hobby or activity, all because someone famous or in the media spotlight has led the way (Vincent, Hill & Lee, 2009).

There may be nothing bad in any of this, provided that celebrities provide positive role models. Where the power of celebrity becomes more problematic is when these public idols display socially undesirable behaviours. Celebrities exposed for getting drunk too often, taking hard drugs, being sexually promiscuous and unfaithful to their spouses and partners, or simply voicing extreme and prejudiced opinions may still possess the power to influence others, but in ways that are not welcome.

Unlocking the secrets of celebrity

Elizabeth Currid-Halkett of the University of South California has tried to understand the nature of celebrity by mapping where celebrities hang out or where they are to be found. She and her colleague Gilad Ravid conducted research looking at photographs of celebrities that appeared in the media and worked out where these images were taken so as to locate where stars spend their time. She obtained the photos from Getty Images, the foremost photographic agency in the world. Over a 12-month period Currid-Halkett found 600,000 relevant images. Over 80 per cent of these photographs were taken in just 3 cities – London, New York and Los Angeles, out of a total of 187 locations represented by these images. A few other locations, such as Cannes, Miami and Park City, peaked in terms of celebrity appearances on specific dates linked to special celebrity events. Throughout the year, however, London, New York and Los Angeles were the places where celebrities hung out most often. Furthermore, within these cities, the photographs were taken in a fairly small number of neighbourhoods.

In Los Angeles, for example, virtually all the images were taken at sites along Hollywood and Sunset Boulevards (Currid-Halkett, 2010).

Hanging out in the right places does not make a celebrity on its own. Although for celebrities, it is important to be seen at specific events even when they have no special professional reason for being there. In terms of defining celebrity status, Currid-Halkett argues that there is a link between talent and fame. She believes that real status is underpinned by having real talent. There are 'celebrities' who enjoy that label because they have an ability to attract publicity to themselves in the media. She gives examples here such as Paris Hilton and Katie Price. These individuals receive extensive media coverage week in week out. In contrast, there are actors such as Dame Judi Dench and Daniel Day-Lewis – Oscar winners with an impeccable pedigree of film and stage credits. In between, Currid-Halkett places others such as Angelina Jolie, Kate Winslet and Keira Knightley who possess both real talent and a knack for getting publicity. A key factor at play here seems to be the extent to which genuine talents get media attention for their work or for their private lives. For some celebrities, publicity centres on professional performance, for others it centres on their private lives (or so-called professional activities that require them to do little more than show up and be themselves).

There was a link between the talent status of a well-known person and the kinds of locations in which they were pictured. Stars who, for Currid-Halkett, represented genuine talent tended to be pictured in unusual places around the world, whereas those who were famous simply for getting their pictures in magazines and newspapers tended mostly to be seen hanging out in a few hotspots in London, New York and Los Angeles.

One important, indeed it seems quite crucial, aspect to being a celebrity is that you must be plugged into the right social networks. Celebrities hang out at a few locations because they get invited to the same parties and other exclusive events. Thus, it is not enough to be pictured strolling down Hollywood Boulevard. It is much better to be seen emerging there from a party to which only a select few have been invited. If those others include celebrities with genuine talent, then some of their distinctive attributes may rub off at least temporarily even on the 'celebrity' known only for being photographed. More than this, celebrities need to be seen not just by the public but also by the movers and shakers behind the scenes who can determine who in the future gets work. This 'success by association' strategy operates through a process that some social scientists have labelled as 'preferential attachment'. Success in terms of celebrity profile is generated less by what you can do, and more by who you know.

The impact of drawing in media attention and through that the attention of the public is that it can arouse a sense of natural curiosity in ordinary people who then develop a need to know more about the icons they see in pictures in the papers and magazines. These days, celebrities of all kinds can cultivate this parasocial relationship with their public more directly through the use of social media and micro-blogging tools. Facebook and Twitter have become the most widely used vehicles in this context through which celebrities can construct tighter links to their fan bases.

Are there different types of celebrity?

The objective of this book is to examine the notion of 'celebrity capital'. This refers to the value that celebrity status can have for the individual celebrities themselves and for others who associate themselves with celebrities. The common sense idea of celebrity generally associates celebrity status with a certain degree of fame. In other words, celebrities are distinguishable from ordinary people because they have a public profile. Whereas ordinary, everyday folk may be known to their family, friends, work colleagues and sundry acquaintances with whom they interact on a day-to-day basis (e.g. the server at the restaurant where your often eat out, the teller at your local bank, the shopkeeper at your local convenience store, the plumber or decorator you hire for home improvements and so on), celebrities have a much wider circle of people who know about them, and who often think they know them personally even though they may never have met.

Hence one form of value (or capital) that celebrities have over ordinary people is the extent to which people know who they are. Another type of personal capital that a celebrity can acquire is the value they have in terms of the reasons why they have achieved celebrity status in the first place. Traditionally, celebrities – who have a wide public profile – have tended to be people who have displayed some kind of special ability or talent or have a high status occupation. They are people who through their professional activities attract a lot of public attention. Early examples of celebrities, before the era of modern mass media, were individuals who produced important scientific discoveries or works of art, wrote literature or became political leaders. The emergence of the mass media in the twentieth century created platforms for more diverse forms of entertainment and news that in turn cultivated a broader range of public figures that became fashion icons, opinion leaders and role models. Hence, movie stars, sports stars, stage entertainers, musicians and singers, and television personalities came to dominate popular contemporary celebrity (Leslie, 2011). Many of these types of celebrity are connected to the mass media that emerged from the start of the twentieth century. Prior to this era, celebrities still existed and were associated with the arts of the time. Hence, artists, musical composers and writers dominated the world of celebrity. Celebrities continue to derive from these fields even today.

In addition, figures that have attracted a high public profile have derived from other areas. The worlds of business, journalism, politics and science have yielded individuals with outstanding abilities who have attracted public attention and acclaim. The modern mass media have helped to broaden the range of celebrity types still further. With the growth of a more consumer-oriented society, the worlds of design and fashion, and providers of luxury lifestyle accessories and activities have joined the celebrity community. Latterly, specialists in fields such as cookery, home maintenance, and personal therapy and self-improvement have attained celebrity status equivalent movie and sports stars. All these different types of celebrity acquire 'capital' based on what they know, what they can do and how adept they are at attracting public attention. Their fame can bring value to their own lives and the lives of others.

Other attempts to categorize celebrity have focused more on its genesis at the level of the individual. Historically, figures that achieved high public profile that comprised fame and sometimes also a degree of worship were people who had achieved something spectacular within their community or society, while others achieved that kind of status through association with others that already had fame (Inglis, 2010). In the modern media era, celebrity status can be gained without achievement other than a talent for getting media attention.

A number of writers have tried to define taxonomies of 'celebrity' that draw upon these historical precedents and the new forms of fame production associated with modern mass media. Monaco (1978) identified three types of celebrity: hero, star and quasar. The 'hero' was a figure who had achieved something of great significance, not specifically in the field of entertainment or the arts.

The 'hero' historically might have been a great military commander and this might be also in the contemporary era but today might also include adventurers and scientists. The 'star' category was reserved more for high achievers who captured the public's attention from the fields of acting and entertainment, and also possibly the highest performing sports men and women and even charismatic business people and politicians.

Finally, the 'quasar' comprised a group of people that had attracted public attention sometimes accidentally through their involvement in significant events such as disasters, criminal activities, or scandals or perhaps through a process of association with others who were famous. The latter category could occur without the help of the media but had probably become a more prevalent and prominent celebrity category because of the mass media.

Rojek (2001) differentiated three forms of celebrity status which he called: ascribed, achieved and attributed. Ascribed status derives from being born into a family that is already famous. Hence, the celebrity status attached to a senior member of the British Royal Family derives from the fact that they are 'royalty'. Their celebrity status could then be further enhanced by the media attention they attract and even by personal achievements (e.g. Princess Anne winning an Olympic Gold Medal as an equestrian). In the first instance, however, their celebrity derived from their bloodline.

Achieved celebrity status is status that is earned through talent and effort. Thus, famous actors, entertainers and sports stars become celebrities through their personal achievements. David Beckham is a major international icon through his wide-ranging sponsorships, but has obtained these contracts and the contingent publicity they have captured because he reached the highest levels of competition as a professional footballer. He also built up a lot of celebrity capital credit as a stand-alone brand such that he has continued to attract sponsorship across multiple brand spaces even after his star as a footballer faded (Vincent et al., 2009). As such he serves as a prime illustration of how lasting celebrity can depend upon the creation of a celebrity 'brand' (Lawrence, 2009).

Attributed celebrity comprises the accrual of celebrity capital that derives from mass media attention. An individual might have limited or no special talents, but has nonetheless attracted media attention through specific actions they have perpetrated. This type of celebrity status might result from appearing in a television reality show, being seen a lot with established celebrities, or entering into a relationship with an established celebrity, or because they were involved in an activity that initially attracted media attention to them. In the United States, for example, Monica Lewinsky was a White House intern who subsequently attained a high public profile after her sexual relationship with

President Bill Clinton was revealed. She subsequently achieved a temporary celebrity-like status out of the initial media coverage and then fuelled still further by staged television interviews and a book she produced about the affair. For Rojek (2001), those individuals who gain 'attributed' fame simply through regular media publicity should be differentiated from genuine 'celebrities' and he coined the term 'celetoids' to distinguish them.

As we will see, celebrity capital or value can be measured in monetary terms and in a range of non-monetary terms, including consumer, corporate, political, social and psychological capital. Usually, celebrity capital is defined in positive terms with a presumption that celebrity status brings benefits to celebrities themselves in terms of lifestyles of comfort, privilege and wealth. There may in turn be positive spin-off benefits for business operators, politicians and members of public through their association to or identification with celebrities.

There can be a downside to celebrity however both for celebrities themselves and for others who link up with them. Celebrity capital is dependent not just on fame per se but more significantly on the development of the right kind of public profile. Fame is differentiated from infamy by reputation and the fact that famous celebrities tend usually to be liked or even loved by the public. Most often (though there can be exceptions) a successful celebrity can generate positive sentiment among others. Celebrities accumulate value for others insofar as others perceive celebrities to be likable and attractive with integrity. When a celebrity's standing takes a fall because their distinctive talents decline, they engage in activities that bring them into disrepute, or the public simply becomes bored with them, their economic, political, psychological and social capital can evaporate. When this happens they can damage the images of others with whom they have previously been associated.

Measuring celebrity capital

The principal theme being analysed in this book is that 'celebrity' has capital or value. Value in this case can be assessed in different ways. A celebrity's value may be determined by how much money they earn for themselves or by how much money they can earn for other people. It might also be measured in terms of how much influence they have. This 'influence' might be cultural, social or political. Given that celebrity is closely associated with fame their status might also be measured in terms of how much fame they have achieved. Fame is also closely inked to popularity. Hence, the status of a celebrity could also be determined by how well liked they are at any point in time. As we will see later on, various tests have been developed to measure the potential economic, political and social capital value of celebrities. At this point however we will focus on fame and popularity in its own right and without reference to consequences that spin off from it for others.

With emergent celebrities that we witness being born, for instance, in televised talent contests, whether the participants are regarded by viewers at home as a real celebrity depends upon whether they are perceived to be genuine in terms of not pretending to be something they are not. Often, this judgement can be bound up with social class divides which in turn act as mediators of viewers' identity with specific contestants (Allen & Mendick, 2012). Another level of judgement applied by viewers determines whether contestants display the attributes normally associated with major artists that command global fame. It has been observed that when the acts that appear and compete in local versions of a talent show franchise are perceived as parochial, for example, viewers revise down their assessments of whether contestants have the potential to reach the heights of international celebrity (O'Connor, 2012).

Assessing celebrity status and the spin-off capital value that attaches to a celebrity are complex calculations. The subjective views of the public are not irrelevant, but they do need to be systematized if they are to be marshalled to make more formal assessments of celebrity value particularly where questions about the impact of celebrity are being addressed. Formal systems for assessing the celebrity currency of a public figure are important also in business contexts where decision are being taken about whether to employ a celebrity or sponsor them.

A number of metrics have therefore been developed to determine the fame value of celebrities. These measures of celebrity status take place in the two parallel realities that celebrities (and most of the rest of us) currently inhabit – the offline world of everyday reality and the online world. In the offline world, which remains important as a source of celebrity evaluation, a celebrity's capital can be determined by their earning power, the amount of media coverage they attract and how much the public like them. In addition, a suite of metrics have emerged in the online world that can provide continuous tracking of a celebrity's status indicated by numbers of online searches on their names, numbers of hits to their websites, numbers of 'friends' they have on social media sites such as

Facebook and numbers of followers they have on micro-blogging sites such as Twitter.

Media capital of celebrities

One set of indicators about the current profile and potential consumer, cultural, economic, political psychological and social capital of celebrities is the amount of coverage they receive in the mainstream mass media. One metric that has been used in this category is the number of column inches (or centimetres) celebrities receive in magazines and newspapers. Page space is at a premium. The amount of this space that is given to celebrities by print media is indicative of how currently relevant, important or influential they are rated by editors.

According to research by TNS Media Intelligence, Madonna was the most famous celebrity of the first decade of the twenty-first century in terms of column inches of coverage received in British newspapers (London Evening Standard, 2009). Her total score was 45,633 articles. In second place was Robbie Williams who was also the top male celebrity with 27,976 articles. The top ten was as follows:

1. Madonna 45,633
2. Robbie Williams 27,976
3. Britney Spears 27,910
4. Brand Beckham (Posh and Beck together) 26,561
5. Kate Moss 26,494
6. Victoria Beckham 25,204
7. David Beckham 24,631
8. Michael Jackson 22,426
9. Simon Cowell 22,263
10. Sir Paul McCartney 20,347

It is clear however that if you aggregated over Brand Beckham, Victoria Beckham and David Beckham that the Beckhams would hold the lead comfortably with a grand total of 76,396 articles.

What was also apparent from this type of analysis, however, was that the highest ranked celebrities could change from year to year. The top ten for 2009 contained just four of the top ten for the decade. Michael Jackson held top spot (6,838 articles), followed by Simon Cowell (6,213), with Madonna in third place

(4,612). Kate Moss still crept in at 10th (2,618). Newcomers were Cheryl Cole (3,745), Katie Price (3,700), Susan Boyle (3,170), Jade Goody (3,049), Lily Allen (3,021) and Peter Andre (2,985). Cheryl Cole had 884 articles written about her in 2007, which increased to 2,241 in 2008 and then to 3,745 in 2009. This type of analysis shows that some celebrities have more staying power than others. Much depends on whether there are significant new developments taking place in their professional lives and in their private lives.

Cataloguing the quantity of media attention a celebrity receives indicates the standing of specific public figures in the opinion of media professionals who often use subjective criteria to decide which celebrity is in the ascendancy and which is on their way down. Is this really a valid indicator of a celebrity's current capital? Although the amount of space occupied by celebrities in the media appears to be a precise measurement, the metrics that have been published are based on selective samples of media publications, tend not to reveal anything about the quality of coverage being given, and may provide only limited insights into the wider potential capital of a celebrity. For some corporate marketers that are contemplating entering into endorsement agreement with specific celebrities, for instance, the scale of their media coverage might present a misleading impression of their potential capital in this context. Corporate brands seek not only to raise their public awareness through association with famous celebrities, but also need to ensure that consumers develop a positive image about them.

To assess whether a celebrity makes a good fit for a corporate brand, marketers need to know whether the celebrity they are targeting represents values they would wish to associate with their brands. At the very least therefore it is important to know whether consumers like the celebrity in question. In addition, it may be useful to know also whether the celebrity is perceived to be a credible endorser. Credibility can depend on judgements about the celebrity's perceived relevance to a corporate brand in terms of expertise, experience and personal image. It can also be affected by whether the public regard the celebrity as trustworthy.

Public popularity capital of celebrities

The level of media interest in celebrities gives an indication of whether celebrities are generating stories through events in their lives that are deemed by media professionals to be newsworthy. Newsworthiness judgements are based on evaluations about events and their likely level of interest for the public. They can also be swayed by observations of what events other news suppliers are covering. Hence if one newspaper has a story about a celebrity, others will follow suit if they believe there is some mileage in doing so in terms of public interest.

The amount of media coverage obtained by a celebrity however does not necessarily provide a precise indicator of their popularity. Popularity is linked to how much people like a celebrity. A disliked celebrity can still attract news coverage if they engage in events that news professionals judge to be newsworthy. The likability of a celebrity is a different type of performance indicator and is important because disliked celebrities can lose capital value in other respects, such as for any sponsors with which their names are connected. As we will see later, celebrities have value for sponsors if they believe that celebrity value will rub off on their brands.

There is also a need for other employers of celebrities to keep track of their popularity with the general public. Unpopular celebrities may be bad choices as news anchors, reporters, presenters or actors in television shows. Audiences might turn away from shows if they do not like the people appearing in them. In this context therefore it is useful for broadcast and movie executives and commercial sponsors to know how likable the public find particular celebrities. Since likability is an opinion and since opinions can change dramatically over time as events occur that cause them to re-evaluate celebrities, it is useful for employers of celebrities to keep a continual eye on their public popularity.

One system that was developed to provide this type of metric was the 'Q-score' which was created by Marketing Evaluations, Inc. 'Q' stands for quotient. The Q-score however is based primarily on the familiarity of a celebrity to the public. Q-scores can also be generated for commodity brands. Other agencies have developed alternative metrics designed to assess the appeal, likability or popularity of celebrities (Marketing Evaluations Inc, 2011).

The Marketing Evaluations system uses a panel of American consumer households that were surveyed by mail. Respondents answer a questionnaire that invites them to provide personal indications of their familiarity with a celebrity and their feelings about that individual. The familiarity and favourability indicators are actually combined within a single scale: A. One of my favourites; B. Very good; C. Good; D. Fair; E. Poor; F. Never heard of them. Marketing Evaluations claims the measure is useful because it assesses both awareness of the celebrity and whether the target is liked. The company has stated that it has compiled a database on over 25,000 personalities dating from 1964 (Marketing Evaluations, Inc, 2011).

One could argue that this scale provides neither of these measures very effectively. Awareness or familiarity is a distinctive measure that depends upon how long a member of the public has known about and held an interest in a particular celebrity and possibly also the frequency with which they are exposed to that individual as a performer or in terms of the news coverage or media publicity they receive. The likability of the celebrity is a measure of positive versus negative feelings about them. This is a construct that is quite different from familiarity although it is entirely possible that the two constructs are inter-correlated.

A celebrity can obtain a high liking score even only after limited public exposure because of the way they have performed or otherwise behaved when not performing. A different celebrity may attract only a low likability score despite receiving extensive media coverage and repeated exposure to members of the public. In fact, greater familiarity in this case might breed greater contempt for the celebrity if their continual appearances are a source of annoyance for the public. It is therefore likely to be more informative for employers and sponsors of celebrities to have access to celebrity evaluations that identify specifically what people feel about these public figures and to have independent measures of familiarity. More than this, it might be important to know whether there are specific attributes displayed by celebrities that are the primary sources of public animosity or negativity towards them.

The Q-score has become an established currency for evaluating celebrities and brands. These scores have been widely used in advertising, marketing and broadcasting to measure the popularity of actors, entertainers, sports men and women, and television presenters. The Q-score is actually computed by dividing the percentage of respondents endorsing a celebrity as 'one of their favourites' by the total percentage who indicate some degree of familiarity with the celebrity (that is all respondents except those giving value F, never heard of this person on the Q-scale).

The computed quotient is based on calculations both of 'liking' for a celebrity and how widely known he or she might be. Thus, if a celebrity is known by 90 per cent of the population and 45 per cent state that he is 'one of their favourites', his Q-score would be 45 per cent divided by 90 per cent or 50. If he is known by only 10 per cent of the population and 10 per cent say he is 'one of their favourites', he would receive a score of 100. Could we actually conclude here, however, that the second celebrity is twice as popular as the first? The answer would be 'yes' if comparing between those people who stated they were familiar with each celebrity. However, should we not also give some weight to actual numbers of people who have any awareness of these celebrities at all?

There is also a risk with this system that Q-scores will be produced that are based on sub-samples too small to be meaningful in terms of whether they represent the wider population of viewers in general or only viewers of a particular type. Ultimately though, the value of Q will depend upon whether it can also meaningfully predict other outcomes such as a celebrity's staying power, earning power, impact on audiences for TV shows in which they appear, influence on the sales of brands they endorse, and other indicators of the level of public interest in their lives.

Another rating system for celebrities has been produced by the David Brown Index (DBI) in the United States. It is provided by The Marketing Arm, part of the Omnicom Group, Inc. This index is widely used by marketers to guide decisions about which celebrities scored best on specific qualities. By 2012, the DBI tracked 2,900 celebrities. According to online information provided by The Marketing Arm (2012), its data derive from a consumer panel of 4.5 million people. The consumer panel is also used to evaluate on an ad hoc basis the potential and actual goodness of fit between celebrities and commercial brands.

Celebrities are evaluated across eight attributes: Awareness, Appeal, Aspiration, Breakthrough, Endorsement, Influence, Trendsetter and Trust (see Table 1.1 for definitions of metrics). The DBI awards celebrities scores on each metric out of 100 and provides their overall rank in the population of celebrities that are evaluated within the system. Although many celebrities are widely recognized and

Table 1.1 Celebrity DBI – The marketing arm

Awareness	Percentage aware of celebrity by name or likeness
Appeal	Likeability and merchandizing potential
Aspiration	Celebrity has life to which respondents would aspire
Breakthrough	Celebrity noticed on TV, film or print
Endorsement	Celebrity identified as an effective product spokesperson
Influence	Celebrity is an influence in today's world
Trendsetter	Celebrity's position in regards to trends
Trust	Level of trust placed in the celebrity's words and image

well-liked, they often score far more modestly on the Trust scale (Cresswell, 2008). This finding indicates that although celebrities can be role models with a generally positive image to which many ordinary people aspire, as consumers they may view celebrities' commercial endorsement activities with some scepticism. When we take a closer look as the consumer capital of celebrities in Chapter 3, the processes that underpin this phenomenon will become clearer.

The nature of public opinion about celebrities can vary with the nature of the evaluation. Online survey research conducted among more than 2,000 people in the United States asked respondents to evaluate each of a list of 100 pre-selected celebrities in terms of how much they liked them, trusted them and believed they would be likely to drive up the business of a company they endorsed (see Table 1.2). Veteran actress Betty White was highest rated on all three dimensions. There is extensive celerity overlap between the top ten listings across these evaluations with Sandra Bullock, Tom Hanks, Morgan Freeman and British royalty – Kate Middleton, occupying all three lists. At the other end of the scale, the least favoured celebrities were Paris Hilton (60% found unfavourable), Charlie Sheen (52%), Britney Spears (45%), Arnold Schwarzeneggar (44%), Tiger Woods (42%), Kim Kardashian (38%), Mel Gibson (33%) and Donald Trump (31%).

Among the celebrities best regarded for their business-enhancing qualities were mostly those who had also been rated as most trusted. New entrants here were, unsurprisingly perhaps, business leaders Bill Gates and Steve jobs, whose

Table 1.2 Most highly regarded celebrities

Most liked	Most trusted	Most likely to enhance business
86% Betty White	69% Betty White	44% Betty White
85% Denzel Washington	66% Tom Hanks	43% Bill Gates
84% Sandra Bullock	60% Sandra Bullock	43% Steve Jobs
83% Clint Eastwood	59% Morgan Freeman	42% Tom Hanks
81% Tom Hanks	58% Kate Middleton	40% Sandra Bullock
80% Harrison Ford	57% Oprah Winfrey	39% Oprah Winfrey
79% Morgan Freeman	57% Taylor Swift	39% Denzel Washington
79% Kate Middleton	56% Clint Eastwood	38% Morgan Freeman
77% Will Smith	56% Harrison Ford	38% Taylor Swift
76% Johnny Depp	56% Julia Roberts	38% Kate Middleton

Source: http://www.ipsos-na.com/news-polls/pressrelease.aspx?id=5306. Ipsos Public Affairs.

success in business no doubt meant that people saw them as distinctly qualified to enhance a business brand.

Online capital of celebrities

With the emergence of the internet, two different realities have become established. The world of everyday reality which we all inhabit has become rebranded as the 'offline world' alongside which is a parallel 'reality' – the online world. The dramatic rise of the internet has created a new digital reality that has come to play a prominent part in people's lives and the activities of businesses, governments and a multitude of other groups and organizations. It is also a platform for celebrity. As the online world has grown in prevalence and importance as a source of information, communication and entertainment, it has also emerged as an environment within which celebrities and their status are evaluated.

The value attached to celebrities in the offline world as measured by their earning power, the volume of media attention they attract and by their popularity with the public as measured by opinion polls represent important currencies by which to assess a celebrity's capital. In addition, their standing in the online world has surfaced as carrying just as much weight in determining a celebrity's current capital – whether this is being measured in economic or social or cultural terms. The internet provides a number of barometers of the current standing of celebrities. These include how many search enquiries, social media 'friends' or 'fans', micro-blog 'followers' and online video views they attract.

Table 1.3 presents data for the most popular celebrities on the internet as measured by numbers of Google searches, Facebook fans and Twitter followers they attracted in 2011. There is significant overlap between these lists. Popular music artists such as Lady Gaga, Justin Bieber, Shakira, Rihanna and Katy Perry appear in all three top ten listings. Other celebrities such as Britney Spears and Kim Kardashian appear in two lists. Others appear in just one list. Other factors than celebrity popularity could account for appearances in only one list. For instance, any ranking on Facebook and Twitter is dependent upon being registered with both services as a user. Google search rankings, in contrast, do not require any special registration. Google's search engine measures any requests made to it by internet users using the celebrity's name.

Table 1.3 Celebrity capital online

	Google		Facebook		Twitter	
Rank	Name	N	Name	N	Name	N
1	Lady Gaga	578m	Eminem	56.1m	Lady Gaga	18.4m
2	Justin Bieber	496m	Rihanna	54.9m	Justin Bieber	16.7m
3	Rihanna	384m	Lady Gaga	50.3m	Katy Perry	14.2m
4	Cher	340m	Shakira	49.4m	Shakira	13.0m
5	Nicki Minaj	296m	Michael Jackson	47.9m	Kim Kardashian	12.7m
6	Britney Spears	277m	Cristiano Ronaldo	43.0m	Britney Spears	12.6m
7	Katy Perry	263m	Justin Bieber	42.5m	Rihanna	12.3m
8	Shakira	239m	Katy Perry	42.1m	Tayor Swift	10.6m
9	Kim Kardashian	232m	Linkin Park	41.3m	Selena Gomez	9.8m
10	Madonna	230m	Akon	38.2m	Oprah Winfrey	8.9m

Notes: Google data show numbers of searches or requests; Facebook data show number of fans; Twitter data show numbers of followers

Sources: Google: http://www.society.ezinemark.com; Facebook: http://www.posh24.com; Twitter: http://www.latesttopten.com. All sites accessed on 8 November 2012.

Another factor is that rankings can be artificially inflated on social media sites such as Facebook and there are many commercial agencies established online that offer 'fans' for purchase. In essence, these are web-sites that provide links to a Facebook giving the appearance of fan links. Celebrities may utilize these and other services to inflate their internet profiles as measured by the metrics shown in the table. These tactics are not likely to account for significant proportions of the scores achieved by the highest ranked celebrities on social media sites, however, and the continual measurement updating of links to sites on Facebook and Twitter means that these metrics can provide an extremely current indication of a celebrity's public status. By following changes to these measures from month to month, it is also possible to use these metrics to track fluctuations in a celebrity's popularity over time. In this way, an upward track from month to month or year to year can indicate growing popularity and a downward track can indicate declining popularity.

Another measure that has attained currency is celebrity power. Each year, Forbes, the business news and financial information service publishes a list of the 'most powerful celebrities' in the world. The list includes actors, athletes, authors, comedians, models, musicians and other media personalities. Forbes state that their assessment of power is based on the fame and wealth of celebrities. Their power index takes into account the pre-tax income of celebrities together with their visibility in print, television, radio and on the internet. As well as web presence indicated by search volumes, Forbes also takes into account the profile of celebrities on Facebook and Twitter (Pomerantz, 2012).

The ten most powerful celebrities identified by Forbes for 2011 contained some familiar names from the other lists we have just seen. In rank order from the top these celebrities were: Jennifer Lopez, Oprah Winfrey, Justin Bieber, Rihanna, Lady Gaga, Britney Spears, Kim Kardashian, Katy Perry, Tom Cruise and Steven Spielberg. These celebrities differed in terms of the specific ratings that contributed most to their overall rank. For Oprah Winfrey and Steven Spielberg, for example, it was their annual income that was a major factor, although Oprah was top rated for her TV presence and as we saw above crept into the top 10 in terms of Twitter following. Lady Gaga had a middle ranking income among the top 10 overall, but she had high visibility on TV and radio and in the social media. Justin Bieber was a consistent performer across all the key metrics – income-related and media visibility. It is not clear from the level of detail disclosed about its methodology what, if any, differential weightings it gives to component metrics. It is also unclear whether other factors are included in addition to the six metrics listed in the data they publish online. Certainly, the rise of Jennifer Lopez to number one spot for 2011 is difficult to understand from her average rankings on these metrics which average less than those for others in the list (see www.forbes.com/celebrities).

Composite celebrity status

Since 1999, the business and financial information company Forbes has produced an annual list of the 100 most powerful celebrities of the year from around the world. Its overall power rating is calculated by an algorithm that draws together a number of different types of data. These include annual pre-tax gross income, print media mentions in newspapers and appearance on front covers of magazines, mentions on radio and television, hits on Google and volume of followers or fans on Facebook and Twitter. Under the heading of celebrity, Forbes includes film and television actors, television personalities, comedians, models, musicians and writers. In 2012, the top ten celebrities in terms of overall power rating were Jennifer Lopez, Oprah Winfrey, Justin Bieber, Rohanna, Lady Gaga, Britney Spears, Kim Kardashian, Katy Perry, Tom Cruise and Steven Spielberg. Only one celebrity had appeared in the top ten every year since this list was introduced and that is Oprah Winfrey.

Ultimately, while these lists can make interesting reading and attract media interest in their own right, whether they have real meaning and applicability in terms of judging celebrity capital depends upon whether the power rating is predictive of other performance outcomes. There is evidence that current status of a celebrity is related to the amount of media coverage they receive following public appearances at live events. Celebrities who, in the words of one celebrity watcher, tend to have the greatest 'star currency' as measured by the Forbes power rating. These are the individuals who, for example, tend to be photographed more in the media than those celebrities whose status is lower. In an analysis of photographs of celebrities that appeared in the media, the so-called A-list celebrities, with highest power ratings, exhibited a higher quotient of media visibility to live appearances than did B- or C-listers. In others words, each live appearance of a top-rated celebrity would generate more media interest than a similar appearance by a lower-rated celebrity (Currid-Halkett, 2010).

This alternative analysis may give us some confidence in the credibility of the rating used by Forbes, but a correlation of this sort needs to be further deconstructed for us to be sure. Since parts of the Forbes power index are based on an evaluation of print and broadcast media visibility we might expect it to correlate significantly with an independent analysis of press photographs because they are both measuring the metric. There is a distinct possibility of redundancy therefore in this type of relational analysis.

In the end, these various celebrity rankings and league tables may have little relevance beyond making interesting reading in terms of determining the true value of celebrity. This is because the ratings are tied to a specific methodology that could run the risk of adding together measures that are effectively as different from each as 'apples' and 'oranges'. The final results are little more than artefacts of the analytical formulas used to generate them. A better and more relevant set of insights into the value or the 'capital' that can be attached to celebrities can be derived from a more systematic investigation of whether celebrities can add genuine premium value to people's lives as well as in terms of measurable business, political and social outcomes. In the chapters that follow, we will examine a range of evidence on a variety of topics gathered from around the world to see if this is indeed the case.

Key points

- 'Celebrity' was initially linked to the idea of 'celebration'.
- Early celebrity status was linked to political or military power, but later celebrity status also emerged from having special abilities or know-how in the arts, literature and science.
- By the twentieth century, celebrities were created by the modern mass media of radio, film and television.
- Celebrities can emerge simply through publicity and being seen in the right places with other established celebrities.
- Digital media technologies have provided platforms and fast-track routes to celebrity status.
- The value of celebrity status can be measured in terms of the individual wealth of celebrities, how much the public like them, the amount of media attention they receive and increasingly by the numbers of online searches or social media followers they attract.

Topics for reflection

• Is it easier to become a celebrity today than at any time in the past?
• What are some of the methods that might be used to measure the current status of celebrities with the public?
• What is the measure of a true celebrity?
• The term 'celebrity' has become more loosely defined and used far more liberally than it should be. Present a case that supports or rejects this proportion.

Further readings

Currid-Halkett, E. (2010). *Starstruck: The business of celebrity*. New York, NY: Faber and Faber.
Inglis, F. (2010). *A brief history of celebrity*. Princeton, NJ: Princeton University Press.
Leslie, L. Z. (2011). *Celebrity in the 21st century*. Santa Barbara, CA: ABC-Clio.
Rojek, C. (2001). *Celebrity*. London, UK: Routledge.

2

The Psychological Capital of Celebrity

The status of celebrity is defined in part by the acquisition of a popular public profile which can take on a condition akin to religious worship. In fact, psychologists often talk about fans engaging in 'celebrity worship'. When a celebrity attains this social status they can become role models and opinion leaders whom others follow. When this happens, celebrities can gain what we might call 'psychological capital' in that they have value to us as in terms of how we think and feel about ourselves. As we will see, many of us use celebrities as benchmarks in defining who we are. Carried to an extreme, we may hold celebrities in such high regard that we adopt an almost worshipful relationship with them. For some individuals, this can take on the form of an obsession that takes over their lives.

Whether celebrities can be regarded as good or bad as role models is open to debate. Celebrities do not always behave well. As we saw in the last chapter, some celebrities are liked and trusted more than others. Even bad celebrities can appeal to some of us. Moreover, we may be more willing to forgive celebrities their misdemeanours than we would people we know personally. Celebrity influence at a psychological level can often begin with ordinary people talking about them. Celebrities are sources of conversation or gossip (De Backer, Nelissen, Vyncke Braekman & McAndrew, 2007). As we will also see, some people vicariously engage with celebrities as if they are real friends. These 'parasocial' relationships can serve as a substitute for real relationships, though our involvement with celebrities is probably driven more by the amount of media attention they receive than by our own social isolation (De Backer et al., 2007).

The important psychological (and social) role of celebrities as a source of gossip is that conversation with others about celebrities itself acts as a kind of social glue. It is an essential aspect of our survival and growth and development as a species that we are able to get along with other people and forge alliances and friendships with them (Dunbar, 2004). We achieve these outcomes through social communication of different kinds. Engaging in conversations with others is therefore crucial to the social bonding process that forges social cohesion. Celebrities can provide aspiration targets for us but also, when they have misadventures, they can appear more human and this can render them even more relatable. Gossip about celebrities can thus provide a source of social learning. By comparing notes with each other about the conduct of celebrities we make assessments about them that could be relevant to decisions we may have to make in our own lives when confronted with similar scenarios (Baumeister, Zhang & Vohs, 2004).

There are of course risks associated with getting too involved with celebrities. They can provide the wrong kinds of role models in some settings. One interesting illustration of this point was the warning issued by UK High Court judge, Sir Paul Coleridge, that celebrities provide poor role models because their marriages are twice as likely to end in divorce as those of ordinary people. Sir Paul chastised celebrity magazines such as *Hello* for presenting unrealistic lifestyle expectations and particularly expectations about marriage from their coverage of celebrity weddings.

Research by the Marriage Foundation, based on data from the UK's Office for National Statistics, corroborated this view following an analysis of marital breakdown rates among a sample of 572 celebrity couples who had married between 2000 and 2012. The study found that the divorce rate among these couples once they had been married for 10 years was 40 per cent compared with 20 per cent for the general population. Further analysis showed that celebrity couples were much more likely than ordinary couples to get divorced after five years (25% vs 7%). It also emerged that celebrity marriages were about twice as likely as non-celebrity marriages to end after only about a year. Sir Paul commented: 'There is a disconnect between the nature of real long-term relationships and the dramatised and apparently more exciting versions portrayed on screen. And this is surely exacerbated by the huge expensive fairytale weddings attended by the icons of the day. This must create a false expectation within the participants that in some way their relationships will be better, easier and, above all, more exciting than the average . . . Unfortunately all men and women, glamorous or not, are riddled with the same weaknesses and shortcomings which surface even quite soon after the excitement of the wedding has died down' (Leppard, 2012).

In terms of whether the claims made about celebrities here have any scientific currency remains an open question. The Marriage Foundation presents two lists each with 11 celebrity couples. In one list the celebrity marriages lasted between just 55 hours and up to 14 months while in the other they lasted between 15 and 58 years. Thus, even though celebrity couples have demonstrated an above average propensity for entering marriages of very short duration, there are famous couples for whom marriage was a very long-term commitment. What this report did not say however was whether in the marriages with longevity the partners remained faithful to each other. A number of the famous celebrity couples listed were known in media circles for the tolerance one showed towards the other's repeated infidelities.

Although the suggestion here that celebrities provide poor marriage role models and that this may in some way influence ordinary couples was not backed up by empirical evidence, this commentary by a High Court judge provides useful insights into where celebrity marriages might go wrong and why ordinary couples should therefore not presume that marriage will be a fairytale for them either. Very often the psychological capital of celebrity derives not just from their value as social role models, but from more deep-seated and personalized attachments that ordinary people can forge with them. Celebrities can become virtual friends and in the extreme, as we will see later in this chapter, take on an almost spiritual status commanding worshipful respect of adulation.

Celebrity capital starts young

The perceived value of celebrity starts at an early age. For today's children and teenagers, a celebrity lifestyle is one they aspire to even after they have just started school. Indeed, the widening popularity of child beauty pageants that take entrants who have not yet even started nursery provides yet another illustration of a search for fame and a platform from which it can be sought, with young parents taking the lead (see Tozer & Home, 2011; Wonderlich, Ackard & Henderson, 2005).

Further evidence of the prominence of celebrity in the lives of young people has emerged in the form of the careers children and teenagers say they want for themselves. Whereas past generations wanted to become doctors or lawyers, today's young generation desire occupations that will not bring them a comfortable lifestyle but also fame. One British survey of 3,000 parents with children aged 5 to 11 years that was commissioned by the Watch TV series *Tarrant Lets the Kids Loose* found that children tended to dream of becoming a star in the worlds of acting, entertainment, music or sport. The survey compared the aspirations of the children with those of their parents 25 years earlier. In the top ten ambitions of these children, the three most often chosen were sports star, pop star and actor or actress (Telegraph Media Group Limited, 2009).

The most often chosen professions among the parents when they were kids were teaching, banking or finance and medicine. 'Sports star' finished in seventh place and 'pop star' or 'actor' failed to break into the top ten at all. It is interesting to note a further possible impact of media and celebrity on the eighth most popular contemporary career choice – chef. Top chefs such as Jamie Oliver and Gordon Ramsey, who have established highly successful media careers, along with a multitude of highly popular cookery programmes on peak-time television that have given exposure to many other top chefs have turned their profession into one that challenges movie making and pop music in terms of their celebrity capital (Telegraph Media Group Limited, 2009).

Parents did not share their children's aspirations and instead preferred their kids to go into professions such as law and medicine. Most of the parents acknowledged that the media (73%) and more specially television (52%) were having a big influence on their children's career choices (Taylor Herring, 2009). Reassuringly for parents, however, other evidence has emerged to indicate that even though many young people in the United States said they would like a celebrity career, they nevertheless nominated people closer to home, such as their parents or older siblings, ahead of celebrity icons when asked to name their most important social role models (Lawrence, 2009). Despite this finding, other research among young adults in America revealed a growing sense of entitlement and expectations of a comfortable lifestyle without always giving due consideration to the effort it might take to achieve this. Among this generation, celebrity and stardom had strong appeal as fast-track routes to their life objectives (Twenge, 2007; Twenge & Campbell, 2010).

The attraction of celebrity for young people is a phenomenon that has spread around the world. When 6 and 7-year-olds in Japan were asked what they would like to be when they grow up, boys placed 'professional athlete' in first place and 'television actor' in fourth place. Interestingly, 'cook or chef' also appeared in seventh place for Japanese boys. Among girls, 'singer or celebrity' was placed second (after 'baker' or 'cake or candy maker') (Skeptikai, 2012). The popularity of baking in this poll may also have a celebrity link given the surprise success at the time of the BBC's Great British Bake-Off reality cooking talent series which attracted interest from a broad spectrum of the public.

The explosion of televised 'reality' programmes and talent competitions has opened up a multitude of opportunities for ordinary people to attract the media spotlight and grab some instant celebrity. The idea that celebrity status comes from genuine skill or talent that may have taken years of dedication and hard work to cultivate has been swept aside by new mass entertainment vehicles that provided access to mass audiences and opportunities for instant fame for individuals with minimal or limited talent. Even when television talent shows such as *(America's/Britain's) Got Talent, Pop Idol/American Idol,* or *X-Factor* were won by contestants with genuine talent, often developed unseen by the public over many years, the appearance given by these shows was that anyone could turn up, sing a few songs, and win a lucrative music recording contract and a massive fan base, and be transported into a celebrity lifestyle within a few weeks.

Many of these television shows have contributed more directly to the creation of a hunger for fame and celebrity by reducing the age limits for competition entry. The 'Idol' stable took entrants at 16, while the 'X-Factor' stable has reduced this to 13 years. In the 'Got Talent' shows, which invite applications from people with any 'talent', no minimum age of entry is stated. The *Britain's Got Talent* application regulations state that applicants aged under-18 must be accompanied by a parent or legal guardian, but no minimum age of entry is stipulated (ITV, 2012). For some youngsters whose families are very poor and for whom society seems to offer no significant opportunities to improve their way of life (at least as far as they are concerned), these television talent shows represent a way out. This is not a new social phenomenon because the worlds of entertainment and sport provided pathways out of poverty and depravation for many young people throughout a large part of the twentieth century, even before television became ubiquitous. That kind of celebrity, however, had to be earned through hard work and fame and fortune might take many years to come and then only for a tiny minority.

Perhaps the most famous example that is frequently held up of someone from a disadvantaged background that went on to become world famous and also one of the richest and most powerful people in show business is Oprah Winfrey. She benefited from being in the right place at the right time when there were emergent civil and women's rights movements. These political movements opened up opportunities for her in terms of entry into employment with a TV station in Baltimore where she received her early schooling in the world of media and entertainment (Brockes, 2010). Being a woman and from an ethic minority during that period meant there were openings for entry into the profession for her that may not have been available otherwise. Nonetheless, once on the inside she then worked skilfully and effectively over many years to forge her hugely successful career (Peck, 2008).

Personal psychological capital of celebrity

From the early days of the mass media, it has been known that members of the public can form emotional attachments to actors, presenters and other people featured in the media. These feelings can grow so strong for some people in the audience that they come to believe they really know the people they see in the media, even though in reality they do not. This phenomenon was termed a 'parasocial relationship'. It took on many of the characteristics of a real friendship for the members of the audience who engaged in it, but it was a completely one-side relationship because the celebrity target was usually unaware of its existence and no real social interactions ever took place between the celebrity and audience member (Horton & Wahl, 1956).

Parasocial relationships could be especially potent between members of the public and celebrities who appeared in films or on television. The nature of how these media are experienced by people played a significant part in this phenomenon. According to Horton and Wahl, these media can 'give the illusion of face-to-face relationship with the performer' (1956, p. 215). Further investigation of the parasocial relationship phenomenon has revealed a number of factors that play their part in making it happen.

We have already seen that celebrity gossip represents a form of social and psychological capital for many people. The mass media have contributed towards the distribution and increasingly the creation of this gossip through celebrity magazines and television shows that review the latest entertainment news. Sometimes gossip about people in the media serves a social learning purpose in that it can enable us to discuss the way others have behaved in specific situations. It can also provide sources of conversation through which we can establish interests in common with other people. For some of us, however, celebrities are absorbed into a personal 'parasocial network' of contacts whereby we feel we know them (even though we have never met them face to face) and treat them as we would real friends. There may be lessons for us to learn in our own lives from observing the successes and failures of celebrities not just professionally but also in their personal lives. This learning process is not simply about copying the behaviour of a celebrity. Their personal lives can often become public property as a result of celebrity gossip circulated by the media. By observing and reflecting upon the different publicly reported twists and turns of celebrities' own lives we can learn behavioural 'scripts' that can be internalized – that is, committed to memory for future reference. Celebrities can thus become a source of inspiration and aspiration for ordinary people (Harmsworth, 2012).

A famous celebrity gets divorced, for example, and it becomes the focus of our attention. We talk about it with our families and friends. We exchange opinions about it. We evaluate the behaviour and possibly attribute blame to one or other of the parties involved. For example, what did followers of Brad Pitt think about him when he left Jennifer Aniston and embarked on a new relationship with Angelina Jolie? Prior reputations of these celebrities are examined and explanations sought for their break-up. Sympathies might be expressed for one party and antipathy voiced towards another. Perhaps we empathize with what has happened. Perhaps we simply want to find out whether our own feelings about what happened are shared by others. The gossip might also have a social cohesion function. It represents a common source of interest we share with others around us. It gives us something to talk about with others (Caughey, 1984). It possibly enhances a sense of group membership or identity because we are able to talk in an informed way with others about a subject they also seem to be interested in. Gossip can therefore create and maintain social bonds (Riegel, 1996; Tannen, 1991). Those who keep up with the latest celebrity gossip (and media events in which celebrities are involved either as themselves or as fictional others) can enhance our experiences of friendship with others by making us feel more socially connected (Kanazawa, 2002).

Psychologists have coined the term 'celebrity worship' to describe behaviour displayed by people who develop strong preoccupations or even obsessions with specific celebrities. The term 'worship' here implies some kind of spiritual dimension to this experience. There is plenty of anecdotal evidence that individuals who gain celebrity status are regarded as a breed apart from people in general. They are regarded as possessing special qualities that render them attractive as role models for the rest of us. The attention that celebrities receive from mass media serves further to fuel the idea that they have some special status that places them above everyone else, whether or not they actually deserve such accolades. As a social and cultural phenomenon 'celebrity worship', although not referred to in such terms, pre-dates the modern mass media. Nearly 100 years before Welsh balladeer Tom Jones rose to world stardom, in the nineteenth century, classical music composers such as Frederic Chopin and Franz Liszt had women throw underwear at them as they performed live concerts (Steel, 2011).

More recently, science has committed systematic analytical techniques in an attempt to define and measure the celebrity worship phenomenon. Psychologists have developed clinically verified scales to measure this human characteristic. The display of curiosity leading to deeper psychological attachments to celebrities has been formalized as 'celebrity worship syndrome'.

Initial research derived from an extension of the 'parasocial relationship' idea that had first been identified in the 1950s. It was already known that members of the public could forge 'friendships' with celebrities from the worlds of entertainment and sport even though they may never have had socially interacted with their idols. For some people, these *para*social relationships were every bit as real as direct social relationships and represented core motivations that shaped their media consumption habits (Rubin, Perse & Powell, 1985). These virtual relationships with celebrities could be intense and deeply personal. Fanatical followers (or 'fans') followed the lives of the celebrities they idolized and could become genuinely moved by events in those celebrities' lives.

Further research on the adulation given to successful people examined the nature of the appeal of celebrities from the entertainment industries and began to develop specific instruments to measure this phenomenon. Stever (1991), for instance, developed a Celebrity Appeal Questionnaire that focused on the role model qualities of celebrities.

There was subsequent psychological research that focused on sports celebrities. What was the nature of sports fandom and how could fans be defined in terms of their motivations to get involved with sports stars. One psychological test identified and measured eight distinct motivations for becoming psychologically involved with successful sports personalities (Wann, 1995). Being a sports fan was underpinned by social status/self-esteem needs, escape from everyday problems, pure entertainment, conformity with family sporting interests, identity with social reference groups, the aesthetic appeal of a sport and sports celebrity, excitement, and economic reasons (i.e. betting).

Finally, a Celebrity Worship Scale emerged that attempted to quantify the nature and strength of this disposition as a generic characteristic in individuals. A number of versions of this type of scale were designed to assess the relationships individuals might develop in their own minds with celebrities whom often they have never met in person. Lynn McCutcheon and her colleagues of DeVry University, Orlando, Florida produced a Celebrity Attitude Scale which measured orientations towards celebrities including empathy for a celebrity, excessive identification with a celebrity and ultimately a total obsession with a celebrity. According to McCutcheon, these responses were all points along a single dimension (McCutcheon, Lange & Houran, 2002).

Further research by UK psychologist John Maltby of the School of Psychology, University of Leicester and his colleagues found that celebrity worship was a more complex syndrome than this and he and his co-workers identified three different components. In addition to confirming that members of the public could develop a curiosity about celebrities and use them as source of conversation in their everyday lives, some people could develop much more extreme and rather negative relationships with celebrities (Maltby, Houran, Lange, Ashe & McCutcheon, 2002).

On one level, celebrities were admired for their talents and ability to entertain. In this vein, they also frequently provided a source of conversation with other people. On another level, individuals could go beyond simple admiration coupled with a broad interest in following the celebrity to a more intense emotional connection with this public figure. At this level, they begin to feel as if they know the celebrity as a personal friend and will often claim to share the celebrity's pain when something unfortunate happens to them. Finally, an even more extreme relationship can develop with a celebrity that takes on a more obsessive nature. An individual may admit here to having constant thoughts about their favourite celebrity, imagine being with him or her in different scenarios and spending disproportionate amounts of their time following the life of the celebrity.

Extreme forms of celebrity worship have been associated with general mental health problems. Those fans that move from simply admiring their favourites to a deeper emotional attachment that takes over their lives tend often to display other symptoms such as being generally anxious or depressed in their own lives (Maltby et al., 2001).

Celebrity and self-identity

One aspect of the psychological capital of celebrities is to be found not simply in the joy they might bring to the lives of their fans, but also in the degree of influence they can exert as role models. Over many years there has been interest in and sometimes concern about the role played by media role models in helping to shape the way young people develop their own self-identities. One important aspect of self-identity is how people feel about themselves. Do they like themselves? This self-feeling is often manifested in terms of personal opinions about one's body shape. This is an area of concern for both sexes, but has mostly been examined in relation to girls and young women. Dissatisfaction with one's own body shape can often result from being inclined to make comparisons between oneself and other people (Dittmar et al., 2000; Harrison, 1997, 2000). Very often in these cases, the primary points of comparison are media celebrities. A tendency to develop a strong attachment to a celebrity may render them an even more powerful role model in the context of satisfaction with own body shape (Maltby et al., 2005).

Maltby and colleagues (2005) found a relationship between celebrity worship and body image perceptions. Female adolescents aged 14 to 16 years were more susceptible to influence from celebrity role models than non-celebrity role models in terms of their body image aspirations. Girls who held a particular female celebrity in especially high regard in respect of her body shape were also likely to display greater dissatisfaction with their own body shape. There was an expectation here that celebrities could provide especially powerful role models in this context because it was already known that teenage girls turn with increasing intensity to media figures as reference sources when defining various outward aspects of their own identity such as the way they appear and the way they should behave towards others (Giles, 2002).

Maltby and his colleagues (2005) recruited three different samples of male and female teenagers (14–16), young adults who were students (18–30) and other adults (22–60). All respondents completed the Celebrity Attitude Scale to assess their orientations towards celebrities and public figures, and further instruments concerned with their perceptions of their bodies. The propensity to worship celebrities was significantly related to being more body conscious, but only among teenage girls. When teenage girls were more concerned about their body shapes, this disposition was distinctly related to a kind of celebrity worship in which they developed an intense fantasy personal relationship with a celebrity. Simply being interested in or admiring of a celebrity for their talent did not represent a powerful enough parasocial relationship to generate the kind of identification with this public figure that rendered them an important role model.

A further important result was that the relationship that did emerge between celebrity worship and body consciousness was confined to teenage girls and did not recur among college women or adult women. This suggested that there may be a critical window in young girls' psychological development when they are most susceptible to celebrity influences and that once they have passed through this stage, this susceptibility starts to disappear.

Maltby and Day (2011) examined the mediating effects of celebrity worship upon decision to have cosmetic surgery. Once again, women who held a particular celebrity in high regard in terms of their body shape displayed a stronger tendency to have elective cosmetic surgery.

It is axiomatic that not all celebrities are the same and equally it would be wrong to presume that all celebrities therefore have the same impact upon members of the public. Celebrities gain their high public profile for many different reasons and display many different talents. Some celebrities, it can be argued, display no specific talent at all except for having a knack for attracting media attention to themselves. One academic commentator on celebrity issues has coined the term 'celetoids' to distinguish ordinary people that attain a certain degree of celebrity status despite displaying no special talents (Rojek, 2001).

The cultural phenomenon of 'reality television' that creates entertainment out of the lives of selected members of the public observed in their workplace (e.g. *Airport*, ITV, 2004–5; *Club Reps*, ITV, 2001–4; *The Hotel*, Channel 4, 2011) or in the everyday lives (e.g. *Jersey Shore*, MTV, 2009–12; *The Hills*, MTV, 2006–10; *The Only Way Is Essex*, ITV2, 2010–; *Made in Chelsea*, E4, 2011–) has also bred a new category of celebrity with some of its members eventually entering the celebrity mainstream.

We have also seen that members of the public become psychologically attached to celebrities in different ways. The attachment may be a perfectly healthy one whereby a person admires a celebrity for their talent or the way they present or conduct themselves in public and develops an associated curiosity about the celebrity but not one that takes over their life. At another extreme, members of the public can develop deep-seated emotional attachments to celebrities and even become obsessively preoccupied with them. What researchers have also found is that different levels of celebrity attachment are also often associated with different types of celebrity.

People who forge attachments to celebrities that are milder in nature and demonstrate an appreciation of celebrities' special talents tend to orient their attention towards actors, musicians, fashion models and other in the entertainment industry. Individuals who form deep emotional attachments or disproportionate preoccupations with public figures are more likely to identify with political and religious leaders and others associated with major world events (including newsreaders). This set of relationships is interesting because the most powerful effects of celebrity role models are most likely to occur among members of the public who forge the deepest attachments to public figures. Since these kinds of attachments are less likely to develop in relation to popular entertainment figures, the latter may represent weaker potential social role models (Sheridan, North, Maltby & Gillett, 2007).

Further evidence that celebrity worship tendencies have displayed statistical relationships with addictive and criminal dispositions begins to shed further light on the value that might attach to specific categories of celebrity for particular types of people. People with the strongest addiction tendencies may display such predispositions in the types of celebrity worship they adopt. Intense attachments to celebrities that take on a pathological profile, for example, may be underpinned by a wider predisposition to show addictive orientations in relation to other behaviours and relationships. Furthermore, a proclivity towards criminal behaviour, together with an addictive personality, could underpin a tendency to develop obsessive preoccupations with public figures and a preference for figures that represent socially negative role models.

Sports celebrities have been found to exert especially strong attraction for young people. The top athletic performers are often idolized by their fans and can serve as powerful role models for their younger admirers (Jones & Schumann, 2000). Adolescents admire top sports performers for being famous and not only for their sporting prowess (Stevens, Lathrop & Bradish, 2003).

Young people can become infatuated with celebrities particularly in popular music (Raviv, Bar-Tel, Raviv & Ben-Horin, 1996). Ultimately, to achieve 'idol' status, a celebrity must be sufficiently attractive and display sufficient achievements and talents (Yue & Cheung, 2000). Choices of celebrities as preferred role models can depend upon the nature of the aspirations held by particular fan groups however and their aspirations in turn may reflect whether celebrity worshippers seek out role models that will have practical lessons to provide that are relevant to their current living environment or whether they seek to identify with more idealistic and ambitious goals that lie beyond where they currently live. Yue and Cheung (2000) conducted a survey among high school students in Hong Kong and Nanjing and found that students in these two locations differed in the types of idols they chose as role models. Young people in Hong King tended to relate to celebrities in an idealistic and romantic fashion, whereas those on mainland China identified with celebrities that provided role models linked to more everyday, practical and realistic aspirations.

Further research in Malaysia among indigenous Malay and Chinese populations found that most of those questioned identified with pop stars and movie stars and were far more likely to be attracted to Western artists than to ones from their own country (Swami et al., 2011).

These qualities can underpin the development of a close parasocial bond between the celebrity and their fans. While their talents must be sufficient to put them above ordinary mortals in terms of their social status for fans, if they possess other qualities that their followers value, their social capital can grow even further. Feelings for the celebrity can then grow so powerful and so real for their fans that some develop strong desires to become the celebrity's romantic partner (Greene & Adams-Price, 1990).

Celebrity role models can influence young people's social attitudes, lifestyle aspirations and kind of person they want to be (Bush, Martin & Bush, 2004; Lines, 2001). Given the 'social identity capital' they possess it is therefore important that celebrities provide the right kinds of examples of how to behave (Lines, 2001). The bad guys can be as influential as the good guys. Celebrities who are talented and also likable and attractive can contribute in significant ways to adolescents' own identity construction as young people seek to adopt the character of their celebrity favourites (Jones & Schumann, 2000; Stevens et al., 2003). When celebrities go bad and display criminal or immoral behaviour such as drug taking, marital infidelity or tax evasion they send out messages to their young fans that such conduct is acceptable (Stever, 1991). The kind of professional activity in which celebrities engage can be important in determining the extent of their popularity. The celebrity status potential of sports performers, for instance, can be limited by the type of sport they play (Martin, 1996).

There are differences between fans themselves that influence whether they engage in celebrity worship and display healthy or unhealthy degrees of interest in their heroes and heroines. Both girls and boys and men and women can display celebrity worship orientations and there has been some disagreement about whether one gender is more likely than the other to become obsessed with celebrities (Ashe, Maltby & McCutcheon, 2005; Bush et al., 2004; Maltby et al., 2004a, 2004b).

There are different personality factors that are related to celebrity worship. People who are shy in social company may turn to media figures as substitutes for companionship. Although such mediated relationships are not 'real' in the sense of direct social interaction with other human beings, they can nonetheless provide comfort and company that can be fulfilling. People who are not only shy but also lonely and have few real social contacts can however develop an unhealthy degree of attraction to celebrities. Being curious about their lives is not by itself sufficient to fulfil the needs they have to fill the void that exists in their own lives. Such relationships with celebrities are not confined to socially restricted people who lack self-confidence. There are individuals who think very highly of themselves – narcissists – who identify with celebrity role models and believe themselves to have taken on some of their characteristics. They then expect to command the same appeals and popularity as their idols (Ashe et al., 2005).

Leaving aside role modelling effects of celebrities, interesting evidence has emerged from a study conducted among a sample of American university students that thinking about a celebrity they had a crush on could make them feel better about themselves. Shira Gabriel of the University of Buffalo had students complete a self-esteem test and then afterwards she invited them to spend 5 minutes writing about their favourite celebrity. Then, they re-took the self-esteem test. Students who produced low self-esteem scores on the first test and who subsequently spent a little time writing (and thinking) about their favourite celebrity scored much higher on the esteem test the second time around. Gabriel explained these findings as follows: 'Because people form bonds in their mind with their favourite celebrities, they are able to assimilate the celebrity's characteristics in themselves and feel better about themselves when they think about that celebrity' (Park, 2008).

Interesting research has emerged involving pregnant women and how they relate (or not) to magazines articles and accompanying photographs of celebrities who also are pregnant (Hopper & Aubrey, 2011). This research focused on whether celebrities had any capital in terms of effects they could have on how pregnant women perceived themselves. Did they make comparisons between themselves and celebrities? Were these comparisons favourable or unfavourable? Images of pregnant celebrities were found to generate a range of reactions among pregnant women readers of the featured magazines, but these reactions depended on whether an image showed a full boy shot of the celebrity or only a head and shoulders shot.

One of the main concerns about celebrity effects on self-identity, especially among women, is that media images of highly physically attractive celebrities that clearly show off their body shape treat women as objects and can lead women who see these images to adopt a more objectified impression of themselves. This notion of objectification usually tends to take on a sexual aspect. If famous women in the media are treated as sex objects, women may come to see themselves in a similar fashion. Because the media also show a strong preference for featuring celebrities with thin body shapes concern about an objectification effect is often wrapped up with concern about causing women to become increasingly worried about their own body shape (Aubrey et al., 2009; Harper & Tiggeman, 2008).

The research of Hopper and Aubrey (2011) was at odds with earlier research concerning the effects of pictures of female celebrities on women's self-perceptions in that it found that these effects could be triggered by head and shoulder shots rather than being confined to full body shots. One explanation of this effect could have been that the celebrities in question were so well known that women magazine readers conjured up their own full body image of a celebrity having seen a shot covering only their head and shoulders. This effect was most pronounced however for inexperienced pregnant women in the early stages of their first pregnancy.

There is also a theory that has received research backing that ordinary people make comparisons between themselves and celebrities. Some people have stronger tendencies to make these 'social comparisons' than do others and the strong social comparison makers are forever comparing themselves to other people – both celebrities and non-celebrities. Friends can be important points of comparison, but celebrities have also featured as primary sources of influence (Heinberg & Thompson, 1992). When people who wish to be like others who are important role models to them perceive a gap between their own self-image and the image of these important 'others' they will strive to close this gap (Wood & Taylor, 1991). Such tensions between how members of the public perceive themselves and the appearance of celebrities (or the characters they play on television, for example) can motivate people to change their own image for one that – in their own minds – more closely resembles that of their favoured role model. This psychological process can be particularly important in terms of enhancing the influence that thin female celebrities seen on television have on female viewers' striving to lose weight and change their own body shape (Botta, 1999, 2000).

Despite the potential of the objectification mindset to cause women to think of themselves as objects rather than as human beings (Aubrey et al., 2007; Noll & Frederickson, 1998), some pregnant women were found to distance themselves from female celebrities sufficiently that this influence was less likely to occur. While pregnant women might perceive some similarities between themselves and pregnant celebrities – namely their state of being pregnant – some also realized that celebrities lead different lifestyles from themselves and that celebrity gossip magazines often tend to present an artificially glossy or rosy impression of a celebrity's life or appearance that does not represent the reality. In this way, even though celebrities retained some entertainment capital, they did not invariably cause pregnant women readers of glossy magazines to change their impressions of themselves or indeed to want to do so (Hopper & Aubrey, 2011).

Strong forms of celebrity worship may lead to even more extreme behaviour patterns, some of which stray into criminality. Celebrity worshippers who develop an unhealthy attachment to specific celebrities are more likely to believe there is nothing wrong with trying to find out where their idol lives or works or socializes. In seeking out celebrities in this way worshippers can become stalkers (McCutcheon et al., 2006). We will return to this aspect of celebrity worship later in this chapter. Before doing so, however, what do we know about the factors that underpin and can explain celebrity worship syndrome?

Explanations of celebrity worship

The influences of celebrity on audiences operate through a number of mechanisms. Attractive celebrity figures represent role models whose actions and characteristics are admired and copied. Fans enter into quasi-real emotional relationships or parasocial relationships with celebrities. They come to regard a celebrity as if he or she is a member of their social circle and feel that they know the celebrity personally. This type of relationship can be further enhanced when fans display strong social comparison tendencies. Some people are especially sensitized to how they appear compared to others. They may actively seek to emulate the attributes of others. This propensity may become particularly acute with role models which they find especially attractive. Such influences can reach their zenith among adolescents and young adults who are still actively trying out different self-identities. Celebrities provide identity models that can be trialled to assess whether they make a good fit.

In cases of extreme celebrity worship, individuals can become totally absorbed by a celebrity and virtually addicted to finding out about him or her. They may lose sight of their own identity during this process and begin to redefine themselves in terms of characteristics they believe their favourite celebrity to possess (McCutcheon et al., 2002). Such individuals may even develop fantasy beliefs of a delusional nature about their celebrity target and most especially about their presumed relationship with that celebrity.

Maltby and his colleagues Loraine Sheridan and Raphael Gillett at the School of Psychology, University of Leicester examined this phenomenon of delusional relationships with celebrities. They surveyed over 1,100 people aged between 13 and 72 years from the United Kingdom, United States, Canada and Australia. Respondents were recruited through publicity about the project placed on media websites, radio programmes, newspapers and magazines. Two-thirds of the respondent sample was female (Sheridan, Maltby & Gillett, 2006).

All respondents were invited to complete an instrument called the Public Figure Preoccupation Inventory. Respondents began by identifying a favourite celebrity who had to still be alive at the time of the survey. They then responded to 50 statements by indicating their level of agreement or disagreement along five-point scales. These statements included: 'I have tried to phone my favourite celebrity'; 'I have followed my favourite celebrity in a car or by foot'; 'I know my favourite celebrity's home address'; 'I have written letters or emails to my favourite celebrity'; 'I would travel thousands of miles to see my favourite celebrity'; 'I feel I constantly desire my favourite celebrity with all my body'; 'I have fantasies of an intimate nature about my favourite celebrity'; 'If my favourite celebrity ignored me then I would feel angry' and 'I would stalk my favourite celebrity if I had the means to do so'.

Statistical tests were run to find out if there was a coherent pattern to the way respondents replied to these statements. Four clusters of perceptions emerged that were interpreted as indicating a disposition to establish contact with the celebrity, a tendency to collect material about the celebrity; a tendency to have thoughts of a sexual nature about the celebrity; and finally a potential to stalk their favourite celebrity.

Having identified these clusters of orientations towards celebrities, Maltby and his colleagues conducted a further study with a smaller sample of 215 people aged 18 to 50 years which was restricted to the United Kingdom. This new sample again completed the Public Figure Preoccupation Inventory. In addition, they filled out two further personality tests designed to measure whether participants displayed a tendency to become dissociated from their everyday lives or whether they display tendencies to become completely absorbed with one train of thought to the exclusion of everything else. It has been hypothesized that in becoming psychologically involved with celebrities, members of the public can display either of these two tendencies.

Maltby and his colleagues confirmed these hypotheses again but found that different forms of celebrity worship were linked to each of these psychological dispositions. Having a tendency to become separated from one's own identity or to lose sight of what it is was predicted most powerfully by the 'establishing contact' aspect of public figure preoccupation. Being inclined to get absorbed with one thought to an obsessive degree was most strongly predicted by public figure preoccupation characterized by sexual thoughts and stalking proclivities (Sheridan et al., 2006).

These findings were not all that surprising given the types of items that defined the public figure preoccupation factors. A tendency to display fantasy connections with a celebrity such as saying you believe you have a psychic connection with them or that you often cry about your favourite celebrity because your feelings are so intense – two of the establishing contact items – would suggest a potential to become dissociated from everyday reality. At the same time, admitting to strong sexual thoughts about a celebrity or saying you would stalk this person if you could displays a degree of obsessive focus that characterizes individuals who score high on the absorption scale. All these data were of course based on information volunteered by survey respondents and this needs to be validated in terms of actual behaviour towards celebrities.

A number of relationships have been discovered between the different types of celebrity worship identified by the Celebrity Attitude Scale developed by Maltby and his co-workers and core personality characteristics. Celebrity worship defined mainly by general entertainment and social needs was found to reflect features of an extravert personality type. Outgoing individuals developed interests in celebrities as an extension of their social lives. Rather than using celebrities as a substitute for real personal relationships, any parasocial relationships they established with celebrities were simply an extension to their social networks and used as social currency – that is sources of conversation, fashion tips and so on.

Those fans who formed more intense emotional attachments to celebrities, but not to the point where their lives were totally dominated by these feelings, tended to score higher on the neuroticism scale. Such individuals tended to be more emotional and perhaps less sure of themselves in real social situations. At the most extreme end of celebrity worship where fans became completely obsessed with specific celebrities, they displayed pathologically oriented traits associated with the higher end of the psychoticism scale (Maltby, Houran & McCutcheon, 2003).

In a further study with adolescents living in the United Kingdom, Maltby and David Giles investigated the nature of teenagers' attachments to celebrities and how these relationships were positioned alongside other important social relationships with parents and friends. Celebrity attachments occurred at a time when attachments to parents were undergoing a process of change as teenagers sought greater independence. For the most part, though, teenagers liked being entertained by their favourite celebrities and used them as a source of gossip. In this respect, celebrities represented an extension of their normal social networks. Teenagers who felt less secure emotionally and socially and less certain about their own identities could become more intensely attached to celebrities as they sought greater autonomy from parents. There is then a risk that the transition from a world defined by parental standards to one that is independent of this might run less smoothly if dependencies are formed instead with celebrities who will never form part of teenagers' real lives (Giles & Maltby, 2004).

Extreme celebrity worship

While fans maintain a sense of proportion with their emotions and their behaviour, celebrity worship can be a harmless and even psychologically and socially beneficial, activity. There are occasions, however, when some fans stray from healthy into unhealthy behaviour patterns. A fan can become obsessed by celebrity to the point where their idol not only preoccupies their thoughts but where a remote parasocial relationship is no longer sufficient. Instead, the fan seeks to make direct contact with the celebrity and to turn a fantasy relationship into a real one. Such fans take to writing frequently to celebrities and may seek face-to-face contact with them.

Stalking is a clinical disorder in which a person becomes obsessively preoccupied with a desired target. Clinical psychologists have called this condition erotomania. The usual outcome of this behaviour tends to be unsatisfactory for the stalker. The object of their desire is generally unattainable – no physical or social contact and certainly no romantic contact is ever likely to occur. Such people often already lead empty and unfulfilling lives and getting knocked back by the celebrity of their desire causes further emotional discomfort that becomes compounded with the frustrations they already experience (Fujii, Ahmed &

Takashita, 1999; Zone, Sharma & Lane, 1993). Once this frustration reaches an intolerable level, it can spill over into violent outbursts that are sometimes targeted against the celebrity (Ferris, 2001).

The stalking of celebrities can take different forms. The most usual understanding is that obsessive fans follow celebrities around, spy on them when they are going about their everyday lives and find out where they live. Obsessive behaviour can also take the form of repeatedly trying to communicate with celebrities most often by writing to them over and over again. This correspondence might be relatively harmless and express admiration or undying love for the celebrity target, but it can also take on more threatening tones. Park Dietz of the University of California Los Angeles and his colleagues carried out an extensive analysis of letters to Hollywood celebrities that had been sent during the 1980s. They examined around 1,800 letters that had been sent to 22 celebrities by 214 people. Dietz and his co-workers were especially interested in letters that contained threatening or inappropriate remarks.

They focused on letter writers who presented a clear impression in their correspondence that they might at some point try physically to approach the celebrity they had written to. There were 170 letter writers known to have tried to make physical approaches to a celebrity. Cases were located through Gavin de Becker, Inc., a Los Angeles-based security company that provided advice to clients about problematic mail. The company had identified from its archive those letter writers known to have attempted to visit the location of the home of a celebrity, visited any agency believed to represent the celebrity, visited a location believed to be the home or business address of a friend, relative, business associate or acquaintance of the celebrity, approached within 5 miles of the above locations, or travelled at least 300 miles to see the celebrity or others who were believed to know the celebrity.

The letter writers on which Dietz and his colleagues focused their attention had averaged eight letters apiece. The number of mailings ranged from 1 to 146. More than four in ten letter writers (42%) had sent just a single letter, and just over one in ten (11%) had sent twenty or more. Letters could vary significantly in duration from a single side to length tomes. Some letter writers posted more than 2,000 pages of text to their target celebrity and some letters were over 6,000 words long.

Nearly one in five of the letter writers (18%) examined by Dietz were simultaneously harassing a second celebrity. Four letter writers were found to be writing to at least five celebrities at the same time. Over half of those

(54%) known to have made attempts physically to approach the celebrity expressed such a desire in their letters. One in five of these letter writers (20%) expressed sexual interest in the celebrity. Six per cent were even more explicit in their desires wanting to marry or have children with the celebrity. Nearly one in five who those known to have attempted physical approaches to a celebrity also identified specific locations (18%) or times (17%) where and when something might happen to the celebrity. More than one in five letter writers (forty-nine specific cases) made at least one threat to do some kind of harm. These comprised explicit death threats, veiled threats and conditional threats that would be carried out unless the celebrity met the letter writer's terms. Some, but not all, of these threats were aimed at the celebrity. Letter writers also threatened other individuals or groups, other public figures and even people from the letter writers' own lives. A few also threatened self-harm.

Negative celebrity psychological capital – impact of celebrity suicides

The idea of people harming themselves over their relationship with a celebrity might seem strange, but it is phenomenon that has been known about for a long time. For many years, there has been evidence that major events that involve the reporting of the deaths of famous people can cause widespread public grief and affect suicide rates (Bollen & Phillips, 1982). Both media news reports and real-life deaths and the depicted deaths of fictional film and television characters have been linked to changes in suicide rates (Hawton & Williams, 2002; Phillips, Carstensen & Paight, 1989; Stack, 2000).

In an attempt to understand the causes of suicidal behaviour, health and medical researchers have identified an important role for the media. Across a range of studies, evidence has emerged that around one-third of suicide cases have occurred close in time to media reporting of suicides. This 'media effect' has been explained within the framework of social learning theory. The presumption here is that media descriptions of suicides provide examples that can be copied by those looking on (Bollen & David, 1982; Pirkis & Blood, 2001a, 2001b; Stack, 2000). This observation has led many experts to conclude that the mass media can convey suicide scripts to the public (Jonas, 1992). Furthermore, individuals who already display suicidal tendencies might be at greater risk of influence than anyone else (Hawton, Simkin, Deeks, O'Connor, Keen & others, 1999; Ostroff & Boyd, 1987; Simkin, Hawton, Whitehead, Fagg & Eagle, 1995).

The research on media news reporting or dramatic fictional representation of suicide effects has not always produced consistent findings. One of the earliest studies reported that the suicide of actress Marilyn Monroe was followed by a 12 per cent increase in suicides in the United States (Phillips, 1974). Another analysis that focused on television stories about suicide, in contrast, could find little evidence for imitation effects whereby the trigger and inspiration for real-life suicides had apparently derived from fictional televised depictions of suicides (Kessler, Downey, Milavsky & Stipp, 1988). A more recent comprehensive review of 42 studies that investigated relationships between news reports or fictional representations of suicide and real-life suicide behaviour revealed that zero relationships were as common as significant relationships between these variables (Stack, 2000).

The evidence concerning the role that might be played by media descriptions or depictions of suicide seems therefore to undermine the likelihood of negative celebrity capital in this context. This is a conclusion we should not rush to make. Inconsistent research findings suggest that so far we do not really know whether celebrity suicides have a behavioural impact on general suicide rates. The reason why we need to look closer at the evidence here is that in many of the studies of news reports, non-celebrity suicides are often mixed up with celebrity suicides. Meanwhile, many televised depictions of suicides involve fictional characters rather than real people and their impact on viewers' own behavioural tendencies might depend upon the nature of any emotional connections they have forged with these characters and how relevant such depictions are to people's own lives. In fact, there is evidence that members of the public will identify more with suicides of real people than those of fictional characters (Gould, 2001; Schmidtke & Schaller, 2000).

In a wide-ranging review of 55 published studies that investigated non-fictional media stories about suicides, Stack (2005) found that significant statistical relationships between coverage of these events and subsequent real-world suicide rates were more than five times as likely to occur when the media suicides involved a celebrity figure. While this result cannot be taken as totally conclusive evidence for negative celebrity capital in relation to the influence of celebrity suicides on public suicide rates, it does begin to unravel why media 'effects' studies that have combined celebrity and non-celebrity suicides have not always produced consistent findings. If there is a modelling or imitation influence at play here, this is likely to be strengthened by an incident that consists of a number of critical characteristics with which observers might identify. One of these critical elements could be that the behaviour is performed by someone that the person watching or reading already relates to in a relevant psychological way. In what follows, we will try to flesh out this idea with some specific case examples.

The suicide of rock idol Kurt Cobain, lead singer of the band Nirvana in April 1994 received widespread media coverage. During the 24 hours after his death had been announced, the Seattle Crisis Clinic received more than 300 phone calls which was 100 more than usual. Many thousands more callers flooded similar helplines across the United States (Toltz & O'Donnell, 1994). This anecdotal evidence does not provide scientific proof of an imitative social impact of celebrity death on the public but it does indicate a level of emotional response – at least in the short term – that warrants closer inspection. Graham Martin and Lisa Koo of the Flinders Medical School, Adelaide, Australia conducted a study of young people in Australia – where Cobain and Nirvana had a big following – across a 30-day period after the news first broke. Their sample comprised teenagers and young adults aged between 15 and 24 years.

Data were examined for male suicide rates for this period and over an identical period in each of the previous five years. Martin and Koo found no evidence of a significant impact of media publicity of Cobain's death on suicide-related death rates among young Australians. For young men in the age range selected suicide rates increased steadily over the five years prior to the post-Cobain death period. Male suicide rate fell during this period compared with the average over the previous years and by a significant margin from the year before. Cobain killed himself with a single gunshot to the head. Deaths from firearms accounted for about one in four young male suicides and the rate of occurrence rose slightly in the post-Cobain suicide period. The actual numbers of firearm fatalities were too small however to draw any conclusions (Martin & Koo, 1997).

The death of Diana, Princess of Wales on Sunday 31 August 1997 had a massive effect on public emotions the world over. There was an unprecedented outpouring of grief during the week following her death in the United Kingdom. Hundreds of thousands of people made a pilgrimage to London to lay wreaths around her home in Kensington Palace in central London. Professor Keith Hawton of the Centre for Suicide Research at the Warneford Hospital in Oxford was interested in whether this public grief was translated into any behavioural outcomes, in particular whether it affected the propensity to commit suicide.

Hawton established baseline average suicide rate data for England and Wales over the period from 1992 and 1996 prior to Diana's death (Hawton, Harris, Appleby, Juszcak & others, 2000). He and his colleagues found that suicide rates during the week between her death and her funeral were no different from usual. However, during the 4 weeks following the funeral, the average number of suicides per week was more than 17 per cent higher than expected. This was a statistically significant change. The margin of increase was especially high for females (+34%) and much lower for males (+13%). Looking at suicide rates for females in the Princess's own age group (25–44 years) during the month after the funeral showed an even higher increase in average weekly suicide levels (+45%).

Hawton also reported that there were increases in incidents of deliberate self-harm following Diana's death. During that first week, the number of episodes of this kind increased by more than 44 per cent. Again, the rate of increase was far higher among females (+65%) than among males (+20%). Curiously, during the four weeks after Diana's funeral there was no evidence of any change in self-harming rates among females or males. More evaluative clinical evidence arose from the case notes of 116 patients who presented themselves to Professor Hawton's hospital in Oxford during the 5 weeks after Diana's funeral. Of these, nine cases made explicit reference to Princess Diana's death, and going against the prevailing trends, two-thirds of these were male. The wider population evidence showing that suicide rates had increased most especially among females in a similar age bracket to the Princess was consistent with a modelling explanation of this behaviour (see Bandura, 1973).

On 1 April 2003, Hong Kong's best-known pop star Leslie Cheung died after jumping from a high-rise building following a bout of depression. His death received extensive media coverage and his loss was mourned by his fans. Research carried out after this incident indicated that it may have triggered many people to consider committing suicide. One study found a significant increase in the number of suicide cases immediately after Cheung's death in 2003, compared with the previous 5 years, especially among men aged 25 to 39 who used the same method of suicide as Cheung (Yip, Fu, Yang, Ip, Chan, Chen, Lee, Law & Hawton, 2006).

King-wa Fu and Paul Yip of the University of Hong Kong followed up this initial research with a further investigation that tried to understand more about various personal factors that render some people susceptible to celebrity influences in this context. They conducted a survey with more than 2,000 Hong Kong residents aged between 20 and 59 years (Fu & Yip, 2007). They were interviewed in their own homes and they answered questions about their personality, values, anxiety levels, whether they had received psychiatric treatment, and about their risk levels in terms of having a propensity to commit suicide.

Questions explored their reasons for living which included their responsibilities to their families and especially their children, moral obligations and ability to cope with problems that life might throw at them. They were also asked more direct questions about whether they had considered committing suicide or paid attention to celebrity suicides. In relation to celebrity suicides, respondents were asked whether they had ever been disturbed by news of a celebrity suicide. They were then asked if a celerity suicide had changed the way they had thought about suicide and whether it had led them to consider suicide. They were then asked if a celebrity suicide had made suicide more or less acceptable to them. Finally, they were asked if they had ever tried to commit suicide in the past 12 months.

Nearly four in ten respondents (38%) admitted that they had been influenced by a celebrity suicide. This admission was more prevalent among women (43%) than among men (32%). It was also more prevalent among people aged under 40 (40%) than those aged 40 and over (35%). On the question of whether celebrities might have any influence over the propensity of people to think about committing suicide, Fu and Yip conducted complex statistical analyses that revealed that strength of acknowledgement of a celebrity influence was independently and significantly related to the degree to which respondents exhibited strong tendencies to generate thoughts about suicide. This relationship persisted even when various personality factors, anxiety symptoms, irrational values, reasons for living and prior suicidal behaviour measures were all controlled. Even more seriously, those individuals – there were 44 of them only – who scored at a level of high clinical risk on the scales designed to measure 'suicide ideation' (i.e. showing propensity to think about committing suicide) displayed a very strong relationship between saying they were influenced by celebrity suicides and the extent to which they thought about suicide.

Further research of this kind was completed in Taiwan following the death by hanging of a well-known television actor, Min-Jan Nee. The reporting of this incident began on 2 May 2005 and lasted for around 17 days. Researchers at the Institute of Biomedical Sciences, Academia Sinica, Taipei reported a series of investigations of the potential impact of this celebrity suicide story on suicide rates in Taiwan and further investigated whether known suicide attempters in the country attributed any influence to media reporting of this suicide. Further research also examined patients with depression who presented suicide risk profiles to find out whether they had exhibited any sensitivities to this celebrity suicide.

Controlling for seasonal variations, weather conditions and unemployment rates – all known suicide risk factors – a marked increase in suicide rates was found during the four weeks after the celebrity entertainer's death compared with the previous two years. The most pronounced increase in risk of suicide occurred among men and there was a significant increase in suicides by hanging – the method used by the celebrity. The findings indicated that the celebrity's death did seem to trigger a spate of copy-cat suicides in the short-term after (Cheng, Hawton, Lee & Chen, 2007).

The same research group identified 124 suicide attempters from known cases that occurred in 2 areas of Taiwan during the first 3 weeks after reporting of this celebrity suicide began. Nearly a quarter of these cases, when interviewed, said that the celebrity's suicide had influenced their own suicidal behaviour. This self-attributed modelling effect was most likely to be mentioned by male suicide attempters and was also linked to cases with a history of suicide attempts. The findings here confirmed what had been observed elsewhere and that is that it is people who already have a predisposition towards suicide who appear to be most at risk of celebrity suicide modelling influences (Cheng, Hawton, Chen, Yen, Chen, Chen & Teng, 2007).

This conclusion was confirmed in a third investigation in Taiwan that focused on depressive patients and their attention to news stories about this celebrity's death. Patients with depression who had recently already tried to commit suicide displayed the strongest risk of trying to repeat their behaviour as a consequence of exposure to media coverage of a celebrity's death by suicide (Cheng, Hawton, Chen, Yen, Chang, Chong, Liu, Lee, Teng & Chen, 2007).

Fu and Yip (2009) provided further evidence of a celebrity-specific effect on suicide rates across three different countries following the deaths of well-known celebrities to suicide in each country. Two of the celebrities have been discussed before – Leslie Chung from Hong Kong and Min-Jan Nee from Taiwan. In addition, FU and Yip looked at the case of a popular actress from South Korea called Eun-ju Lee who killed herself by hanging on 22 February 2005. Extensive media coverage followed each one of these deaths. The researchers also collected suicide data for Hong Kong, Taiwan and South Korea for the year of the celebrity's suicide and for the preceding two years. Weekly suicide rates were examined throughout these periods to determine whether they had changed following each celebrity suicide.

Overall, weekly suicide rates during the whole study period for each country were 21.5 for Hong Kong, 69.7 for Taiwan and 219.8 for South Korea. During the four weeks after the celebrity suicide in each country, the weekly rates increased to 31.5, 107.8 and 291.8 respectively. Further analyses produced results that were consistent with modelling effects for celebrity suicides. There was a 40 per cent elevation in risk for suicides among people the same gender as the celebrity, but a non-significant change for the opposite gender. While the opposite gender were unaffected, for the same gender there was a 63 per cent increase in likelihood that the same method of suicide would be used as that used by the celebrity. There was also an age-related dimension to suicide behaviour. There was a 49 per cent increase in suicide rates among people in the same age group as the celebrity, compared with a 21 per cent increase among other age groups. The celebrity suicide effect was felt mostly within the first four weeks after the celebrity's death, and then gradually fell away after that. Even so, suicide rates remained 14 per cent higher even 18 weeks after the celerity committed suicide.

Conclusion

Drawing this chapter to a close it is clear that celebrities can have different kinds of psychological capital. This capital can be both positive and negative. Celebrities offer us role models and can represent targets for our own aspirations. In finding out about their lives, celebrities offer us social scripts we can try out in our own lives as well as providing sources of conversation through which we can connect with others. Celebrities can also become objects of our affection to a point where they displace ordinary relationships. When this happens, our involvement with them can get out of proportion and in the extreme our dependencies on these virtual relationships can lead us to display obsessive behaviour that can lead us to become socially marginalized in everyday reality. The loss of a celebrity can be deeply felt and where a celebrity's life has ended, we might experience genuine grief. If our favourite celebrity took their own life, for some of us, this can be a trigger to think about doing the same thing.

For most of us, thankfully, celebrities are a light-hearted distraction from our everyday lives. In a social and psychological sense, they have some value but to a point where they motivate us to make radical changes to our own lives – even though we may often be envious of theirs. In other settings, however, there is evidence that attaining celebrity status has real value. It can enhance the attractiveness of goods and services, enhance the value of companies, promote greater awareness of health and social issues, and even make politicians seem more electable. In the remaining chapters of this book, we will look at all these different kinds of celebrity capital to find out just how significant they are.

Key points

- Celebrities are key social talking points and sources of gossip.
- For some people, celebrities become part of their extended social network.
- The attraction to celebrity starts in childhood.
- Celebrities can create an illusion of real friendship for susceptible individuals.
- Psychological feelings for celebrities can become so powerful that they come to resemble a form of worship.
- Powerful psychological relationships with celebrities can encourage their fans to want to be more like them.
- Celebrity attachments can serve as substitutes for real attachments.
- Extreme celebrity attachments can result in tragic consequences when celebrities die.

Topics for reflection

- Celebrities often provide poor role models. Discuss this premise with reference to specific case examples.
- A celebrity can become your 'best friend'. Explain how this can happen for some people.
- Can celebrity worship be measured? Critique the methods that have been used to investigate this phenomenon.
- How far will fans go to be like their favourite celebrity? Use the scientific research to explain some real-life examples of extreme celebrity worship.
- Is celebrity worship a good thing or a bad thing?

Further readings

Dunbar, R. I. M. (2004). Gossip in evolutionary perspective. *Review of General Psychology*, *8*, 100–10.

Fu, K., & Yip, P. S. F. (2007). Long-term impact of celebrity suicide on suicidal ideation: Results from a population-based study. *Journal of Epidemiology and Community Health*, *61*(6), 540–8.

Giles, D. (2000). *Illusions of immortality: A psychology of fame and celebrity*. New York, NY: St Martin's Press.

Giles, D., & Maltby, J. (2006). Praying at the altar of the stars. *The Psychologist*, *19*(2), 82–5.

Maltby, J., & Day, L. (2011). Celebrity worship and incidence of elective cosmetic surgery: Evidence of a link among young adults. *Journal of Adolescent Health*, *49*(1), 483–9.

3

The Consumer Capital of Celebrity

Celebrities have been used worldwide to endorse products and services. This is not a new phenomenon. The earliest use of celebrities to promote products can be traced back to the nineteenth century. Even royalty got in on the act. Queen Victoria herself had an endorsement relationship with chocolate manufacturer, Cadbury (Sherman, 1985).

As brand marketing and mass advertising grew during the early decades of the twentieth century, with the emergence first of cinema and then radio broadcasting, and then television, the opportunities to use celebrities to promote products and services grew rapidly. The use of celebrities became so popular so quickly that the market soon found that the pool of relevant talent was limited (Erdogan, 1999; Kaikati, 1987).

In the early stages of development of the kinds of celebrities as product endorsers to which we are all accustomed today, there was a limited pool of endorsers to choose from. Advertisers found that initially many established celebrities from the worlds of film, stage and even television were reluctant to 'lower' themselves to making public appearances as brand promoters. There was a deeply ingrained feeling among stars of the 1930s, 1940s and 1950s that their public image could be damaged if they lent their names as endorsers of commercial products (McDonough, 1995).

As the television and movie industries continued to grow, the former in particular cultivated new 'stars' who also became more comfortable with the idea of lending their names to commercial endorsements, advertisers found they had more choice (Thompson, 1978). By the end of the 1970s, celebrity endorsement was commonplace (Howard, 1979). In the United States, the prevalence of celebrity endorsers increased from around one in six commercials in the 1970s to more than one in five from the 1990s (Motavalli, 1988; Shimp, 1997; White, 2004). By the mid-1990s, it was estimated by one writer that advertisers were spending $1 billion a year just to sports endorsers (Lane, 1996).

The public became increasingly accepting of celebrity endorsers as a cultural phenomenon. An American survey carried out by Adweek/Harris Interactive asked consumers whether they felt their opinions about brands could be swayed by celebrity endorsements. Respondents were asked, if they would be more or less likely to buy a product after it had been endorsed by a sports, start, movie star or other celebrity. An overwhelming majority of respondents (77%) said that they would be no more or less likely to buy a product under these circumstances. Among the minority of consumers who felt that their inclination to buy a product could be influenced by a celebrity, many more (14%) said they would actually be less likely to buy it than more likely to do so (4%). Older consumers, aged 55 and over (19%) were especially inclined to say that celebrity endorsement would put them off buying a product. Such findings must be treated with caution however (Chapman, 2011).

This survey did not allow consumers any options to make comparisons between celebrities nor to consider goodness of fit between the celebrity providing the endorsement and the nature of the product or service being advertised. This evidence indicates that although the public did not oppose the use of celebrity endorsers in principle, the challenge for advertisers was in making the right choices of celebrity for the brands they sought to promote. This objective became increasingly important as the cost of hiring celebrity endorsers escalated over time.

The consumer capital of celebrities stems to a significant degree from the social and psychological identity influences they have as role models. As well as being social role models celebrities are cultural icons who set trends and fashions. This is often manifested in terms of the way celebrities style their outer appearance. Children and teenagers can be especially strongly drawn to celebrities in this context as they explore and try on different identities for themselves. Pop stars and sports stars are particularly influential in terms of fashion trends. Although parents are important consumer role models for children, young consumers also nominate their favourite entertainers or favourite athletes as being just as important to them in this context (Martin & Bush, 2000). Through their identification with these celebrities children internalize associations between commodities and being a certain type of person. Celebrities are not all powerful however. There is a process of negotiation that goes on in which young consumers judge not only whether a particular style of clothing looks good on the celebrity but also whether it is appropriate for them to wear as well. Hence if a celebrity such as Avril Lavigne or Beyonce wears revealing outfits that expose a lot of flesh some teenage girls will take a lead from this in their own fashion choices, while others will reject what these icons wear despite respecting them as artists (Boden, 2006).

The same principles apply in terms of sports stars and their influence over children's sportswear brand choices. Styles worn by favourite sports performers might be adopted as trendy, but this tends to happen after a process of negotiation that frequently involves discussion of specific styles and brands with peers. Peer pressure might reinforce the branding activities of celebrities, but can also limit the impact of specific brands (Elliott & Leonard, 2004).

One particularly important decision was whether to use an expensive celebrity endorser or to develop a non-celebrity endorser instead. Some marketing experts argued that advertisers could actually do well by creating their own 'celebrities' whose profiles become established through their appearances with popular brands that were given widespread and repetitive airing via different mass media to mass consumer markets (Tom et al., 1992). The advantage of adopting this marketing strategy was that advertisers could control the image of a non-celebrity endorser to ensure that it represented a good fit with the image of the promoted brand. The risk in using celebrity endorsers was that although they brought some initial consumer capital with them in the form of their existing fan base, their own 'brand image' was pre-formed and might not always match the type of image being sought for the commercial brand they were hired to promote.

Elsewhere, empirical evidence surfaced that celebrity endorsers were found to be no better than non-celebrity endorsers in terms of enhancing consumers' attitudes towards a brand or their intentions to purchase it. In addition, there was another risk that emerged that in the presence of a celebrity consumers paid less attention to the sales message about the brand (Mehta, 1994).

Celebrity endorsers have generally been associated with commercial brands in two ways. There is the standard endorsement of a product by a celebrity usually in return for payment. In addition, there is the celebrity license arrangement whereby the commercial brand becomes a brand extension of the celebrity and the celebrity's name is integrated with the name of the product (Mistry, 2006). One example of this is the George Forman Grill in which the former world heavyweight champion boxer gave his name to a kitchen appliance. Perhaps one of the most prolific exponents of celebrity licensing is the TV cook Jamie Oliver who has given his name to a wide range of food products, including, meat, fish, cheese, pasta and herbs and spices (http://www.JamieOliver.com/products/food).

Another celebrity licensing arrangement was signed between rap artist Sean 'P Diddy' Combs and Diageo, the spirits company. This deal took the form of a profit-sharing arrangement whereby Mr Combs also became brand manager of Diageo's Ciroc vodka line. Within this partnership, the corporate sponsor and celebrity took joint ownership over the brand and steered its development.

Some celebrity licensing agreements have taken place at the very beginning of an artist's career with the corporate sponsor contributing to the developing public profile of a budding celebrity as well as benefiting from their emergent celebrity status. One illustration of this phenomenon was the commercial agreement between Totes Isotoner, a modest Cincinnati company that manufactured umbrellas and the singer Rihanna. The artist was signed to the company on the strength of her debut hit record, 'Umbrella' even before it was released and the celebrity, her management team and the company worked together on a line of products, under a profit-sharing arrangement (see Cresswell, 2008).

Celebrity endorsements are much more widely used than celebrity licensing arrangements. This is not a surprise given that licensing deals entail a different level of commitment on the part of the celebrity to the commercial product and a more complex level of integration between celebrity and commercial brand meaning that the goodness of fit is likely to be more closely scrutinized by consumers. Nevertheless, celebrity licensing tie-ins are becoming more prevalent.

The decision for marketers about using celebrity endorsers therefore should never be regarded as a simple and straightforward one. Well-known celebrities can help brands to stand out in a crowded marketplace, but the really important question here is whether they also effectively get the promotional message across and cultivate a suitable image for the commercial brand. There are occasions when simply using a very famous and popular celebrity can work effectively for products. Equally, there are many occasions when consumers expect to find some degree of relevance of the celebrity to the brand being endorsed. This 'relevance' may be judged in terms of the perceived expertise of the celebrity in the context of giving advice or information about a product or at least a perception that the celebrity seems to be a feasible user of the product (Speck, Schumann & Thompson, 1988). Consumers need to believe that there is at least half a chance that the celebrity really likes the product and that this opinion has derived from the first-hand experience with it (Silvera & Austad, 2003).

There is certainly a trade view that celebrity tie-ins can enhance the profile and images of commercial brands and that it will ultimately play an important part in persuading consumers to buy the product (License!, 2007). The opinions of consumers themselves however do not always offer support to retailers' perceptions. Research carried out among consumers in Britain found that celebrities did not invariably persuade them to purchase endorsed products. Indeed, many consumers said they did not trust celebrity endorsements (Datamonitor, 2006).

In some countries, most notably the United States, the use of celebrity endorsers was even greater (Stafford, Spears & Chung-Kue, 2003). Advertisers believe that celebrities can add significant value to a brand (Erdogan, Baker & Tagg, 2001a). Although there is evidence from consumer research to reinforce this belief (Agrawal & Kamakura, 1995; Mathur, Mathur & Rangan, 1997), there have also been cases where celebrities can damage brand reputations when their own reputations take a nose dive, perhaps through loss of popularity with wear-out over time or because they have been involved in a public scandal. As we will see in the next chapter, Chapter 4, celebrities who turn bad can have toxic effects on the corporate value of their sponsors as well.

Celebrity endorsements can take different forms. Celebrities are used as spokespersons for a product or service, as demonstrators of its use, or are simply presented in association with it. Marketers must think carefully about choosing the right celebrity. It is not simply a case of selecting a public figure that currently has a high profile. Celebrities are brands in their own right and the celebrity's brand must fit with the commercial brand of the sponsor. Hence, even if the use of the celebrity is restricted to simple association with the product or service being promoted, without any verbal endorsement of it or demonstration of its use, the celebrity must possess the kind of reputation that will enhance the value of the advertised brand.

An alternative strategy is for marketers to find non-celebrity endorsers over whom they may have more control. With enough exposure these initially unknown spokespersons can acquire some celebrity status of their own but this is defined by the commercial brand with which they are associated. The movement of attributes occurs in the opposite direction from that which occurs when a famous celebrity is used. Evidence has emerged that created endorsers can prove to be a better fit for many products and may produce a more effective campaign (Tom et al., 1992).

How does celebrity consumer capital work?

Celebrities are used by marketers for a number of reasons. One reason for using celebrities to endorse products is to generate extra publicity for a product or service by drawing public attention to it. Vance Packard wrote more than 50 years ago that celebrities made good endorsers for products because of their high social status. Consumers would be persuaded to follow the lead of celebrities because they identified with that status and sought it for themselves (Packard, 1957). By buying products endorsed by celebrities, who they may have presumed were also consumers of those products, they believed that some of the celebrity's stardust might rub off on them. In consuming products endorsed by famous people, consumers could enter an imaginary world in which they believed they had acquired some of the attributes of celebrities through shared consumer preferences (Fowles, 1996).

The reasoning runs like this. A celebrity is a popular figure that ordinary people may like and identify with. They will therefore pay more attention to commercial messages that involve that celebrity than they would otherwise. Hence, the high public profile of the celebrity will transfer to the brand raising its public profile. Not only will a brand therefore attain greater recognition among consumers, but with the right choice of celebrity endorser, positive thoughts and feelings associated with the celebrity will also migrate across to the brand. Hence, the brand will become better known and better liked (Tom, Clark, Elmer, Grech, Masetti & Sandhar, 1992). Marketing experts have drawn upon psychological theories about human cognition, emotion and behaviour to create models to guide the use and selection of celebrities as product endorsers. What are the do's and don'ts associated with adapting the consumer capital of celebrities?

The consumer capital of celebrities cannot be presumed to magically emerge simply because they have a high public profile. It is important to make the right choices for specific brand promoting campaigns. Among the important factors to be considered here are whether a source is likable, attractive and credible as a source, whether they make a good fit with the brand they are invited to endorse, and whether the more relevant and beneficial attributes transfer from the celebrity to the brand. In addition, where a celebrity is very popular and has been commissioned to support more than one brand, can multiple brand endorsements dilute their consumer capital?

The effectiveness of celebrities as endorsers in advertising can depend upon a range of personal characteristics that they are known for and bring with them to the advertising setting. Celebrities have more promotional value for advertisers if they are well-liked, attractive, and regarded as trustworthy and credible sources of information and advice. Celebrity credibility can depend upon the goodness of fit between them and the type of product or service being advertised. Credibility can also be determined by the public's perceptions of their relevance to the advertised brand. Are they credible users of the brand? Are they likely to have expert knowledge about it?

According to McCracken (1989) a celebrity endorser is a person who is widely recognized by the public and can use this profile to boost consumers' awareness of a commercial product or service by appearing alongside it in an advertisement. An endorser will work best if he or she is already familiar to consumers, if consumers like the endorser and perceive certain similarities between themselves and the endorser. A celebrity endorser often has additional qualities. If they are successful at what they do, consumers may aspire to be like them even if they are not already. A celebrity's social status may also give them an authority in terms of expertise and trustworthiness than an anonymous or unknown endorser would not possess.

Within the advertising industry practitioners have acknowledged that celebrities can enhance brand images through the transfer of values. Where these values are positive and relevant to the brand, this can work to enhance the brand's distinctiveness in the marketplace and raises its profile and its attractiveness and credibility with consumers. At the same time, it is known in the industry that extremely well-known celebrities could overshadow the brand. This phenomenon is known as the 'Vampire effect' and we will return to it later on. While celebrities can give a new product, with an ill-formed brand image, instant appeal, it is essential that the celebrity's image will be the most suitable one for the commercial brand in the longer term (Dickenson, 1996). The product must be the centre of attention and not the celebrity (Cooper, 1984). Consumers take with them a memory of having seen or heard a particular celebrity, but no recollection of what that endorser said about the brand or even about the type of product or service being promoted (Rossiter & Percy, 1987).

While it is important for the celebrity to be well-liked not just because of their physical attractiveness but also for the kind of person they seem to be, if there is a further story linked to them that renders them especially relevant to the advertised brand, then they are more likely to be contracted. For example, it makes sense to use a current and successful sports star to promote a sports product. At the very least, there should be a sense that the celebrity is also a genuine brand user. There is nothing worse for the credibility of a celebrity endorsed campaign for evidence to surface publicly that the celebrity is not a brand user and even that they actually use a rival brand (Erdogan & Baker, 1999).

The values espoused by a celebrity endorser must also resonate with the dominant values of a specific national market. The idea of using rich and successful people as endorsers who deliberately flaunt their affluent lifestyles might go down well in the United States among consumers who identify with similar aspirations, but would jar with consumers in some Asian markets where such boastfulness is defined culturally as inappropriate.

A number of models of celebrity endorsement have emerged that attempt to explain why it can enhance the impact of brand advertising. The most prominent explanations derive from the source image, product match-up and meaning transfer models. The image of the source of a promotional message comprises a number of sub-components. Message receivers make judgements about sources in terms of their physical attractiveness, the likeability of their personalities, and their credibility in terms of whether they are seen as trustworthy and have relevant expertise (see Ohanian, 1990).

In summing, up, these different attributes underpin what we might call the reputation of the endorser. It is important that a celebrity endorser is regarded as having a reputation that consumers admire and that this reputation can then benefit an advertised brand with which the celebrities' name is associated (Fombrun, 1996).

Celebrity-brand matching and meaning transfer

A brand image comprises a range of attributes that are perceptually connected to the product or service being promoted. The brand itself can be regarded as a hub within the individual's memory with multiple links to different attributes that characterize that brand. Hence, a brand of soap powder might be defined by having a distinctive smell, colour, texture, ability to get items clean, and price. If a celebrity endorser is used to promote it, he or she becomes yet another defining attribute linked to the brand name (Keller, 1993). Consumers can then create further attribute associations with the brand based on their own experiences with it (Barich & Kotler, 1991).

Celebrities can also be thought of as 'brands' as well. Like all brands, they are defined by various attributes that reflect their physical characteristics, personalities, lifestyles and talents. Such attributes may be rated as positive or negative by consumers. According to the 'match-up hypothesis', the trick for marketers is to choose the right celebrity with the right appeal for the right brand. This is achieved when there is maximal attribute congruence between the celebrity endorser and the brand being endorsed (Kamins & Gupta, 1994). Sometimes, the fame of a celebrity alone can be enough to get a good result in terms of enhanced brand awareness. If this was always true, then all marketers would need to do is select the most famous celebrities and they would be guaranteed great results. In reality, this does not always work

Thus, having a high profile or a good reputation is not by itself sufficient to ensure a winning combination in the context of celebrity endorsement of specific brands. There must also be a good fit between the celebrity and the type of product or service and more specifically with the brand. The product match-up model comes into play here and effectively requires that for consumers there is an obvious relevance of the celebrity endorser's attributes and the attributes for which the brand stands (Kamins & Gupta, 1994). A further element that can come into play here also is the reputation of the company that is advertising the brand. Insofar as that company also has a distinctive corporate image, the celebrity 'brand' image must also display congruence with it. The most obvious link-up here is between sports products and top sports performers (Shimp, 1997).

While a good celebrity-brand fit might be located at a surface level, whether this partnership makes a good lasting fit can depend upon whether the celebrity's core defining attributes and values are congruent with those for which the advertised is already known or would like to be known. The importance of a productive relationship at this level is embodied by the meaning transfer model. Consumers must be able to identify with a celebrity on a number of levels and at least some of these should mirror different levels at which they also relate to brands.

These models have been presented as specific explanations of the celebrity endorsement effects. In fact, they do not represent separate processes but touch on a range of factors that can interact with each other. Meaning transfer can depend upon whether celebrity attributes and brand attributes make a good match. In general, since a brand will seek to benefit from positive attributes associated with the celebrity as a source, the perceived attractiveness, trustworthiness and expertise of the celebrity will be important in term of whether a good match can be achieved. If the source is well regarded in ways that are relevant to the advertised brand, then the conditions are set in place for appropriate transfer of meanings to occur from the celebrity to the brand.

Finding a good fit between celebrity and the endorsed brand can depend on the type of product. For products that are judged mostly in terms of their functional value – that is their ability consistently to do what they say they do on the tin – it is important to use endorsers who are regarded by consumers as having relevant expertise or who simply get on with demonstrating in practical terms what makes a particular brand good. For brands defined in terms of the lifestyle or social status value, the use of a celebrity who possesses relevant attributes can be a great advantage because consumers are not buying into the functionality of the brand but more into what association with the brand says to others about them.

Thus, if a celebrity is perceived by consumers to possess attractive and valued attributes and is someone they can identify with, they will consume brands endorsed by that celebrity in the hope that some of those qualities will be transferred to them (McCracken, 1989). In principle, this explanation seems to make perfect sense. As consumers, we often adopt celebrities as social role models or as people were would like to be like. One of the ways we can be more like them is if we purchase and use the same brands of products or services. In practice this is not always how things work out. Sometimes sponsors choose the wrong celebrities for their brands. At other times, a good choice can turn sour if the celebrity's own standing takes a tumble (Kaikati, 1987).

Celebrity as credible source

We have seen that it is crucial that celebrities convey the right meanings and messages to consumers and make a good fit with the images of the commercial brands they endorse. What we need to know next however is what are the right kinds of meanings and how can a good match-up be achieved? Such questions bring us to an analysis of how celebrities work as sources of information and advice about products. A central concept here is that of 'source credibility'. In the history of social psychological research into the way people form beliefs and attitudes about different things, the role played by techniques of persuasion in this process has been centre stage. An important aspect of being persuaded to adopt a specific point of view is what the message receiver's perceptions are of the source of that persuasive communication (Hovland & Weiss, 1951; Hovland, Janis & Kelley, 1953).

Evaluations of sources of persuasive messages centre primarily on the attractiveness, likability, expertise and trustworthiness of the source. There may be other factors that can come into play such as the demographic or personality characteristics of sources, but it is important that sources are liked and seen as credible (Ohanian, 1991). Where celebrity endorsers are concerned, judgements are also made on the basis of their performance and their status in those spheres for which they are known (e.g. that sports stars continue to win; that movie stars keep getting major roles in top grossing movies and so on) and that they maintain a positive public image (e.g. do not attract negative publicity for activities in their private lives). In the business of marketing, all these elements have been embraced in a strategy model called FRED, which stands for familiarity, relevance, esteem and differentiation (see Miciak & Shanklin, 1994) (see Table 3.1).

A number of evaluations of celebrity-brand match-ups have found that even the best-known celebrities do not always make the right endorsers for particular brands. When invited to express in their own terms the values of celebrity endorsers, consumers place credibility centre stage. They expect the product being endorsed to be genuine or authentic in terms of the claims made about it in advertising with the same standards applying also to a celebrity endorser

Table 3.1 Celebrity endorser attributes

Likeability
Celebrities attain their status by gaining social capital among the public who place value on them for the achievements for which they are known or because their high public profile in its own right creates degree of familiarity that breeds curiosity. Repeat exposure to these public figures via the mass media, whether through their specialist achievements or because the media have adopted them as focal points of attention for reasons other than having a special talent, can result in ordinary people wanting to know even more about them. If celebrities have interesting characters, the public may warm to them and grow to like them. The likability factor can be sufficient in its own right to enable celebrities to add value to brands with which they are associated.

Attractiveness
The physical attractiveness of celebrity endorsers can often be a critical attribute that strengthens their position as a source of reference in relation to a brand. Regardless of other attributes that might characterize endorsers or spokespersons, if they look good and sound good, their ability to influence others in enhanced. In a brand image context, the attractiveness of the celebrity rubs off on the brand and consumers believe in turn that their use of the brand will mean they take on some of these qualities themselves.

Expertise
The credibility of sources can be significantly mediated by whether they are perceived to have relevant expertise. When celebrities are hired to present arguments in favour of using a brand, their impact can depend upon whether consumers regard them as qualified to make these arguments. This point becomes particularly important for products and services that consumers think carefully about buying.

Trustworthiness
Ultimately, consumers must be able to trust the endorser of a brand. Celebrities can command trust, even where they may not be experts in relation to the product or service being promoted, because of their reputations in their professional and personal lives. If the endorser is perceived to be a person of integrity, he or she will be trusted by consumers simply because they believe such a person would never deceive them.

Performance
Celebrity value can depend upon the level of their personal performance. Are they celebrities because of special talents they possess? Have they demonstrated sustained high-level performance or been one hit wonders?

Negative behaviour
Celebrities have value for sponsors if they can sustain a good reputation with consumers. This depends not just on their performance within their field, but also on how they conduct themselves in their lives in general. If they engage in anti-social and amoral activities or are found to demonstrate a lack of integrity in the things they do, their image can become damaged.

---

of the product. One analysis of the way a small groups of consumers expressed their opinions about a campaign run by Reebok, the sports merchandise manufacturer, alongside other campaigns they had selected themselves, the value of a celebrity endorser clearly depends upon whether consumers perceive a good match between the celebrity and the product, whether they feel the celebrity can be trusted particularly when he or she is being paid by the advertiser, and whether previous experiences have taught them that celebrity endorsers in general represent a trusted source (Temperley & Tangen, 2006).

In a report on celebrities' impact on branding, Christina Schlecht of the Centre on Global Brand Leadership, Columbia Business School showed that despite their national and international fame, some celebrities failed to enhance the images and performance of the brands they were contracted to endorse (see also Till & Busler, 1998; Walker, Langmeyer & Langmeyer, 1992). Match-ups between Liz Hurley and Estee Lauder, Cindy Crawford and Revlon and Pepsi Cola, Michael Jordan and Nike, Jerry Seinfeld and American Express and Milla Jovovich and L'Oreal were also judged to be success stories. In contrast, endorsements of Bruce Willis for Seagrams, Michael Jordan for WorldCom and Whitney Houston for AT&T were unsuccessful.

One reason for the failure of some well-known celebrities to enhance commercial brand images is that their consumer capital is not dependent purely on their fame. It also depends on the celebrity' personal brand attributes being relevant to the type of image a commercial brand seeks to create or in many instances already has among consumers. Coupled with the notion of a good 'match-up' is the idea of meaning transfer. What this refers to is a process whereby the attributes associated with the celebrity are transferred across to the commercial brand they are hired to endorse. This idea is backed up by psychological theory. Associative learning theory proposes that there can be a transfer of meaning from the celebrity to a brand that the celebrity endorses (Till, 1998). Through repeated exposure, consumers learn to connect the attributes of the celebrity with the commercial brand. Cognitive theorists propose that concepts as such are stored in the brain as inter-connected networks. The more often two entities are experienced together the stronger will be the neural link that exists between them in the brain (Till et al., 2008).

Match-up and meaning transfer can be seen as working together. Sponsors seek to enhance consumers' awareness and liking for their brands. To achieve these objectives, not only must specific attributes successfully transfer from the celebrity to the commercial brand, but also these attributes must be ones that are seen as relevant to the brand. An admired celebrity endorser might therefore produce positive thoughts and feelings about the brand(s) they endorse.

According to Grant McCracken, meanings that define the celebrity transfer across to the product being endorsed and are then absorbed in turn by consumers. Famous people are not usually defined by a single attribute (McCracken, 1989). There may be a number of features, including their gender, age, social status, the profession for which they are known, and any special abilities or talents they display. Film actors may be defined both by what members of the public have managed to find out about them in their private lives as well as by the types of roles they have played. Sports stars are known for their skills and performance in the competitions in which they take part. With many established brands, a brand image has already been firmly conditioned in the minds of consumers. Celebrity endorsers will therefore be judged by consumers in terms of whether their attributes make a good fit with the attributes of a commercial brand.

The importance of celebrity likability

If a celebrity is well-liked, this positive image may rub off on the brand being endorsed by them. The likability factor has been known about for a long time (McGuire, 1985). The public can warm to celebrities as they get to know them over time. The emergence of a positive opinion about a celebrity can depend upon the way they behave in their own lives and this is often driven also by their physical attractiveness (McCracken, 1989). Technically, this effect has been called the 'transfer of meaning' (Belch & Belch, 1998). The way it works is like this. The celebrity has positive attributes such as being very talented, very attractive and very successful. These attributes then attach themselves to the brand with which the celebrity is associated enhancing its brand value to consumers. This type of effect is increasingly important in crowded and competitive marketplaces, in which brands must fight ever harder to stand out, the use of a celebrity endorser is believed to lend the brand more distinctiveness (Biswas, Hussain & O'Donnell, 2009; Keller, 2008).

This theory seems on the surface to make sense. In practice, however, celebrities can vary in the nature of the support they can offer to brands. Marketing researchers have found that using a likable celebrity endorser does not guarantee enhanced sales or even brand image. The sensitivity of consumers to the presence of a popular celebrity in an advertisement can depend upon the importance of the advertised product or service. With products that are important to consumers, for example, the presence of a likable celebrity can make little difference to their perceptions of the advertised brand. In contrast with products that consumers do not give a great deal of thought – usually everyday items that are relatively inexpensive to buy and which feature as regular purchases in their weekly shop, a popular celebrity endorser can make a difference (Kahle & Homer, 1985).

This effect may occur because for 'low involvement' items, the marketplace can be crowded and successful brands must find a way to stand out from the rest and attract the attention of consumers who normally do not devote a great deal of mental effort to thinking about the different brands available. In this context, the association between a brand and a popular celebrity could make all the difference in making the brand stand out from the crowd. In contrast, with commodities that command more attention from consumers in terms of which brands to buy – such as luxury items that are expensive and require a significant financial commitment – decisions about whether to buy or not will not be swung simply on the say-so of a famous person. Instead, consumers want to reflect on the qualities of the brands available and weight them up in terms of which will make the best buy for them in terms of functionality, social status statement and value for money.

Celebrity attractiveness, credibility and trustworthiness are important attributes if a celebrity endorser is to enhance brand image (Dean & Biswas, 2001; Seno & Lucas, 2007). Attractiveness is usually based on judgements about the physical appearance of an endorser, although it can also derive from their perceived status and confidence. For most consumers however that attractiveness judgement is a physical attractiveness perception (Kahle & Homer, 1985).

A celebrity's attractiveness can play an important part in determining how popular they are among members of the public. As with general likability, however, when advertisers use celebrities because they are seen as being prize physical specimens, this does not always equate to having higher consumer capital. Researchers who examined the impact of celebrity attractiveness of the appeal of razor blades found that it did enhance the image of the advertised brand (Kahle & Homer, 1985). This finding was restricted to one product type however and in this case the product was one linked to looking good (i.e. having an extra clean shave) and linking this brand with an attractive male celebrity probably represented a very credible fit. This explanation was reinforced in other research that found that celebrity attractiveness was no guarantee of enhanced brand image. This outcome was most likely to emerge when the celebrity's attractiveness represented a quality that had distinctive relevance to the product being advertised (Silvera & Austad, 2004). The value of celebrity attractiveness does not always emerge with immediate effect. It can sometimes take some time and repeat exposure before consumers respond by developing a positive brand image (Eisend & Langner, 2010).

Physically attractive endorsers can be more effective at changing beliefs about products and services (Chaiken, 1979; Debevec & Kernan, 1984) and increasing consumers' intentions to make specific purchases (Friedman et al., 1976; Petroshius & Crocker, 1989). 'Attractiveness' in this context usually means physical appearance. In other words, does the celebrity have a handsome or pretty face, do they have a shapely body or good physique? Attractiveness can also be defined by other personal qualities such as whether they are very intelligent, very funny, very rich or very successful at what they do for a living.

Marketers' expectations are that endorsers who possess these kinds of attributes will provide them with spokesperson or demonstrators who have more authority and credibility with consumers, more believability, and who will provide endorsements that are more memorable and better liked. These reactions should then in turn encourage consumers to buy the brand. Certainly evidence has emerged that by using physically attractive celebrities to endorse products, commercial brands are liked and remembered better, and the promotional campaign is regarded as more convincing (Kahle & Homer, 1985).

When consumers were probed in depth for their reasons for liking the American singer Cher as the endorser of Scandinavian Health Spas, they noted that she was characterized by a number of relevant attributes such as being attractive, healthy and sexy. By linking these attributes which derived from Cher's personal brand to the product brand in this case set the right tone as far as consumers were concerned (Langmeyer & Walker, 1991a). A further investigation in the same series of studies explored the impact specific celebrities might have when linked to a range of potential product types including bath towels, video-recorders and blue jeans. The celebrities being considered on this occasion were the model Christie Brinkley and singer, recording artist and actor Madonna. It emerged that when these celebrities were combined with the different product types, the images that young student consumers articulated about the products changed from those described when the products were considered independently (Langmeyer & Walker, 1991b). In each instance, the product acquired some of the perceived qualities of the celebrities.

The importance of relevant credibility

A celebrity can also make a good fit for an advertised brand when he or she has had life experiences that display special qualities that a sponsor wishes to have linked to their brand. The celebrity's life might represent a story of success despite having to overcome adversity, for example, which demonstrates to people at large that anyone can attain their dreams if they apply themselves in the right way. By associating itself with this type of narrative, a commercial brand might hope that consumers will believe that it can help them to achieve their aspirations in this way. Not only must a celebrity be seen by consumers to possess product-relevant qualities, but they must also be regarded as a source that can be trusted. Trust can be a woolly term to define but in this context it really centres on whether a celebrity has a reputation for honesty and integrity in the way they live their life and also on judgements concerning a sense that they genuinely believe in the product and/or that they possess relevant knowledge or expertise to endorse it.

Ultimately, consumers must trust a celebrity endorser. Trust operates at a deeper level than qualities such as attractiveness and likability. In this case, the presence of a celebrity who consumers believe can enhance the effectiveness of specific arguments being made about a brand in its advertising (Priester & Petty, 2003). Advertisements can vary in any case in terms of the strengths of their arguments in favour of buying a specific brand. Using a celebrity who is regarded as a trusted source because of their general reputation or because of specifically relevant expertise they bring to a particular sales context can render weak arguments stronger and strong arguments even more compelling for consumers (Siemens, Smith, Fisher & Jensen, 2008).

In general, more credible celebrity endorsers are known to have consistently positive effects on a brand's image (see Goldsmith, Lafferty & Newell, 2000; Lafferty & Goldsmith, 1999; Lafferty, Goldsmith & Newell, 2002). Highly credible celebrities can be especially effective in enhancing the corporate image of a company behind an advertised brand (Lafferty & Goldsmith, 1999). As we will see later, when a celebrity's own image takes a tumble because of a loss of form or involvement in scandal, the images and sales of associated brands and the stock value of linked corporations can also fall – sometimes dramatically.

One aspect of the effectiveness of advertising is the strength of arguments it makes in favour of the advertised brand. What is it that makes this brand special compared to others in the marketplace? Why should the consumer choose this brand? What can they expect to gain from it that will be relevant to their needs? What makes this brand such good value? These questions can be answered through product-related arguments presented within its advertising. This information can be presented anonymously or it can be backed up by a well-known public figure.

Marketing specialists have called this phenomenon the consumer's likelihood of elaborating on an advertisement. According to the 'elaboration likelihood model' consumers may devote considerable attention and cognitive effort to an advert and the information it provides about a product or they may choose not to do so. The likelihood that 'deeper processing' of an advert occurs is often determined by the nature of the product and its wider importance to the consumer. Products that have greater personal importance and products that carry greater costs of acquisition (and therefore risks in the event that the consumer makes the wrong purchase decision) tend to invite more involvement on the part of the consumer (Petty & Cacioppo, 1981, 1983, 1986a, 1986b).

Arguments can vary in their potency. Some arguments make fundamental claims about a product's performance and value, while others might simply refer to relatively superficial or cosmetic attributes. Hence, a promotion for a car might talk about its engine capacity, fuel efficiency and various enhancements designed to make it easier to drive. Equally, it might focus on the range of colours in which it is available and its exterior design features from a purely cosmetic perspective and without any reference to the relevance of these features to the way the car handles or performs.

In the first instance, consumers are being invited to consider arguments in favour of this brand based on careful reflection about its operational characteristics. This requires a degree of mental commitment on the part of the consumer in thinking through what these arguments really mean in terms of the type of vehicle being offered and its functional advantages over its competitors.

In the second instance, the colour of a car might be conceived as a relatively superficial feature that requires less mental commitment on the part of the consumer. With high expense items such as motor vehicles, most consumers generally observe greater caution and reflection before committing to a purchase, because making the wrong choice could prove to be costly.

Using a celebrity to endorse a brand of car might initially draw in the consumer's attention, but whether it will affect the brand image, intention to purchase or actual purchase decision will depend upon how the celebrity is perceived. The likability of the celebrity might be sufficient to influence a purchase decision where that decision is based on relatively superficial features of the product.

With high risk items where the wrong purchase decision can prove to be costly, however, consumers will be more likely to process arguments based on the fundamental performance-related aspects of the product. In this case, a celebrity generally has to be regarded not only as likable but also as trustworthy and as possessing relevant knowledge to be a credible source of expert information about the product and its performance characteristics. Research evidence has indicated that the presence of a celebrity endorser in an advertisement interacts with the level at which consumers process the commercial message to influence the outcome of the advertising. A celebrity can influence consumers' attitudes towards a product for a low involvement campaign, but this celebrity effect does not materialize in high involvement campaigns. Similarly, celebrities can enhance consumers' ability to remember a product under low involvement conditions but not under high involvement conditions (Petty, Cacioppo & Schmann, 1983).

The importance of expertise is underpinned by ensuring that the celebrity endorser is a relevant choice for the particular brand. Do the brand and celebrity make a good fit in terms of the perceived relevance of the celebrity's known expertise? (see Martin, 1996). The expertise of the endorser may derive from their intrinsic qualities which, in the case of a celebrity, may be publicly well known. Hence, the use of a top sports performer to endorse sportswear makes sense in that the celebrity is expected to have specialist insights into what types of sports clothing is best suited to particular sporting activities (Kamins, 1989).

The goodness of fit can also be established if the celebrity is known for a particular talent and this activity is related to the functions of the product being endorsed. The most straightforward example of this type of relationship is the use of a sports star to endorse sports merchandise – clothing or equipment (Hsu & McDonald, 2002). Where sports stars are used to promote other product categories, such as cosmetics, motor vehicles, financial products, their credibility may progressively diminish the larger perceived gap between the nature of the advertised product and the activity for which the celebrity is known (Daneshary & Schwer, 2000).

Of course, stereotyped celebrity-brand associations can become conditioned among consumers if advertisers adopt repetitive patterns of endorsement. One manifestation of this phenomenon is the discovery that male celebrities tend to be used more with products that have specific functional benefits and require not just visual demonstration but also verbal explanation. Female celebrities, in contrast, are used to endorse products designed to produce certain physical or social benefits. These female endorsers are therefore used to demonstrate the outcomes of using the products but do not provide an explanation as to why the endorsed brand is best (Stafford, Spears & Chung-Kue, 2003).

The price of multiple brand endorsements

Some celebrities are extremely popular and therefore find themselves in considerable demand from sponsors. Where a celebrity has many endorsement contracts or sponsor associations running at the same time, questions have been raised about whether this dilutes their consumer capital? Before a major sexual scandal tarnished his public image, champion golfer Tiger Woods had many sponsorship links to global brands, including American Express, Nike and Rolex. During the early part of the twenty-first century, film actress Mila Jovovich had several concurrent brand endorsement contracts with L'Oreal, Banana Republic, Christian Dior, Calvin Klein and Donna Karan. Marketing researchers have produced mixed evidence on whether it is better for a celebrity to endorse lots of products or to stick to just one brand.

Research by Carolyn Tripp and her colleagues a few years earlier indicated that once a celebrity had passed a threshold of four concurrent brand endorsements, their consumer capital declined (Tripp, Jensen & Carlson, 1994). She conducted in-depth interviews with consumers to probe their opinions about celebrities who endorsed many different products as compared with those who endorsed only one product. There were some indications that consumers questioned the trustworthiness of celebrities who promiscuously endorsed multiple products. This finding however was then undermined by further insights from the same consumers that they did not ordinarily pay much heed to how many products a specific celebrity did or did not endorse. Indeed, it seems likely that this is something most consumers are not consciously registering in terms of their evaluations of whether a specific celebrity represents a credible endorser.

The last observation has been reinforced by research conducted in Australia by Andrew Redenbach of Griffith University (Redenbach, 1999). He invited undergraduate students to give their opinions about two advertisements with celebrity endorsers. One of these advertisements for Vodaphone featured American actor Michael Richards (who played a prominent character in the popular US situation-comedy Seinfeld). The second advertisement promoted Gatorade a sports drink and was endorsed by Michael Jordan, the Famous American basketball star. Jordan was known to be an endorser of multiple products at this time, while Richards was known only to endorse one product. Initial findings indicated that the fact that Michael Jordan endorsed many products in no way diminished his capital as a celebrity endorser for these young Australian consumers. Indeed, as a source, he was rated more highly than was Michael Richards. When probed about it, these students also estimated that Jordan endorsed a significantly larger number of products than did Richards. Even so, many members of the sample had no accurate impression of how many products either of these two celebrities actually endorsed, and the estimates they did provide were therefore based largely on guesswork or perhaps were influenced by different public profiles of the two celebrities which in this instance had not been separately controlled.

Advantages of one or multiple celebrity endorsers

Some campaigns use more than one celebrity in a single campaign. These may be featured in a series of distinct promotional messages or they may appear together within the same message. Reebok launched a campaign of this sort in 2005 that featured famous sports personalities from different countries (Allen Iverson, Kelly Holmes), though mostly from the United States. They also included music stars and movie stars (Jay-Z, 50 Cent, Lucy Liu).

One reason for multiple celebrity campaigns can be a presumption that specific celebrities will vary in their appeal to different consumer sub-groups within the overall target market. Another presumption is that multiple well-known celebrities will make the campaign more memorable. Psychological theory about human memory would seem to support this presumption. Often the trick in memory is not in the strength of the original learning, but in whether specific memories can be retrieved at a later date. Memories for entities such as brands may be stored as images and verbal descriptions. Hence, specific descriptive terms or images can later serve to trigger memory when they appear in our environment. The richer and more varied the array of such trigger points, the greater the likelihood that the associated brand will spring to top of mind compared to its competitors (see Martindale, 1991; Meyers-Levy, 1989; Sheth, Mittal & Newman, 1999).

Celebrities might represent potentially powerful memory triggers because they also have a rich array of attributes associated with them, many of which may represent qualities that consumers admire or value in themselves. The use of more than one celebrity with this memory triggering potential might create a wide array of brand-related associate attributes rendering the brand very memorable (see Wells, Burnett & Moriarty, 1989).

Breaking into new markets

Using a well-known celebrity can also help brands to enter new markets where they are unknown. Through association with a celebrity who already has a high and positive profile in a new market, the brand's marketers will hope more quickly to attain a high profile for the brand (Erdogan, 1999). One prime example of this approach was the global advertising strategy adopted by Pizza Hut in the mid-1990s, in seeking to establish a worldwide profile, in using such diverse celebrity endorsers as American power couple Ivana and Donald Trump, models Cindy Crawford and Linda Evangelista and former Russian premier Mikhail Gorbachev and his grand-daughter Anastasia. In one commercial, Crawford and Evangelista were seen engaging in a squabble over a pizza in the catwalk.

This technique of seeking to have a celebrity's qualities rub off on a brand is used by many large multinational corporations. Nike's marketing strategy, for instance, has been fundamentally characterized by their use of famous sports personalities as endorsers of their brands. Nike seeks to persuade consumers of sports merchandise to buy into the brands that are linked to their favourite sports heroes and heroines. In this way ordinary consumers can seek to become a little more like their sports role models – even if they cannot display their sporting talents, they can adopt part of their persona by wearing the same clothing brands or using the same branded sports equipment. There is also a strong emotional component to all of this. Famous sports stars can evoke the emotions experienced by their fans at sports events at which these stars compete. Marketing campaigns then often feature these same sports stars in action sequences that mirror their competitive performances in order to trigger those emotions in direct association with the featured advertised brands (Katz, 1994; Willigan, 1992).

Another spin-off benefit to sponsors of their association with celebrity endorsers is that they may often benefit from free publicity linked to the popularity of these endorsers. If an ingrained mental association of a celebrity to a brand develops in the public's consciousness – such as, for example, that between former footballer Gary Lineker and Walker's Crisps – non-marketing-related public appearances by that celebrity could have brand value for the sponsor. If that additional publicity enhances the overall popularity of the celebrity, the brand will accrue additional 'rub-off' effect merely through association, even if actual promotional appearances of that celebrity with the brand tail off (Copeland, Frisby & McCarville, 1996).

The manifestations of celebrity consumer capital

Amos, Holmes and Strutton (2008) conducted a meta-analysis of 32 studies concerned with celebrity endorsement effects. The effects covered by these studies included purchase intention, attitude to brand, attitude to advertisement, believability of brand-related endorsements and brand recall or recognition. Some of this research also examined effects on actual purchase behaviour. A meta-analysis takes the original studies and aggregates across their findings to estimate the overall average strengths of relationships between specific celebrity endorsement characteristics and consumers' reactions to brands. In other words, Amos and his colleagues tried to measure the average effect size of specific celebrity attributes.

Most important of all to the outcome of celebrity endorsement for a brand was the occurrence of negative information about the celebrity. If a celebrity's image became tarnished, this could override any other celebrity attributes in terms of how consumers subsequently responded to a brand endorsed by the celebrity. The second most important celebrity factor was trustworthiness, followed by expertise, and attractiveness. Much further behind in the size of their effects were celebrity credibility, familiarity and likability. The performance of the celebrity was the least important factor.

Celebrity endorsement and consumer awareness of the brand

Part of ensuring that an advertised brand stands out is to make it more memorable to consumers. Celebrity endorsers have been found to enhance advertising message recall (Friedman & Friedman, 1979). Celebrities can also help consumers remember brand names (Petty, Cacioppo & Schuman, 1983). The effect of celebrity endorsers on making brands stand out can be especially effective with younger adult consumers. Those aged 18 to 25 years seem to have their attention drawn to adverts by the presence of a celebrity endorser more than most (Biswas et al., 2009). Older consumers tend to have their attention drawn more to product-related information that to the person speaking on behalf of it. This varying sensitivity to celebrities in advertisements among younger and older consumers might signal variances on the importance of image with increased age. Younger consumers are drawn to brands that are defined as having image-relevant features, whereas this type of image consciousness is no so acute among older consumers.

These processes differ in the mechanisms through which celebrity endorsement works can be further explained through one widely recognized model of consumer persuasion – the elaboration likelihood model (Petty & Cacioppo, 1986). According to this theory, there are two pathways to persuading consumers to like and eventually to consume a brand: the central route and the peripheral route.

The central pathway involves providing consumers with rational information about why a particular brand is worth buying over others. It presents a series of arguments designed to persuade consumers that this brand is best because of its intrinsic qualities. Hence, if the brand is a washing up liquid, what makes it more effective than other brands of its type? Does it wash the dishes more effectively? Do you need to use less of it to get the same results? Is it kinder to your hands – assuming you have not got a dish washer? Is it cheaper? Thus, at a practical or functional level, there are reasons for choosing this brand over others. Research has shown that the central pathway to persuasion works best with highly motivated consumers who go to the effort of making comparisons between brands at this level of detail. For consumers who are not motivated to take such factors into account, detailed factual information about products goes over their heads and has little effect on their decision making.

The peripheral pathway takes a different approach and makes different assumptions about consumers. It assumes that consumers for some products are less attracted and persuaded to buy because of their functional qualities and more interested in a product if it enhances their social image or lifestyle. Hence, presenting a brand alongside a celebrity endorser for instance might be sufficient to make the brand stand out. There is less interest in whether that brand is actually better than others in a functional sense and indeed this is rendered unimportant as a factor if the brand conveys subtle messages about social or lifestyle success that consumers covet.

The peripheral pathway can be especially significant to certain classes of brand such as luxury brands. This effect can cut across product markets. This approach has proven to be particularly effective with luxury fashion brands that have liberally linked themselves to major celebrities including global film stars, music artists and sports personalities. In some cases, celebrity and brand become tightly inter-connected with the brand being named after the celebrity. Thus, the Italian fashion designer Armani developed a blazer named after soccer player David Beckham. Rival fashion group Dolce and Gabbana then used Beckham as an inspiration for their own luxury men's range (Dolce & Gabbana, 2005). Some consumer research indicated however that Beckham was not always perceived to make a good fit, image-wise, for this luxury brand. There was no doubting his fame and success both in his primary sport and off-field activities. He was seen however as a sportsman made good from a lower socio-economic status background and who therefore did not have the social status of the type of young professional males usually associated with this type of brand (Schroder & Mai, 2006).

Celebrity endorsement and brand identity

Celebrities not only raise the profile of brands, but can also help brands establish a distinctive identity (McCracken, 1989). The main factor underpinning successful use of a celebrity in an advertising campaign is the reputation and credibility of the celebrity in question. If a celebrity is well known and has widespread popularity advertisers hope that some of that positive public opinion will rub off onto any brand with which the celebrity is connected. If the celebrity also has expert status that is relevant to the brand, then brand image can be further enhanced and it might be hoped by advertisers that their advertising message is likely to be taken more seriously by consumers. For example, a famous and well-respected chef may be regarded as having special credibility in relation to an advertisement for a food brand. Even where there is no expert relevance, the general likability of the celebrity alone might be enough to make consumers take more notice of any advertisement in which that icon appears.

A lot of focus has been placed on the direct transfer of celebrity attributes to the brand. This direct link between celebrity and brand is not the only route through which celebrity endorsement might have positive impact on the brand. Ronald

Goldsmith and his colleagues at Florida State University constructed a test in which consumers' responses to different versions of a Mobile Oil Corporation advertisement were measured (Goldsmith, Lafferty, & Newel, 2000). Goldsmith began by extracting a genuine advertisement for Mobile that had appeared in the Wall Street Journal. Mobile was regarded as having a distinct corporate brand identity, separate from that of its products, based on its reputation as an oil company that had become established over any years. Interest here therefore centred on the potential influence on consumers' perceptions of the brand and the way it was advertised if the company was an endorser and what would happen if a celebrity endorser of trusted status was also used alongside the company name. Goldsmith and his co-workers constructed a celebrity version of the Mobile advert that featured an endorsement by noted news broadcaster Tom Brokaw.

A sample of students and adults related in some way to the students was split between these two conditions. All participants gave a number of verbal ratings via a questionnaire of the brand and the advertisement they had seen. The researchers found that more positive evaluations of the Mobile brand in the advertisements were predicted by longer established positive opinions of Mobile as a company. The image of the celebrity endorser did not enhance perceptions of advertised brand, but they did lead to more positive opinions about the advertisement. A higher corporate image predicted not only more positive impressions of the Mobile brand as it appeared in the advertisement, but also for the advertisement. Furthermore, having better established impressions of Mobile was significantly linked to stronger purchase intentions regarding Mobile products. Celebrity endorsement did not directly predict stronger purchase intentions, but was believed to have an indirect influence here in that liking of the advertisement (which the celebrity did enhance) is known to make consumers more likely to want to purchase advertised brands.

What is clear then is that celebrities can add value to brands, but this is not guaranteed through simple association. Sponsors must choose the right celebrity for their brand and then the celebrity should be used in the most effective way (Misra, 1990). Some celebrities make a better fit than others for specific brands. This matching of celebrity to brand is in turn associated with the type of product or service being advertised and the typical level of involvement consumers normally have with it. If the product or service is something consumed on a regular basis and that is relatively inexpensive and therefore presents minimal risk to consumers, it may invoke little mental effort in purchase decision making (Petty, Cacioppo & Schumann, 1983).

With promotions for such products and services consumers are more likely to engage in some form of peripheral processing. In this setting, the mere presence of an attractive celebrity may be sufficient to add value to a brand. In contrast, if the product or service represents a commodity that consumers need to think about because it costs more to purchase or because to make the right brand decisions has potential social capital for the consumer, central processing of arguments to purchase is more likely to occur. In this case, the celebrity must be used to do more than simply appear with the brand. He or she must be able to present compelling arguments for its use. To do this effectively, consumers must believe that the celebrity represents a credible source in this setting.

Finding a celebrity who makes a good fit with a brand can magnify the potentially positive effects on consumers' feelings about the brand, memories for its attributes and intention to purchase by enhancing the credibility of the endorsement message (Kamins & Gupta, 1994). Finding the right match-up between celebrity endorser and the advertised commodity has to be thought through at more than one level. In the first place, the advertiser must have confidence that the celebrity is the right type of person to endorse a product or service of a particular type. The celebrity's reputation is founded in whatever activity he or she is known for. While some celebrities may be so famous that their fame transcends the need to be concerned about match-up, this is not true for most of them. A celebrity known for their success in sports might be seen as entirely appropriate to endorse sports equipment. They may also be seen as suitable endorsers for certain lines of clothing brands and cosmetics. They might be regarded as less relevant as source of financial advice. In contrast, a successful business entrepreneur might make a perfect fit as an endorser of financial products, but why should they have any special credibility as endorsers of cosmetics?

Once a good fit has been found, a commercial brand can experience significant benefits in terms of its own public profile and the strength of its position in the marketplace. A bad fit can have the reverse effect. Where there is congruence between the celebrity and the advertised brand, consumers are likely to develop more positive opinions about the brand. Where the fit is seen as poor, not only can the brand's image suffer, but so too can that of the celebrity. This is because consumers might begin to ask why the celebrity has endorsed a product they would seem to have no special expertise about (Kamins & Gupta, 1994; Till et al., 2006).

Whether celebrities prove to be more effective in persuading consumers to make purchases that involve high cost as opposed to ones that are inexpensive remains unclear. Evidence has emerged that celebrity endorsers were effective and may be better placed promoting products that carried high financial or psychological risk for consumers (Friedman & Friedman, 1978). This practice can work well with products such as computers and services such as management consultancy (Kamins et al., 1989), Elsewhere researchers found that consumers are more influenced by celebrity endorsers when products are relatively inexpensive (Callcoat & Phillips, 1996).

Within the advertising industry, practitioners make a range of judgements about celebrities before deciding to use them. Advertising professionals weigh up celebrities in terms of a range of attributes and generally seek out those public figures who not only have many positive characteristics, but who also seem to make the best for the type of product or service being marketed (Erdogan, Baker & Tagg, 2001b; Miciak & Shanklin, 1994).

For advertisers it is not simply a matter of deciding whether a celebrity is attractive or credible, although these are important factors. They also need to be sure of two other crucial factors. The first of these is that the celebrity makes the right fit in terms of product or service type and the aspirations that advertiser has for the brand image that will best ensure the brand stands out from its competitors. The second factor is that the celebrity's own brand strength has not been diluted by endorsing lots of other products or services.

If all these conditions are in place, then advertisers have greater confidence about using a specific celebrity. There is a presumption here that brands can be thought of in similar terms to people. That is, brands have personalities defined by their specific qualities, some of which are functional and others reputational or symbolic. The functional qualities of brands can be described and brand reputations grow among consumers who as brand users find that the brand delivers what was promised in its advertising. Other symbolic attributes can be important in helping the brand develop distinctiveness in the marketplace by associating it with specific values or lifestyles that consumers hold in high regard (Fortini-Campbell, 1992). Celebrity endorsers, when chosen skilfully, can play a critical part in the development of distinctive symbolism around a brand (Domzal & Kerman, 1992; McCracken, 1989).

Choosing the celebrity with the best consumer capital for the brand

It is important that advertisers make the right choices when deciding to use celebrities within their advertising campaigns. Either the celebrity in question must be regarded as having brand capital that derives from their expertise or because they are currently famous and well-liked. Some negativity might be tolerated, but this will depend upon the behaviour associated with it. A bad boy soccer player for example may attract attention because of his on-field antics, but this might not undermine his brand value if he is known to behave properly off the field. A celebrity who engages in scandalous or criminal activity, however, might become too high a risk.

If a celebrity is perceived by consumers to have a background or character that makes them relevant to a particular product or service, this will enhance their effectiveness. If an endorser – no matter how well known – is used who is regarded by consumers as lacking in relevance to the brand being advertised, the outcome can be the reverse of what the advertiser hopes for. Instead of making consumers more likely to buy the brand, they may be less likely to want to do so (Till & Busler, 1998).

When celebrity endorsers are perceived by consumers to have relevance – whether in terms of communicating convincingly about brand functionality or its social image significance – they also become seen as more credible as spokespersons. This credibility may then extend to the advertised brand which is in turn regarded as more credible for making an appropriate choice of spokesperson (Till & Busler, 1998).

It is important that advertisers understand that negative celebrity information can stick in consumers' memories more powerfully than positive information (Folkes, 1988; Kensinger & Corkin, 2003; Ybarra & Stephan, 1996). Moreover, if a celebrity has enjoyed positive public opinion and then falls from grace, the new negative image may be more negatively evaluated than if that public figure had not previously enjoyed high status as people feel let down.

Finding the right match between celebrity endorser and brand leads to considerations about what types of endorsers are likely to work best. Many celebrity endorsers tend to be from the world of sport. Other celebrity types include actors, comedians, fashion models, musicians and singers, other entertainers, television presenters, and other public figures. The appeal of top sports performers derives from their fame, their special abilities and the fact that they often look really good physically. In their professional lives they also often already have the status of role models. This means that ordinary people want to be just like them. They also have a significant degree of versatility in terms of their relevance to a range of product types. Apart from their expert relevance in the context of advertising sports-related products, they also have relevance across other domains such as cosmetics, toiletries, clothing, certain foods and drinks, and other lifestyle-defining products. Indeed, looking even further, sports celebrity endorsers could add value to just about any product or service domain where brands are promoting themselves in terms of their excellence (Miciak & Shanklin, 1994).

Sports performers can be differentiated in terms of the sports in which they compete. Potential fan bases could vary here depending upon the relative popularity of the sport among people in general. Sports popularity for some sports is defined in terms of the numbers of ordinary people that participate themselves but is more usually defined according to the traditional support fan base that is often linked to the media coverage a particular sport usually attracts (Martin, 1996). Another approach to the classification of sports-related endorsers is to differentiate between those who are well known and also liked and those who are well known but disliked. In other words, there are heroes and anti-heroes (Stuart, 2007). Joshua Stuart of the Sacred Heart University in Connecticut developed a Celebrity Hero Matrix in which sports performers were classified in terms of being high or low in celebrity status and high or low in hero status. He argued that being high on both scales was the secret to finding an effective celebrity endorser (Stuart, 2007).

One problem with sports celebrity endorsers is that a few of the highest profile among them have become over-used. This runs the risk of a dilution of their impact for individual brands. As with other classes of celebrity, any scandal in their private or professional lives can damage their public image which in turn can reduce their added value as endorsers. Another risk factor with sports performers however is that their brand capital can be significantly and irreparably damaged if they suffer career-threatening injuries or a substantial dip in form.

Consumers' decision making can be influenced by their attitudes towards the product and the advertisement. It can be shaped by the perceived value of the brand being promoted which can be further defined in terms of its intrinsic qualities and reputation and perceived relevance to the consumer in terms of functionality and personal image. Research carried out among 400 American college students asked them to make a series of judgements about the goodness of fit between a sports personality endorser and a brand. In this case, the sports celebrity was female tennis star Maria Sharapova and the advertised brand was Canon PowerShot Cameras (see www.youtube.com/watch?v=sW8z4qa7boU). The extent to which the endorser was perceived to be a good fit for the brand was not influenced by the degree to which the respondents were interested in tennis, but it did have some relationship to the perceived value of the brand. When the brand was perceived to have personal value, this in turn enhanced intentions to purchase. Thus, there was some evidence here that using a celebrity perceived by consumers to be a relevant and credible product endorser could positively influence the personal value of the advertised brand and indirectly influence the likelihood of future purchase (Braunstein & Zhang, 2005a, 2005b).

Dix, Phau and Pougnet (2010) reported a self-completion questionnaire survey among young people in Australia that found that sports celebrity endorsers could influence young consumers' intentions to purchase specific brands. Celebrity endorsers could encourage brand switching to the endorsed brands, promote positive word-of-mouth endorsements among consumers and enhance brand loyalty.

Braunstein-Minkova of Towson University, USA and her colleagues (2011) investigated celebrity endorser-brand congruence. Their focus was placed on the use of different sports star endorsers and their perceived relevance to the products being marketed in terms of expertise and credibility. Was endorser relevance a critical factor underpinning its effects on consumers' intention to purchase specific brands? They developed a five-factor model that derived from consumers' responses to a 42-item scale that measured perceptions of identification with specific athletes and sports, perceptions of product attributes, value and likelihood of purchase. This model was regarded as being useful in relation to determining whether a sports celebrity made a good fit in terms of endorsement of non-sports brands (Braunstein-Minkova, Zhang & Trail, 2011).

Another choice advertisers make is between whether to use male or female endorsers. Sometimes the choice may be easy because the product being advertised is gender specific in its target market. Assuming it is a female product, the question then remains with some female celebrities – those from sports for example – whether to focus on a performance angle or a beauty angle in the way they are used. Some marketing experts have argued that the focus on feminine beauty with female sports celebrity endorsers will only be effective where this is relevant to the type of product being advertised (Kamins, 1990). Thus, this approach may work well for beauty and body-care products. For other product types however it might be safer to use female sports celebrities in achievement-related or performance-related narratives (Thompson, 1990).

Celebrity endorsers do not always produce the outcomes that advertisers hope for. In a study with young Belgian consumers, Roozen and Claeys (2010) found that an anonymous, non-celebrity endorser could prove to be just as effective, if not more so, for some products. They compared the use of no-endorser, a non-celebrity endorser and a celebrity endorser for a confectionery brand, a beauty product and a laptop computer. A celebrity proved to be more effective than no endorser in enhancing attitudes towards the brand and the advertisement, but was not better than a non-celebrity endorser. This result pre-tested whether the celebrity endorser was rated as a good or poor product match. A similar result emerged for the beauty product. Although in this case, the researchers noted that the non-celebrity endorser in this case was an attractive female model and that image used showed part of her body only, including part of her breast, whereas with celebrity endorsers, the whole body was visible. The sexual objectification of the non-celebrity model might therefore have introduced a new variable into the mix that drew in consumers' attention.

For the laptop product, which because of its technical nature was also regarded potentially as a higher involvement item for consumers, meaning that they would be more likely to pay attention to detailed product-related information, neither the celebrity nor non-celebrity endorsers enhanced consumers' attitudes towards the brand or the advertising of it.

Celebrities and brand purchase

The ultimate impact of celebrity endorsement is that it will encourage consumers to purchase and use the brand. The purpose of advertising is to convert the firm's investment in promotional messages into increased consumer interest and purchase that in turn enhances brand equity. The use of celebrity endorsers is believed to add further value to this process (Keller, 1993). This is the theory but in practice some celebrity endorsers simply do not work out. Sometimes even the most popular of sports celebrities fail to deliver. One example of this outcome involved Shaquille O'Neal who was dropped by Reebok for delivering poor sales returns despite enjoying a continuing positive media profile (Bhonslay, 1997).

Despite the belief by many advertising practitioners that celebrity endorsers bring brand benefits culminating in increased purchases, the research evidence has not always supported this proposition. The use of celebrity endorsers may be less significant than are the types of argument made in favour of a brand. Strong arguments can enhance brand attractiveness regardless of the fame of the endorser (Sanbonmatsu & Kardes, 1988). Further, some celebrity endorsers can actually have the opposite effect from that desired and can put consumers off buying the brand (Tripp et al., 1994).

Martin and Bush (2000) surveyed 13- to 18-year-olds in the United States. Respondents were asked to estimate the degree of influence exerted on their consumer purchase intentions by their father, mother, favourite athlete and favourite entertainer. The study examined different kinds of purchase behaviours. Both family and media role models were identified by these teenagers as having some influence in this context. Parents were regarded as most important, but other role models were not without influence.

Dix (2009) ran an investigation in Australia that was originally conducted by Bush, Martin and Bush (2004) in the United States. Bush and colleagues studied teenagers aged 13 to 18 years. Dix studied a young adult sample aged 17 to 25 years. The Bush sample was recruited from high schools and junior high schools in the mid-south of the United States. The Dix sample was drawn from students registered at a large university in Western Australia. Thus, both samples were convenience samples and were not representative of the wider population of either country.

Three original hypotheses were established by Bush et al. These hypotheses predicted that teenagers' athlete role model influence would be related to product switching and complaint behaviour; and to favourable word-of-mouth opinions about a product; and to brand loyalty. Data were collected via a self-completion questionnaire. A role model influence scale was adapted by Bush and colleagues from an earlier study. This scale required respondents to indicate their level of agreement with a series of attitudinal statements about 'their favourite athlete'. A further derived agree–disagree scale was used to measure behavioural intentions regarding products and brands. The original items were modified to include a specific reference to 'my favourite athlete' with respondents being asked to attribute influence of that role model in relation to described product or brand-related behaviours.

Both scales were subjected to factor analysis which attempts to find whether there is a specific structure to a list of evaluations in terms of how they are inter-related. This analysis confirmed that the role-model-influence items loaded onto a single factor while the behavioural-intentions items clustered into three distinct factors. These factors represented the following constructs: favourable word-of-mouth; complaining and switching behaviour; and brand loyalty and price sensitivity. These factor analysis results were confirmed by Dix in his replication study.

In the original study, Bush et al. used regression analysis to link athlete role model influences to each of the three purchase intentions and behaviour factors. Role model perceptions emerged as significant predictors of positive word-of-mouth and brand loyalty factors, but not of complaining behaviour. Dix found significant relationships between role model perceptions and all three factor-dependent variables.

Bush et al. discuss their results as if they have uncovered evidence of specific effects of sports celebrity role models on teenager's brand perceptions and intended behaviours. However, it is debatable as to whether they have even come close to demonstrating such links. The weakness of this study (and of the replication run by Dix) drives primarily from its core measures. We need more precise measurement of favourite athlete. In this study, the measure that is used is too generic. The dependent variables are equally questionable. The items used in this scale measured intentions which may have not validity in terms of predicting or representing actual behaviour. Not only this, but their wording required respondents to make a causal attribution. A typical item was 'my favourite athlete influences me to buy fewer products from certain companies'. How does the average respondent even know this? What is the magnitude of this effect, even if it does occur?

Zahaf and Anderson (2008) tested the effects of an advertising campaign in which a local celebrity was used as the endorser. They were especially interested in the goodness of fit between the celebrity and the advertised product. In this study, 198 students were randomly assigned to view a TV commercial for an MP3 player that was produced in different versions, with and without a celebrity endorser. In the celebrity version the endorser described the product and its different attributes and functions.

The researchers established whether participants already owned an MP3 player and had them provide a psychographic profile that provided more information about their music interests and involvement with the product. Evidence emerged that both versions of the commercial made these students more willing to buy the MP3 product. The presence of a celebrity endorser however strengthened this effect and made these young consumers even more likely to say they wanted to buy the product. This was true in particular if the celebrity was regarded as a credible source. The perceived attractiveness, similarity to self and expertise of the source were important factors here also, regardless of whether the spokesperson for the product was a celebrity or not.

Makgosa (2010) surveyed the purchase intentions of 200 Botswana teenagers to investigate the potential influence of celebrity role models from television. Television celebrities had strong consumer capital and their association with specific products was sufficient to reinforce the attractiveness of these items to a point where these young Botswana consumers would even switch from another brand.

Cross-cultural celebrity consumer capital

When celebrities were first used to endorse commercial brands, there was a largely intuitive presumption that positive benefits would occur. There was little systematic testing of the impact of celebrity endorsers. As celebrity endorsement became more widespread and as the emergence of a competitive market for the acquisition of the best known celebrities pushed up the costs of hiring them, more sponsors sought evidence that this was money being well spent in terms of the achievement of business objectives. Questions started being asked about whether a celebrity endorser did enhance brand image and attract consumers' attention? Did such endorsers trigger increased sales and market share (McDonald, 1991; Marshall & Cook, 1992)?

Even at the level of the individual consumer, evidence emerged that using celebrity or non-celebrity endorsers made little difference to what consumers felt about an advertisement or about the advertised brand and did not make much difference either to their intentions to purchase the brand (Mehta, 1994).

There has been much debate about the power of celebrities to enhance the images of advertised brands with which they are associated. In some countries, such as China, regulators have become so concerned about the influence of celebrity endorsers that they have banned their use for some categories of products such as pharmaceuticals. One reason for doing this was that many drugs' companies used well-known Chinese celebrities to speak positively about the beneficial effects of drugs that in some instances proved to be gross exaggerations of the truth (People's Daily Online, 2007).

Despite these concerns, celebrity endorsement has continued to be widely used in most national markets, China included (see Chan, Hung, Tse & Tse, 2008). Chinese marketers have exhibited a strong preference for celebrity endorsers in advertisements targeted at the youth market (Chan, 2008). There is a strong belief in China that celebrities can enhance the effectiveness of advertisements through the process of 'value transfer'. This means that celebrities, such as well-known sports stars, are characterized by strong values of personal courage, striving and success. Where these have relevance to a brand, through association with the right celebrity, such values can rub off and define the brand as well. The risk associated with this marketing strategy is that if the celebrity suffers damage to their own image through poor performance or scandal or reduced visibility through injury and illness, the brand can also experience an image downturn (Gu, Hung & Tse, 2008).

The values capital of celebrity endorsers can also be linked to broader strategies of indigenous values maintenance. In markets such as China in which collectivist values are held in higher regard than individualistic values, celebrity endorsers are selected for marketing campaigns that represent those values the advertisers seek to promote among its young people (Hung & Li, 2007; Hung, Li & Belk, 2007).

Celebrities can thus be used to endorse traditional values or to introduce and promote new values. As the Chinese economy has grown, for example, the emergence of an affluent and large middle class has created a bigger market for luxury goods and premium brands (Zhou & Belk, 2004). These commodities are particularly attractive to young professional people who have become increasingly global in their outlook and materialistic in their aspirations (Hung et al., 2007).

The goodness of fit between the celebrity and brand can also be determined by type of promotional messages being presented. Advertising messages that play to traditional values of the national market, for example, are best presented by celebrities from the same domestic culture (Choi et al., 2005). Of course even the use of local celebrities can run out of steam for local consumers if a particular celebrity endorses a lot of different brands (La Eerie & Sejung, 2005).

Kineta Hung and his colleagues of the Hong Kong Baptist University surveyed more than 1,000 Chinese consumers recruited from a national panel of more than 200,000 registered participants. They measured respondents' level of identity with two well-known Chinese celebrities – Andy Lau, an entertainer and Yao Ming a sports star. In each case, respondents were questioned about the extent to which they had a curiosity about each of these celebrities and enjoyed finding out more about their lives and then whether they felt more deeply connected to these celebrities and empathized with their successes and failures. In another part of the survey, respondents were asked to evaluate brands that each celebrity had endorsed. The findings showed that interest in these celebrities can occur at a fairly superficial level of expressing a general curiosity about their lives or at an emotionally much more involved level. Strong feelings at either level about each celebrity rubbed off also on the opinions consumers held about the brands endorsed by these two public figures (Hung et al., 2007).

It was also hypothesized that if consumers liked a celebrity more and that this then enhanced their opinion about brands endorsed by that celebrity this would also increase the intention of consumers to purchase those brands. Hung and his colleagues found that this was true. However, the effect of celebrity endorsement on intention to buy a brand was reduced if the celebrity in question endorsed lots of brands. The brand promotion capital of the celebrity, it seems, is diluted if that celebrity associates their name with a lot of different brands. Thus, celebrities can over-endorse and in doing so they lose credibility as brand endorsers with consumers. This outcome though can also vary between celebrities. In this study, the over-endorsement effect was much stronger for the sports personality than for the entertainment personality (Hung et al., 2007).

The choice of the right celebrity can become even more critical for campaigns conducted on an international scale. Many large global brands are marketed in countries where cultural value systems differ and where consumers' psychological orientations towards products and services can vary. In global advertising campaigns therefore advertisers must ensure they do not use promotional messages that cause offence. It cannot be presumed that because a campaign worked well in the United States or United Kingdom that it will also be equally well received in China or Saudi Arabia (de Mooij, 2010).

The need to ensure that global campaigns can work equally effectively in markets with different cultural values applies also to the choice of celebrity endorser. This decision does not simply come down to selecting a celebrity who is known in different countries, but also one who represents symbolic values that are important in all the national markets in which a brand seeks to establish a footprint (see Choi et al., 2005).

One of the principal divisions between cultures in the West and those in the East (i.e. Middle East and Far East) is in the relative prominence of individualism versus collectivism. Individualism represents a group of values that place an emphasis on personal striving and achievement, individual self-fulfilment and freedom of opportunity and being successful in life for oneself. Collectivism places greater value on maintaining strong family and community ties, seeking harmony and fulfilment of group needs rather than individual ones. Individualistic communities tend to be political and economically democratic and believe in allowing markets to have freedom to operate openly without heavy government-imposed legislation and restrictions. Collectivistic cultures tend to be politically more autocratic and hierarchical and operate with markets that are centrally more closely controlled (Hofstede, 1984; de Mooij, 2010).

For maximum effectiveness, advertisers must ensure that their commercial campaigns represent or reflect the values of the market communities they have targeted and at the very least that their commercial messages do not offend those communities. Using campaigns in Eastern markets that promote Western values can result in those advertisements being dismissed as irrelevant to local mores and needs. Hence, promoting brands with messages that focus on individual striving may work very well in an open market society as the United States in which personal success is valued, but not in markets such as Korea or Japan where consumers are concerned about family and community harmony and integrity and doing things that benefit their social group before themselves (Belk & Bryce, 1986; Han & Shavitt, 1994).

Are kids influenced by celebrity endorsers?

The answer appears to be 'yes they can be influenced'. However, the power of celebrity endorsement – even with young consumers – depends on how they are used and how they are presented. As we have seen already, celebrity endorsers have 'persuasion capital' if they are regarded as credible and relevant to the sales pitch being made in an advertisement. Hence, if a decision is taken to use a sports star as endorser, this strategy will work best if this type of celebrity appears to consumers to be relevant to the commodity being promoted. Thus, it makes sense when advertising toy cars to use a celebrity who in his professional life is a successful motor racer. As we have also previously seen, the status of this type of endorser can be enhanced further if they are presented in an advertisement doing what they are good at – namely performing the sport for which they are known.

In two controlled experiments Rhonda Ross and her colleagues at the University of Kansas randomly assigned American children aged 8 to 14 years to watch advertisements for toy cars with and without a celebrity endorser who was a professional motor racing driver and with or without footage of live racetrack action (Ross, Campbell, Wright, Huston, Rice & Turk, 1984). In the first study, a commercially made advertisement showed a brand of model race car endorsed by a well-known motor racing driver and included live motor racing footage. In a control condition, an alternative version of this advertisement was shown minus the endorser and real racing footage and simply showed footage of model car racing instead. In the second study a commercially made advertisement for a different brand of model racing car was selected and shown in one of four versions: with celebrity (motor racer) endorser and live footage of real motor racing; with the endorser minus the real racing footage; with the live racing footage and minus the endorser; and finally minus the endorser and racing footage. After viewing the advertisements, all participating children answered questions about the nature of the toy racing product, about the endorser and indicated their preference for this toy over other toys and games.

The presence of real racing footage in the adverts led the children to overestimate the size, speed and complexity of the toy racing car. Simply seeing the product being used on its own did not produce this effect. The boys who saw the adverts felt more strongly that the promotional message was direct at them rather than their parents when a celebrity endorser was present. The presence of the endorser also strengthened the product recommendations made in the advertisement and this effect was most pronounced among the older boys. Part of the reason for this influence could have been that the boys regarded the professional racing driver as an expert source in this context and they therefore took more note of what he said about the product.

Some evidence emerged that the presence of an endorser could increase the extent to which the boys indicated a preference for the advertised toy over other toys. This effect seemed to be mediated by whether the boys identified with the celebrity endorser. If they did not identify with him, the endorser had the greatest impact on product preference when the endorser appeared on their own and without live motor racing footage. From these findings it was clear that celebrity endorsers can alter the impact of advertisements for products aimed at children. This effect however cannot be automatically expected with all children (Ross et al., 1984).

Summary

For a long time, advertisers have adopted celebrity figures to endorse their products and services in the belief that celebrities' fame and reputations will enhance the images of advertised brands. The consumer capital of celebrity, in this context, is mediated by a number of factors of which the likability and trustworthiness of the celebrity in question are critical. A celebrity endorser must also have credibility and this feature stems not just from their professional or personal reputation but also their perceived relevance to the commercial brands with which they are linked. Even with a well-liked celebrity, his or her credentials might be challenged if they are used to promote a product or service that they might not be expected to use themselves. Or, where a celebrity is used in the case of commercial services that require special expertise that the celebrity is not known to possess. For instance, consumers might prefer to have advice about a financial service provided by someone known to have relevant specialist financial knowledge than from, say, a professional footballer who has no track record of business expertise.

Although the use of celebrities as commercial brand endorsers can attract attention to advertising campaigns and raise the public's awareness of them, such endorsements do not invariably translate directly into bigger sales or market share. Care must also be taken to ensure that any downsides to contracting a famous celebrity outweigh the benefits. A famous celebrity who is in demand and endorses many different products and services could experience wear-out in terms of their impact on consumers because they have become too ubiquitous. There is also a risk that where a celebrity is already closely associated with other high-profile commercial brands, that recruiting her or him to endorse one more could result in consumers becoming confused between brands.

The choice of celebrity must also work well across all the different markets in which a commercial brand is sold. This point is especially important for global campaigns that operate across cultures. A celebrity's consumer capital may be high in one market but low or non-existent in another. Finally, a celebrity's reputation can itself be fluid and fluctuate from one day to the next depending upon events in his or her life. When a celebrity's profile and standing professional take an upward turn, the cost of using them as endorsers might increase, but will the value they deliver in return match this increased cost? Equally, if a celebrity's reputation takes a knock, does their consumer capital respond in the same way and how quickly does this happen? Hence, there are benefits and risks that can flow from using celebrities as commercial brand endorsers. As we will see in the next chapter, another type of value can accompany celebrities in sponsorship settings, and this is their corporate capital where they can add (or subtract) value to (or from) companies that use them to promote their commercial brands or integrate celebrity brands with their commercial property.

Key points

- Celebrities have been used by product manufacturers to endorse their brands since before the era of the modern mass media.
- Celebrities are regular features of contemporary advertising.
- Advertisers believe that there is consumer capital in using celebrities in that people will be more likely to notice and to like brands that are endorsed by famous people.
- Research evidence has shown that celebrities can enhance the public profile of brands they endorse, but that this does not always work.
- Consumers need to believe that celebrities' opinions about brands are relevant to their own decision making.
- Not all celebrities are perceived as credible spokespersons for specific brands.
- Repeat exposure can enable consumers to associate specific celebrity attributes with brands being endorsed by them.
- A celebrity needs to be liked by consumers to be effective as a brand endorser, but this is not always enough. Consumers must feel they can believe and trust celebrities as well.
- The credibility of a celebrity endorser is also underpinned by whether consumers perceiver the celebrity and brand to make a good fit.
- Consumers make judgements about whether celebrities have relevant expertise to endorse a specific product.
- A celebrity can sometimes endorse too many brands such that their consumer capital becomes diluted.
- Brand endorsers do not have to be celebrities to enhance likelihood of brand purchase.

Topics for reflection

- Celebrities always represent good value as brand endorsers. Present an evidence-based case in which you argue for or against this proposition.
- Taking three case examples of measures that sponsors might use to decide whether to commission a celebrity, and analyse their strengths and weaknesses and produce a briefing paper that makes recommendations to sponsors about the best way to select the right celebrity endorsers for their needs.
- When do celebrities make poor product endorsers? Present your arguments with relevant evidence.
- What are the psychological principles that underpin consumers' reactions to celebrity endorsers? Examine relevant theories and research.
- In designing an advertising campaign to promote a brand in different parts of the world, consider the key factors marketers should take into account when using celebrity endorsers.

Further readings

Amos, C., Holmes, G., & Strutton, D. (2008). Exploring the relationship between celebrity endorser effects and advertising effectiveness: A quantitative synthesis of effect size. *International Journal of Advertising, 27*(2), 209–34.

Dix, S., Phau, I., & Pougnet, S. (2010). 'Bend it like Beckham': The influence of sports celebrities on young adult consumers. *Young Consumers: Insight and Ideas for Responsible Marketers, 11*(1), 36–46.

Pringle, H. (2004). *Celebrity sells.* Chichester, UK: John Wiley.

Roozen, I., & Claeys, C. (2010). The relative effectiveness of celebrity endorsement for print advertisement. *Review of Business and Economics, 55*(1), 76–89.

Till, B. D. (1998). Using celebrity endorsers effectively: Lessons from associative learning. *Journal of Product & Brand Management, 7*(5), 400–9.

4

The Corporate Capital of Celebrity

In examining the role played by celebrity endorsers in the context of advertising, we saw that celebrities are used to enhance the value of the promotional commercial messages about brands. Celebrities can add value to the advertising process. They have been shown to render advertisements more attention grabbing, more memorable, more credible and to enhance the brand image by rubbing off a little celebrity star dust on the brand itself. Ultimately, users of celebrity endorsers seek an even bigger return than this. If marketing campaigns are successful they will enable a firm to sell more of its products or services. If they do this and enjoy larger turnovers and profits, the capital value of firm will grow. Hence, celebrity endorsers can add value not only to brands but also to the overall value of companies.

Celebrities from the worlds of film, music, sport and television become cultural icons and role models with the power to set fashions and trends across a wide range of consumer commodity markets. Some celebrities make a point of styling themselves in distinct ways as part of their celebrity commodity image. This phenomenon is most often manifest in appearance aspects of celebrity such as clothes, cosmetics, hair care products, perfume, jewellery and accessories. There are opportunities here for celebrities to re-invent themselves stylistically and to refresh the markets in which they operate as endorsers. Perhaps the most famous example of this effect was the renaming of the Hermes Grace Kelly handbag after 1950s film icon Grace Kelly who subsequently became Princess of Monaco. More recently, Mulberry reported a 36 per cent jump in sales after model Alexa Chung was photographed with their Alexa bag, and Modalu experienced a 50-fold jump in sales after Princess Catherine's younger sister, Pippa Middleton was publicly seen carrying one of their bags (and had one named after her) (Urwin, 2013).

For some celebrities their status and prominence as endorsers can become as strong as a defining aspect of their celebrity image as their original special talents as entertainers or sports competitors. A prime example of this type of redefined celebrity image is 'Brand Beckham' comprising footballer David Beckham and his ex-pop-star, fashion designer wife, Victoria. Beckham as the power to set fashions as an endorser not only because he was a star, international professional footballer but also because of the profile attained from both his success as a ubiquitous endorser for many sponsors and from his high media-profile role as husband and father in his private life (Vincent et al., 2009).

Even as his star as a footballer has faded, Beckham has retained his global appeal and his celebrity corporate capital was still expected to be strong enough to move 150,000 shirt and boot kits bearing his name for French club Paris St Germain across a 5-month stint at the club in 2013 (Miller, 2013). Through the totality of this composite brand image, Beckham has not only helped to sell many different consumer products but also ideas about masculinity (Cashmore, 2002; Cashmore & Parker, 2003).

The potency of celebrity brands of this kind can reach a point where even non-posed shots of the famous wearing a specific brand of shirt or footwear, or carrying a branded accessory is enough to render the commercial brand highly desirable and push up consumer demand for it (Lawrence, 2009). Brand owners will pay handsomely to get the right celebrity to use or promote their brands. The big question is, do they get a good return on their investment? In this chapter, we will explore what the evidence tells us about this.

The added value of celebrity endorsements

Research evidence has begun to emerge that celebrities can bring wider business benefits than simply raising the market profiles of specific brands with which they are linked. They can actually add to the capital value of companies. The flipside of this is that where a celebrity's image takes a slide, either because of deteriorating performance or because they are embroiled in a scandal that tarnishes their reputation, the negative image effects can also rub off on the brands they endorse. Sometimes, this collateral damage can extend further and impact upon the image and financial market value attached to the company that produces the brand.

At a fundamental level, there have been calculations of the financial 'return on investment' for large corporations of specific advertising campaigns that featured a well-known celebrity as a central aspect. Jamie Oliver, the TV cook, has been employed in advertising campaigns for Sainsbury, the UK supermarket chain since 2000. By 2002, it was estimated that this campaign generated £1.2 billion of incremental revenue and that every pound sterling spent on this advertising delivered a return on investment of over £27. Walkers Crisps employed ex-professional soccer player and BBC TV sports presenter Gary Lineker as the main celebrity in a series of advertising campaigns (that often featured other celebrities in support to Lineker) from 1996. By the early 2000s, it was estimated that this advertising delivered a return on investment of £1.70 building to £5.10 for every £1 spent on advertising (see Pringle, 2004 for more information about these campaigns and others).

The problem with this type of evidence is that it does not single out the specific effect of the celebrities to the return on investment aside from other aspects of the advertising campaigns in which they featured. The impact of advertising could have been mediated, for instance, not only by celebrity capital but also by the narrative and production treatments used in the advertising and by the location and placement of advertising in different media.

Demonstrations of the economic value of celebrities for companies that hire them have derived from a methodology called 'event study'. What happens here is that marketing experts identify real world events linked to companies and then follow financial performance data used by the financial markets to evaluate their current capital value. An event such as a change in a government regulation that might make life more difficult for a business by restricting its opportunities to trade in specific markets or by placing new tax liabilities on it, that might in turn affect its profitability which will result in financial markets downgrading its future value. Similarly news that a company has made a new product breakthrough or won a massive new order could lead market analysts to upgrade its capital value. In a similar fashion, news that a well-known celebrity is to endorse a company's brands or the launch of a new advertising campaign that features a popular celebrity figure can likewise have an uplifting impact not just on the company's public profile but also its standing in the financial markets.

In studying celebrity endorsers' economic impacts upon their sponsors marketing experts have identified events such as announcements of new celebrity endorser contracts and/or the launch of new celebrity endorser campaigns and examined changes in financial performance statistics for those sponsors that occurred at the time of these events or subsequently.

Jagdish Agrawal and Kamakura Wagner of the School of Business and Economics, California State University took a sample of 110 celebrity endorsement announcements that occurred in major newspapers between 1980 and 1992 in the United States (Agrawal & Wagner, 1995). There were other cases that occurred during the same time period, but the specific dates on which it was first publicly known that a firm was hooking up with a celebrity could not be cleanly established. These cases involved 35 firms and 87 different celebrities. Around one-third of these cases mentioned the contract values to the celebrities. The researchers then obtained stock market data on the companies concerned so that they could track their financial performance after celebrity endorsement deals had been struck. They found an immediate impact in that companies that announced new celebrity endorsement deals experienced significant upturns in levels of investor interest in their stock over the next day compared with average levels of interest. This evidence suggested that investors perceived that celebrity endorsements would bring longer-term improved financial performance for the company.

These findings have been confirmed by later studies. Ding, Molchanev and Stork (2011) analysed 101 announcements of celebrity endorsement contracts made between 1996 and 2008 by firms listed in the US internet. They examined the effects of these announcements on the financial performance of the firms at the time of the announcements and subsequently. Technology industry products seemed to benefit most from these sponsorship arrangements. Some evidence emerged that these endorsement deals worked better when there was a good match between the celebrity and the product being endorsed. Celebrities can often continue to have economic and corporate capital even after their death.

The 'death effect'

Celebrity value can be calculated by the nature of the celebrity's talent, the prevalence of their popularity and also by their simple visibility in the public domain. Celebrities can also transfer value to items with which they are associated. Thus, awards that have been won by celebrities add to the celebrity's intrinsic value and the trophies that represent physical manifestations of awards also have value. Clothing that has been worn by a celebrity might have value above and beyond its standard retail cost if put on sale.

Celebrities can continue to have value after they have died. There are some celebrities that continue to attract public attention and celebrity worship and whose estates continue to make money long after they have passed on. This 'death effect' has been observed as a particularly powerful factor in the world of art and music where the outputs produced by famous artists and musicians grow in value after the death of their creators.

Celebrity worship is an established social phenomenon. Psychologists have managed to measure its strength and diversity and have discovered that its occurrence can be closely linked to specific personality types. People who display the most extreme forms of celebrity worship are often characterized by having weakly defined personal identities or find it difficult to relate to others in their regular everyday lives. Forging an attachment with a celebrity can represent a substitute for something that may be missing elsewhere in their own lives.

The fashion for nostalgia can also play a part here and even mean that some celebrities accumulate more wealth after death than when they were alive. Nostalgia takes the form of a yearning for a past age or era which can become especially acute among people dissatisfied with contemporary life. While we cannot travel back in time, despite what worshippers of Dr Who might choose to believe, we can bring by-gone times into the present through the collection of historical artefacts. When these items have once belonged to or were created by a deceased celebrity of whom we were particularly fond, they can serve to revive memories of that person and in a sense bring them back to life again. Nostalgia can be triggered by states of loneliness (Wildschut et al., 2006), but is also linked to a longing for values from the past (Holak & Havlena, 1998; Schindler & Holbrook, 2003).

Economists have found, for instance, that the worth of an artist's works or a celebrity's memorabilia gains in value after the celebrity's time of death (Ekelund et al., 2000). One reason for this is that no further outputs can generally be expected from that celebrity after death. Another factor is that celebrity-related works have nostalgia capital in that they maintain a sense of the celebrity's presence in the world and for worshippers of that celebrity represent an enduring connection to him or her. The nostalgia factor, however, can be short-lived. Extensive media coverage at the time of a celebrity's death can create a spike of public interest, but over time as the publicity drops away so too does the nostalgia wave (Matheson & Baade, 2004).

Fortune magazine specializes in tracking the rich and famous and the sources of wealth. It has recorded that dead celebrities can generate more revenue than living ones (see www.forbes.com/deadcelebs). Thirty years after his death Elvis Presley earned $52 million in 2009–10 which was more than both Justin Timberlake ($44 million) and Madonna ($40 million) that year.

Robert Evans of Texas A & M International University and his colleagues questioned American college students about their recognition of and opinions about dead celebrities, including a nomination of their favourite among these (Evans, Hart, Cicala & Sherrell, 2010). They were also asked to respond to a series of further items designed to measure their feelings about these celebrities and most especially whether they held some special curiosity about them or identified with them very closely. The research found that identification with dead celebrities was predicted most of all by the degree to which respondents were inclined to take social risks. Those who displayed low risk-taking in their contemporary social lives were also the most likely to display some close connection with dead celebrities. Enjoyment of following news or events about dead celebrities was also closely associated with having a strong orientation towards nostalgia in general. The most liked dead celebrities among this sample were Chris Farley, and then Heath Ledger, Bernie Mac, Bob Marley, Tupac Shakur and Elvis Presley.

Negative celebrity corporate capital

The wrong choice of celebrity for a brand can cause as much damage as the right choice can bring benefits. Celebrity damage to brand images can occur when a non-credible celebrity is selected to endorse a brand, when a celebrity's profile is so strong that it drowns out the message about the brand (also known as the 'Vampire effect'), or when a celebrity's own image takes a tumble because of poor performance or involvement in a scandal.

There are risks also that the value of a celebrity might be diluted if that celebrity is already endorsing many other brands. This can create a market clutter around that celebrity with the association between the celebrity and a newly endorsed brand battling for consumer attention against other brands already in an established relationship with the same celebrity. Whether a celebrity spreading themselves too thinly across many brands is invariably harmful in terms of their consumer capital remains a somewhat open question. Early research indicated that celebrities that engaged in multiple endorsements at the same time lost promotional value (Mowen & Brown, 1981). Later work failed to support this observation (Tripp, Jensen & Carlson, 1994).

Consumers' beliefs that a celebrity truly believes in a brand they have endorsed can be affected by the knowledge that the celebrity is being paid a very large sum of money by the advertiser to offer their endorsement. Does the celebrity really like and use the product or are they only endorsing it because they are getting paid a lot of money? Does the fact that a celebrity is being well paid enough to undermine their credibility as an endorser? Research has been carried out on this question that has indicated that consumers still accept that the celebrity is telling them something worth listening to. Some of the evidence here indicated that the payment of high fees to celebrities as opposed to low fees or no fee made little difference to consumers' perceptions of the brand or the celebrity's involvement with it. Yet, there have also been signs that payment can make a difference to consumers' opinions about a celebrity and the campaign in which they are involved. This difference may derive from a judgement about whether the nature of a promotional campaign warrants voluntary rather than paid endorsement on the part of celebrities.

One aspect of this effect is a phenomenon known to psychologists as 'correspondence bias'. This phenomenon extends beyond marketing situations. It is concerned with whether we make accurate judgements when trying to decide why a person displayed a particular pattern of behaviour. In an initial test of this phenomenon, Jones and Harris (1967) invited students to read essays about the Cuban leader Fidel Castro that were either pro-Castro or anti-Castro. Afterwards they were asked to judge the extent to which each essayist would have been likely to agree or disagree with a series of anti- and pro-Castro attitudes. There was a presumption that the author who wrote the anti-Castro essay held negative opinions about him while the author who wrote the pro-Castro essay was expected to agree with pro-Castro attitudes. Under one set of conditions, the essay writers were presented as writing their true thoughts and feelings, while in another, the research participants were told that the authors had been instructed what type of essay to write. Under the latter condition, therefore, the authors may not have been representing their real feelings about Castro in their essays. Nevertheless, the participants ascribed positive and negative feelings about Castro respectively to the pro-Castro and anti-Castro essay writers even though knowing that the essays they had written may not have reflected their true feelings. Instead, the participants mis-attributed attitudes to the essay writers based on their behaviour. It was presumed that any attitudes they held ought to 'correspond' to the behaviour they displayed.

This same correspondence bias principle has been hypothesized to apply in the case of celebrities who endorse products. There is often a naïve assumption made by consumers that because a celebrity appears in an advertisement as a product endorser, they must really like and use the product. The reality may be quite different. In fact, the celebrity might not be a product user and might even not like the product, and speak on its behalf only because he is paid to do so.

Maria Cronley of the University of Cincinnati and her colleagues conducted an experiment with undergraduate students in which they were shown an advert for a company that promoted healthy eating habits. The model and actress Cindy Crawford appeared as the celebrity endorser in this case. Before exposure to the advertisement, which was shown in a print format, the researchers used different sets of instructions to the participants to manipulate the nature of the business arrangement between Ms Crawford and the advertiser and also to vary the strength of her endorsement for the advertised product. In one condition, participants were told that she had endorsed the product without payment because she believed in the promotion of healthy eating habits. In another condition, participants were told she had been paid $6 million for her services. In other conditions, she provided either modest or very powerful endorsement of the company featured in the advertisement (Cronley, Kardes, Goddard & Houghton, 1999).

After looking at the advertisement, participants were asked to estimate how much Cindy Crawford liked the brand, how often she used it herself and how much she believed in it. The strength of her arguments for the brand had the biggest impact on participants' beliefs that Ms Crawford was committed to the brand herself when they believed she was speaking on behalf of it for no payment. Even when the participants believed Cindy Crawford had been well paid for her endorsement, they were still swayed to some extent by her arguments in support of the advertised brand. The potency of her views however was strengthened by the knowledge that she was speaking voluntarily on behalf of the brand. Moreover, when participants believed that she liked the brand, they liked it more also.

Further research with young consumers in South Africa by Delarey Van der Waldt and his colleagues of the Department of Marketing and Communication Management, University of Pretoria assessed two print advertisements designed to get people to drink more milk that featured Britney Spears and Jackie Chan respectively (Van der Waldt, Schleritzko & Van Zyl, 2007).

Prior to seeing the advertisements, the research participants – all undergraduate students – in one condition were told that the two celebrities had been paid for their services, while in another condition they were told that Chan and Spears had offered their endorsement for free. The researchers measured what difference this prior information made to the way the students evaluated the celebrities as endorsers, the product being promoted and the advertisements. The advance information that the celebrities had been paid or unpaid affected the evaluations of Britney Spears and her advertisements but not of Jackie Chan and his advertisement. Knowing that Spears had been paid for doing this commercial resulted in less favourable evaluation of both her and the advertisement in which she appeared.

According to Van der Waldt these findings are important because they tell advertisers that for some celebrities and in relation to specific types of campaign, the knowledge that a celebrity has been paid can be off-putting. He further observed that 'it is essential for marketers to test potential combinations of products and celebrities' (p. 190) to ensure that a celebrity endorser creates the right impression among consumers when associated with a particular product. However, we can go further than this here and say that consumers expect celebrities – and perhaps especially those who are already wealthy – to give their services voluntarily (and with pay) for campaigns that have a social purpose rather than a purely commercial one.

The importance of 'correspondence bias' to the value that celebrities bring to brands was confirmed among young consumers in Norway. David Silvera and Benedikte Austad of the University of Tromso asked whether the effects observed strongly in the United States would also be present in Norway where a more sceptical attitude towards celebrity endorsers might persist (Silvera, & Austad, 2003). They examined how Norwegian university students judged supermodel Cindy Crawford as an endorser of a luxury brand of wrist watch in a print advertisement. They were invited to assess whether Crawford really liked the brand, used it herself and viewed it as a good product. Prior to seeing the advertisement some of them were told that she was endorsing the product for no remuneration, while others were told that she was being paid around US$6 million for doing so.

Previous research had indicated that under correspondence-bias conditions, consumers will be more likely to believe a celebrity likes a product simply by seeing them associated with it as an endorser. This has been observed to happen even when consumers are aware that the celebrity has been well paid to endorse a product. In this Norwegian study however this effect did not occur. When young Norwegians knew that Cindy Crawford was being well paid to endorse the wrist watch, they did not believe that she genuinely liked the product more than most other people.

Silvera and Austad did not stop there. They conducted a second study in which Norwegian students again were shown a print advertisement showing actor Pierce Brosnan endorsing a brand of cologne. As before, the students were asked to judge whether Brosnan liked the product, used it and viewed it positively. Some students were told before seeing the advertisement that he was paid to endorse it, while others were told he was unpaid. The results confirmed those of the first study. Participants who believed Pierce Brosnan had been paid to endorse the product did not believe he liked the product better than most other people. In other words, they displayed no correspondence bias in their judgements about his orientation towards the brand he endorsed.

Despite these findings, there was further evidence that certain perceptual evaluations of the celebrity endorser on the part of the young consumers in these studies that in turn might mediate the view that the celebrity did hold some affinity with the product would also enhance consumers' opinions about it. Thus, evaluating Cindy Crawford as having a 'sense of style' and as having some knowledge about the product resulted in consumers thinking more highly of the product itself. With Pierce Brosnan, similar results occurred and on this occasion it was his perceived knowledge about the product he endorsed and his attractiveness that promoted positive consumer dispositions towards the product. The fact that the results of these two studies were fully consistent in the kinds of variables characterizing celebrity endorsers that might enhance their capital with consumers, means that we cannot be totally confident in what exactly is going on here. More research is needed to unravel the roles played by specific product and celebrity attributes in determining whether a celebrity's capital in endorsing brands will be positive or negative.

Celebrities can render brands more memorable and more attractive, but they also carry risks for the consumer and therefore in turn for the sponsor. Even before we consider what happens if the celebrity's own image becomes tarnished, the risk inherent in basing brand decisions on celebrity associations lies in the fact that the consumer is openly aligning themselves, in terms of their personal identity, with the celebrity endorser of the brand. The internal rationalizing of a consumer's decision making here goes something as follows: 'If I buy this brand, I will become more like this very successful person.' In addition, however, there is a much broader social statement being transmitted to others in the individual's social setting: 'By wearing this brand, I am publicly endorsing and identifying myself with this celebrity and everything they stand for' (Onkvisit & Shaw, 1987; Solomon, Bamossy & Askegaard, 2002).

Despite the drive towards celebrity endorsement as a solution to brand salience in an increasingly cluttered marketing environment, it is a technique that should not be deployed indiscriminately. As the costs of securing the services of celebrity endorsers escalates especially for the ones with global popularity, sponsors need to be sure they have made the right choice. Will a celebrity spokesperson make a difference? Which celebrity is the best one for the job? For how long can a particular celebrity have sufficient brand value added capital to be worth the expenditure? Are there risks associated with a particular celebrity as far as the security of their own image is concerned? Does a celebrity have a track record of problematic behaviour? Are they at the end of their careers? Is there personal brand so powerful that it will overshadow the sponsor's brand? These are all questions sponsors must ask before using celebrity endorsers.

A number of corporations have had their fingers burned with celebrities. Even the biggest corporate brands in the world are not immune to the effects of a celebrity doing something that attracts public criticism. In 1989, Pepsi had Madonna under contract as a celebrity endorser when she produced her 'Like a Prayer' music video that depicted fields of burning crosses and stigmata on her palms. Catholic groups complained about the video and the offence they alleged it caused to their followers. The public attention their lobbying attracted forced Pepsi to discontinue its campaign featuring Madonna in the United States.

Pepsi ran into trouble again with its long-running arrangement with Michael Jackson. He first signed to Pepsi in 1984 and over the next ten years earned millions of dollars endorsing Pepsi products. Just months before the end of this contract, however, Jackson became embroiled in a highly public scandal after being accused of alleged child sex abuse.

Coulter and his colleagues examined the use of celebrity endorsement by Reebok. They used a method called the Zaltman Metaphor Elicitation Technique (Coulter, Zaltman & Coulter, 2001) that could enable consumers to articulate their thoughts and feelings about brands. The sample was very small, comprising only eight participants, with whom in-depth interview were carried out. They were initially asked to collect a small number of images that represented celebrity endorsements of products to them. They were asked to describe what these images contained, sort them into piles and then to conduct a similarity and difference comparison exercise in which they identified how any two of these images were alike in one respect and different in that respect from a third image. This technique was used to generate a series of constructs that represented evaluative dimensions for the assessment of advertisements and brands. This approach was also used with images of Reebok brands and participants were given the opportunity to identify the kinds of attributes or dimensions that define Reebok and make it different from other brands. All these thoughts and feelings were written down and the transcripts were analysed further to explore the kinds of thoughts and feelings that were used to describe and define Reebok sports footwear.

A range of opinions emerged that reflect both positive and negative reactions to the use of celebrities as brand endorsers. Seeing a sports personality in an advertisement for a brand where they were depicted playing their sport had a kind of authenticity to it in that the celebrity was depicted in the context that consumers were accustomed to seeing them. Taking sporting celebrities out of their usual context and using them in a different type of endorser role could result in a loss of credibility. The consumers interviewed here knew that the relationship between celebrity and brand was ultimately all about money for both parties. Celebrities were used by sponsors to enhance the market profile of their brands in the hope of selling more units. At the same time celebrities loaned their images to brand in return for being well paid.

Knowing that this financial contract was a centrepiece of the arrangement between celebrity and sponsor led consumers to adopt a sceptical position about what was going on here and how they were expected to react. Because of this, it was important that sponsors utilized celebrities in ways that were deemed relevant and acceptable to consumers. Since celebrities were probably not qualified to speak expertly about most products, they should not be used in that type of role in advertisements. On the other hand, it was acceptable for sponsors to associate themselves with celebrities to benefit from the public profile of their famous endorsers, provided they did not use celebrities as experts where such expertise was not proven.

Thus, using famous sports stars such as double Olympic gold medal winning track athlete Kelly Holmes, as Reebok did, was accepted and regarded as positively benefiting the brand. Holmes had an image of someone who had succeeded through hard work and despite adversity along the way. She never gave up on herself, when others had done so. This was the kind of image consumers were happy to identify with. The use of rappers such as 50Cent, in contrast, was not perceived to be effective in that there was no reason to believe in the relevance of his image and his story in relation to the brand. It was recognized that sponsors were like puppet masters and manipulated celebrity endorsements to the benefit of their brands. Consumers generally know that this is the score. What they are less likely to tolerate is being treated as gullible by sponsors who present celebrities as something they are not, rather than as something they are. Whatever it is that defines the persona of the celebrity for consumers must in turn have relevance to the values of the brand (Coulter, Zaltman & Coulter, 2001).

The same qualitative interpretative technique was deployed by Temperley and Tangen (2006) in exploring consumers' open-ended comments about celebrity endorsers. One general concern about the use of celebrity endorsers was that the cost of employing them might eventually be charged back to consumers through the price tag on the product. As one of Temperley and Tangen's participants remarked in relation to the endorsement of Nike products by golfer Tiger Woods: 'I think I might buy a product that is not endorsed by him. That is because I know that Nike pays him a lot of money for this and this money must come from higher prices for me' (p. 101).

Mismatches between commercial brands and celebrity endorsers also surfaced as a problem for these consumers and this could become mixed in with concerns about the impact of using an expensive celebrity endorser on the eventual cost of the product to the consumer. Thus, in relation to footballer David Beckham's endorsement of a Japanese food product, consumers questioned his authority and expertise here. As one study's participant remarked: 'This reinforces my image of him being a commercial person, not sticking to his trade. Going into this world of being a celebrity, popular and seen, I think I would respect him more if he had stuck to football, and not endorsing products like [name of product], which seem to have nothing to do with it. He is only doing it for money, which reinforces my image of him as a shallow commercial person' (Tamperley & Tangen, 2006, p. 101).

The risk of brand association with a celebrity whose image has gone bad is especially acute for new brands because there is no history of brand promotion and no established brand image for consumers to refer to. Instead, a new brand's image may become defined by the image of the celebrity employed to endorse it, and by little else. This risk can be minimized by sponsors doing homework in advance to discover whether a particular celebrity has any skeletons in the closet or a history of public misbehaviour (Charbonneau & Garland, 2005). Sometimes though it may be impossible to predict when a celebrity falls out of favour.

A further important feature in terms of the consumer capital of a celebrity endorser derives from the relevance of any information they provide to consumer judgements about the product and its potential benefits to them. The presence of irrelevant information in a persuasion communication setting can make a difference to the overall effectiveness of the message. The most important effect here is that the presence of irrelevant information can dilute the impact of any relevant information that is also provided (Kemmelmeier, 2004; Zukier, 1982). In an advertising context, this phenomenon could have a significant effect on the overall impact of the commercial message.

Ilicic and Webster of Macquarie University in Australia (2012) tested out the effects of celebrity relevance and irrelevance on consumers' reactions to an advertisement for a financial institution (the Greater Building Society). These were members of the public aged between 25 and 44 years who were invited to view and evaluate 1 of 3 versions of the advertisements for this brand. These different versions were distinguished by the relevance of the brand information provided by the celebrity. On this occasion, the celebrity in question was the well-known American comedian, Jerry Seinfeld. In one version, the advert presents information of relevance about the brand in the form of a customer discussing her experience with the organization. In another version information was provided that was irrelevant in the form of Jerry Seinfeld making a joke about ice cream. In a third version, relevant and irrelevant information were mixed in together.

The findings revealed that the version only with the *irrelevant* information was rated poorest and had the worst impact on consumers' perceptions of the brand and what it could deliver to them. The version only with the *relevant* information was rated highest on all measures. The version that combined relevant with irrelevant information was rated in between. The other important finding here however was that participants were asked to evaluate whether Jerry Seinfeld made a good or poor match with the advertised commercial brand. Among those who felt him to be a poor match, the presence of even some irrelevant information resulted in significantly worse evaluations of the advertisement and the brand. Among those who felt that he was a good match for the brand however, although the presence of some irrelevant information produced a poorer outcome than the relevant information only condition, this difference did not achieve statistical significance. These effects were not only manifest in consumers' evaluative attitudes about the brand, but also filtered through to the intentions to use the brand.

Mismatches and damage to celebrity capital

We have already seen that getting the right match between a celebrity and an advertised commercial brand is crucial. Get this wrong and the commercial brand image can suffer. This may not be the only outcome however. A commercial brand that has poor standing in the eyes of consumers can also be bad for the celebrity's personal brand image. Samuel Doss of the Florida Institute of Technology had a range of commercial brands pre-rated in terms of their standing among consumers. He then pre-selected ones that were the most positive and most negative in terms of consumer opinion about them. Further pre-ratings were made in the same way of a number of celebrities and the most positively regarded and most negatively regarded were chosen for the study. He then subsequently matched positively regarded celebrities with either positively rated or negatively rated commercial brands and did the same thing for negatively regarded celebrities.

College students were recruited and assigned to conditions in which they viewed and evaluated positive–positive pairings and negative–negative pairings or positive–negative/negative–positive pairings. Positively perceived commercial brands did not affect the perceived attractiveness or trustworthiness of celebrities, but well-regarded commercial brands enhanced the degree to which celebrities seemed to have product-relevant expertise. Of greater importance were findings that commercial brands about which young consumers held poor opinions could also damage the image of a celebrity associated with them – diminishing their perceived attractiveness, trustworthiness and expertise. Doss cautioned that his study had a number of limitations, not least in respect of its non-representative sample of consumers and limited celebrity-commercial brand pairings. Nevertheless, the results uncovered a potential effect of ill-conceived celebrity-commercial brand hook-ups that needs to be explored further (Doss, 2011).

When celebrities fall from grace

The emergence of negative news about a celebrity that harms their public standing and reputation can be bad news also for sponsors who have paid those celebrities to promote their brands. Just as positive qualities of the celebrity can transfer to the brand, negative ones can do likewise. As we will see in this chapter, negative publicity about a celebrity can damage the images of brands promoted by that public figure. This impact might have a further knock-on effect on the brand's market share and then in turn on the stock value of the company that produces the brand. We have seen already how through repeated exposure to an advertised brand coupled with a particular celebrity endorser, consumers learn over time to associate one with the other. This associative learning can be very powerful when this pairing is given a great deal of public airing and over a long period. Attributes linked to the celebrity can become intermingled with those associated with the commercial brand, such that one set of attributes can trigger thoughts and feelings about the other (Domjan & Burkhard, 1986; Klein, 1991; Martindale, 1991).

The real danger for advertisers is that if a celebrity's image takes a nose dive, the image of an associated brand can suffer likewise simply through association (Langmeyer & Shank, 1993). As we will see later, it is not just the public image of an advertised brand that can be damaged if a celebrity endorser loses credibility but also the value of the company behind the brand (Louie, Kulik & Jocobson, 2001). Although highly regarded brands can survive this kind of damage, reversal of the impact of negative brand-related information can be difficult (Butler & Berry, 2002).

In an ingenious experiment, US marketing researchers Brian Till of Saint Louis University and Terence Shimp of the University of South Carolina introduced students to a fictitious product and fictitious celebrity about each of which they provided a number of pieces of information (Till & Shimp, 1998). For some participants, only two pieces of information were presented, while others received six pieces of information. The product was a racing bicycle called Avenix. The 'celebrity' was a champion cyclist called Pierre Varnay. The participants were told that the manufacturer was interested in getting students' opinions about their product. After this initial exposure to information about the product, participants were tested to see if they could recall that information correctly. Next they were exposed to a series of ten print advertisements for the product in which the celebrity was seen riding an Avenix bicycle.

In a further condition, participants read three articles about the celebrity, and the third of these contained negative information about him. Two types of negative information were presented to different participants. The first of these disclosed that the celebrity had used steroids to enhance his sporting performance and the second claimed he had multiple drink-driving infractions. Control participants received no negative information about the celebrity.

Finally, all participants were invited to provide a series of evaluations of the celebrity and the advertised product.

The findings revealed that participants' evaluations of the celebrity and of the product declined after exposure to negative information about the endorser. There was no deterioration of opinion about the celebrity or product for those participants who read no negative information about the celebrity. Furthermore, when participants received only two advance pieces of information about the celebrity or product, their opinions of them declined more than when they had received six pieces of information.

In a follow-up study, the same researchers explored other factors that might influence the extent to which negative information about a celebrity could tarnish his reputation and the value attached to the product. On this occasion the researchers were interested to find out whether receiving negative information about a celebrity *after* exposure to an advertising campaign would have more or less impact upon their perceptions of the celebrity and endorsed product than when the negative celebrity information appeared *before* exposure to the advertising. They also wanted to find out whether the strength of association between the celebrity and the endorsed product was important in this context. The strength of association was manipulated by the number of times the celebrity was pictured with the product across ten advertisements for it that were shown to the participating students. In the strong association condition, the celebrity was seen in all ten advertisements with the product, whereas in the weak association condition, he was seen with the product in only three out of the ten advertisements.

Once again, the participants' evaluations of the bicycle product were poorer after exposure to negative information about the associated celebrity. Furthermore, this effect was magnified by creating strong rather than weak association between the celebrity and product. Finally, the negative celebrity information did more damage to the product's standing when presented before exposure to the product advertising than afterwards.

In a third study, Till and Shimp wanted to find out whether the same effects would occur when using a real celebrity as the product endorser. In this, the champion road racing cyclist Greg LeMond was substituted for the fictitious Pierre Varnay as the Avenix endorser. On this occasion, however, there were no significant effects of negative information about the celebrity on the evaluations of the celebrity or the product. What this study indicates is that although negative information about a celebrity can affect their consumer capital, with some well-known celebrities, there may be such a well-conditioned range and richness of positive attributes associated with them that a single exposure to negative celebrity information might not be enough to lower their standing among consumers.

Bailey (2007) and Edwards and La Ferle (2009) conducted investigations in which they manipulated news coverage in a fictional setting about a celebrity endorser to find out whether this would affect consumers' opinions about brands endorsed by those celebrities. In one instance, a story told of a celebrity's involvement in domestic violence and in another about their involvement in child abuse.

The impact of negative information on a celebrity's consumer capital occurs among consumers across different cultures, with some cultures being more sensitive to such disclosures than others. Bruce Money of Brigham Young University in the United States conducted research with American and Japanese students on this matter with Terence Shimp of the University of South Carolina and Tomoaki Sakano of Waseda University in Japan. In this case, the names of real celebrities (movie stars) were used in association with the name of a fictitious brand (a portable high-tech electronic device called a WebPad). Pre-tests resulted in the names of two specific movie stars being selected (Money, Shimp & Sakano, 2006).

The students in both countries were shown a mock magazine advertisement for the WebPad which pictured the product and presented further information about its features and functionality. At the bottom of the advertisements was a photograph of one of the two celebrities (alternated in different presentation conditions). A statement of endorsement about the product was show that was attributed to the celebrity. After exposure to the advertisement, the participants were presented with information about the celebrity they had seen. This information disclosed that the celebrity had been a regular cocaine user. In two further conditions, the consequences of this habit were also disclosed. In one instance, called self-orientation, it was claimed that the celebrity's drug habit had been concealed from the public and his own family and had been a cause of considerable angst for him. In a second condition, called other orientation, it was stated that the celebrity's drug habit was known to his family and had caused them to worry a lot about him. In a third condition, some participants received no negative celebrity information.

The reason for varying the outcomes of the celebrity's drug abuse derived from prior research showing that consumers in the United States and Japan tend to display different value orientations with the Japanese being more sensitive to the impact of one's own anti-social tendencies on others and the shame it can bring. In the United States, in contrast, consumers were more driven by the need to individualistic and distinctive and are less concerned about the collective good. Contrary to expectations, intentions to purchase the product were strongest both in Japan and the United States among participants exposed to self-oriented negative information about the celebrity's drug taking. In the other oriented negative information condition and no negative information condition, there was no significant change in young consumers' interest in the product. It seemed that in the condition in which the featured celebrity had suffered alone with his drug problem, young consumers exhibited more sympathy towards him. This outcome – assuming it is reliable and replicable – means that negative information about a celebrity does not invariably mean that their consumer or corporate capital is lost. Consumers may take into account qualifying circumstances before deciding to give up on a celebrity or in turn on the products he (or she) endorses.

Positive or negative effects on corporate value

Celebrities, as we will see, can have substantial business value for corporations. There is evidence that signing the right celebrity can improve sales and market share and increase stock market value. The use of sports celebrities has been particularly commonplace (Burton, Farrelly & Quester, 2001). At the same time, it is important for companies not to get carried away with using celebrities. Entering into endorsement contracts with celebrities carries various risks. It is important for corporate sponsors and advertising practitioners to assess carefully the probable value of specific potential celebrity endorsers, using relevant empirical data and not to presume that because a celebrity is well known, they will also have corporate capital as endorsers (Brooks & Harris, 1998).

Not all celebrities bring with them the same value. There may be various reasons for this. We have already seen that there are different types of celebrities and the growth of celebrity culture since the last decade of the twentieth century has expanded the celebrity population. Celebrities' intrinsic value in the context of sponsorship and endorsement arrangements can vary with the nature of their celebrity and whether it derives from genuine talent and performance or simply from being able to attract publicity. It can also vary with the type of activity for which the celebrity is known and whether that celebrity is perceived to make a good fit for the brand. Hence, it makes sense for a sports-related brand to be associated with a celebrity sportsperson. In this case, the celebrity might be seen as having relevant expertise as a probable user of the product. Using a sportsperson to sell financial products, in contrast, may be seen as a less good fit because while the celebrity may be well known and well-liked there may be a preference among consumers to receive recommendations from someone they believe to have relevant expertise with such products where the personal risk of use could be high.

When murder charges were brought against O. J. Simpson, drug charges against Michael Irvin and when Mike Tyson was jailed, the consequences were felt by many of their major sponsors that include such household names as Hertz, Kodak, Pepsi and Toyota.

One approach to the study of the corporate capital of celebrities has been event study methodology. This methodology has been used by economists to generate models that describe and explain the potential effects on various measures of a company's value of specific types of events that involve the company. One key measure of a company's worth is its stock value in the financial markets. This value can be indicative of further performance measures such as a company's likely future profitability. Stock prices can fluctuate in the financial markets as analysts monitor market events that could impact upon a company's future business prospects and performance. Market-related events such as a change to the company's name, changes in senior personnel, the introduction of new products, the sales performance of its products, product recalls and any new government regulations that restrict the way the company can operate all represent events that could influence perceptions about its future performance and future value (see Capon, Farley & Hoening, 1990; Chaney, DeVinney & Winer, 1991; Horsky & Swyngedouw, 1987; Jarrell & Peltzman, 1985). The announcement of a new tie-up with a celebrity endorser is another such event.

Some event analysis studies studied announcements of new links between companies and celebrities, and other studies have investigated new contract signing events in which the celebrities already had an established association with the company. Relevant deals include announcements about celebrities signed to corporate sponsorships and Hollywood stars signed to appear in new movies.

Leading movie actors can command fees of many millions of dollars, with the Hollywood stars at the top of the ladder receiving tens of millions in fees and profit sharing agreements. If a star such as Tom Cruise, Tom Hanks or Brad Pitt receives $20 million+ to appear in a movie, how much difference does this make to that movie's performance at the box office? Do these deals also enhance the stock market value of the production companies behind the movies?

There has been mixed research evidence for the effects of star status and movie revenues. Some studies have found little positive impact at the box office, while others have reported that the impact can be considerable, though variable in terms of whether it provides a short-lived or lasting boost to revenues (Ainslie, Dreze & Zufryden, 2005; Albert, 1998; De Vany & Walls, 1999; Elberse, 2007; Litman & Kohl, 1989; Litman & Ahn, 1998; Ravid, 1999; Wallace, Seigerman & Holbrook, 1993).

From a sample of over 1,200 announcements about star signings to movies between 2001 and 2005, Anita Elberse of the Harvard Business School used event analysis to examine the subsequent impact on the revenue returns of the movies (496 in all). A 'star' had to have at least two leading roles in movies released by a major Hollywood studio or a larger number of supporting roles across a range of films on general release. Each star's value was based on an average of the box office gross revenue generated by their last five movies. Where an announcement included the names of more than one 'star', Elberse averaged over their individual, five-year box office averages. She also took into account how many stars were signed to a film and their career history in terms of awards they had won. Elberse found that star power was predictive of a movie's expected and actual box office performance, but made little difference to the stock value of movie corporations. Announcements of star signings led to higher predictions of expected returns, while news that a star signing had dropped out of a movie could have the reverse effect. On average a star could add $3 million of actual revenue to a movie's box office returns. There was no evidence that the valuation of movie companies changed significantly as a result of news of their star movie signings (Elberse, 2007).

Movie stars also tend to get involved in promotional and publicity campaigns for their movies just before and after the movies go on general release. Box office celebrities can then attract considerable media attention. Does these media appearance by celebrities add value in terms of enhancing the box office performance of movies?

One analysis of movie star appearances in the well-known US celebrity, publication *People*, found that while a specific celebrity can have valuable promotional capital through the general coverage they receive, their media appearances as part of specific publicity campaigns did not seem to add much further value. In this instance, the success of a movie was measured in terms of the revenues it generated during its opening weekend and its gross revenues for the United States and Canada. Results were based on a dataset of 273 movies released between 2004 and 2006. The appearances of movie stars in *People* magazine were measured over periods of three months prior to the release date of a move they starred in and over a longer, 21-month period. If the three-month measure had a relationship with the success of a movie, this could be attributed to the effectiveness of a promotional campaign featuring the star actor in the lead-up to its general release. If the 21-month measure was related to the success of a movie star's films, this might be taken as a measure of the star power of this celebrity. This analysis found that the 21-month measure of a celebrity's media coverage was a significant predictor of their movies' successes, but not the 3-month coverage measure. Thus, a popular celebrity might add value to a movie's box office receipts just through association and because of their lasting star power, and not just because he or she also took part in an orchestrated publicity campaign organized by the studio (Treme, 2010).

Turning to celebrity-corporate sponsorship deals, Mathur, Mathur and Rangan (1997) examined the impact of Michael Jordan's return to professional basketball in 1995 on the stock market values of corporate sponsors with which he had endorsement arrangements as well as on the stock prices of nine rival companies. Endorsed brands experienced an average 2 per cent rise in stock value which equated to US$1 billion. It is difficult to determine the significance of this study in terms of our wider understanding of celebrity endorsement effects on corporate stock values because it investigated only one celebrity endorser and a small sample of companies.

Farrell, Karels, Montfort and McClatchey (2000) conducted another similar study that again focused on the impact of one celebrity endorser – the golfer, Tiger Woods. Stock market values of three endorsed companies were examined between 1996 and 1998. It is difficult to establish from this study the extent to which Woods' endorsement caused unusual stock price changes for his sponsoring companies. There was evidence that one of his sponsors, Nike, did benefit from his run of sporting success during this period, but the picture was less clear for his other two sponsors – Fortune Brands and American Express. The authors concluded that in the case of Fortune Brands which owned Titleist, a golf equipment manufacturer, its market position was too small for Woods to make a difference to it. With American Express they question whether consumers regarded a golfer as a credible source of advice about financial services.

Louie, Kulik and Jacobson (2001) investigated the effects on a company's financial performance, measured in terms of stock returns, of negative publicity linked to a celebrity endorser that it sponsored. The effects for corporate sponsors could be serious where the celebrity was apparently to blame for events that damaged their image. Where the celebrity was blameless, the impact on stock market performance was less pronounced. Thus, despite earlier research (Agrawal & Kamarkura, 1995) showing weak market sensitivity to whether celebrities attracted negative publicity, these findings revealed that market analysts and investors can and do make judgements about a company's stock value that are influenced by a wider corporate public image factor. Where this corporate public image is tarnished through association with a celebrity whose own image has suffered, there may be concerns about the knock-on effects this might have on future consumer behaviour.

Next, we turn to studies that included analyses of new deals between companies and celebrities who were working together for the first time. Agrawal and Kamakura (1995) used event analysis to study relationships between publicly floated companies' announcements of new celebrity endorsement deals and their stock value. They identified more than US 100 cases over a period spanning 1980 to 1992. They examined changes in stock returns for the event day (day the contract with a celebrity was announced) and for each of ten days before and after the event day. In that way they were able to compare daily changes in stock price for a company before and after the financial markets became aware of the celebrity tie-in. They found that the event day delivered a significantly higher average growth in stock price. Thus despite the risks that are associated with celebrity endorsers including whether they make a good fit, endorse other companies' products and attract negative publicity that can transfer to the sponsor, the financial markets continued to believe that celebrity sponsorships were generally good for business.

Fizel, McNeil and Smaby (2008) assessed 148 athlete endorsements announced between 1994 and 2000 and found no significant overall effects of these events on stock prices on the day of the announcements or over other time periods.

Christopher Knittel and Victor Stango of the University of California, Davis, reported that the fall from grace of Tiger Woods after his car accident in November 2009 and subsequent revelations about his private life cost his major sponsors dearly in terms of their share value over the next few weeks.

They put these losses at anywhere between $5 billion and $12 billion (Knittel & Stango, 2012).

At the time of his accident Eldrick 'Tiger' Woods was the highest paid sports star in the world bringing in around $100 million a year from endorsements. According to Forbes, Woods was the first sports star to earn $1 billion. Although a highly successful competitor who won a large amount of prize money each year, his personal wealth derived mainly from his extensive commercial endorsements than made him more than four times as much as his golf prize winnings. One of the reasons for Woods' popularity with sponsors was a spotless character – an apparently clean living family man who was dedicated to his sport. Then this very positive personal brand image unravelled as disclosures about his colourful private life emerged after the incident with his car in which his wife had also been involved.

Following the mishap with his car, his personal reputation was left in tatters amidst stories that he had been unfaithful to his Swedish-born wife multiple times during their marriage including while she was pregnant with their children. At the time, media attention focused on the impact this would have on his career as a professional golfer as well as on his personal wealth assuming that his career was finished or that his sponsors would not wish to be linked to him. What was more significant for his sponsors however was whether the damage caused to Mr Woods' reputation also spread to their own brand image by association. At the time that this event occurred, Tiger Woods had lucrative contracts with a number of global corporate brands including Accenture, Gillette, Nike, PepsiCo (Gatorade) and Electronic Arts (EA). These deals alone accounted for 80–90 per cent of his sponsorship income.

Knittel and Stango (2012) sought evidence that the Woods' incident damaged the stock value of his sponsors. They obtained data on stock price movements for all Woods' sponsor companies as compared with broader changes in stock price movements for the financial market as a whole and for close competitor companies with no association with Tiger Woods. Stock market data were examined from the first trading day after the car crash and for the next 13 days. They also looked at aggregated data just for the five sponsor companies and then separately for two sub-sets, the three companies (EA, Gatorade and Nike) that marketed sports-related products and the other two (Gillette & Accenture).

For all sponsor companies taken together, there was a 2.3 per cent decline in stock market value which was calculated to be worth $12 billion. For the Big Five sponsors only, the decline was 2.4 per cent ($8.11 billion) and for the three sports-related brand companies (EA, Gatorade and Nike, the decline was 4.3 per cent ($5.71 billion)).

There is also growing concern in terms of determining the value of celebrity endorsements of a dilution effect among the most popular and current celebrities who endorse many different brands. The cost of signing celebrities has also grown and for the most successful performers in their fields, contracts can run into many millions of dollars or other currencies.

Despite the apparent fall in stock value of Nike documented above, other research has shown that the company financially benefited in very significant ways from its association with Tiger Woods and that this effect persisted even during the period when he attracted negative publicity over his marital infidelities. Chung, Derdenger and Srinivasan (2013) found that Woods delivers Nike's golf ball division $60 million in profits over a 10-year endorsement contract. The company acquired 4.5 million new customers as part of this effect. Chung and his colleagues estimated that Woods' infidelity lost Nike 105,000 customers to its golf ball division and cost the company around $1.3 million in profit. More widely the scandal cost the company 446,000 customers and $6.2 million across its other divisions.

Nike's decision to stand by Woods, when his other sponsors terminated their contracts with him, turned out to be financially beneficial even though the company's stock price may have taken a temporary tumble. There was a residual Tiger Woods effect over the period between the scandal breaking and his return to competitive golf after a temporary withdrawal from it. This was estimated to deliver a $1.6 million profit to Nike across a number of product ranges. This finding is rendered less surprising by other consumer research (reviewed later in this chapter) that found that for many consumers Woods' behaviour in his private life was nothing out of the ordinary and should in any case be divorced from any judgements made about his qualities as a golfer (Akturan, 2011).

Ding, Molchanev and Stork (2011) conducted another event analysis on 101 corporate announcements about celebrity endorsement deals that occurred between 1996 and 2008. This analysis examined statistical relationships between the timings of these announcements and day-to-day movements in the stock prices of the companies concerned. The researchers inspected news stories about these celebrity deals and stock prices for ten days either side of the day when the contract was formally announced. In contrast to the findings reported by Agrawal and Kamakura (1995), their data provided no evidence of any announcement day effects on stock prices. A further set of analyses examined stock price movements over four-week periods after the event day and again found no evidence of celebrity effects. These zero effects persisted when the celebrity endorsed companies stock prices were compared over the same time periods with stock prices of rival companies in their sector.

Further modelling was then computed on stock prices and celebrity contract announcements taking into account various characteristics of the celebrities and companies such as whether the celebrity was an athlete or not, whether a contract was signed with a single celebrity or a group of celebrities, whether the celebrity endorsed multiple products, whether the company used multiple celebrities, the celebrity's age, the size and value of the company, whether the company was a technology firm and whether the celebrity endorser and company represented a good fit. Virtually all these factors made no difference to the relationship between the celebrity endorsement contract signing and the company's stock price. Celebrity-company match-up had a marginal effect on this relationship, with celebrities making a good fit having the most beneficial effect on stock price.

The researchers concluded that despite the potentially positive benefits of celebrity endorsers in terms of drawing attention to a company and its brands and in enhancing brand image, there are also risks that include the celebrity overshadowing the brand, and the possibility that a celebrity might attract negative publicity that would affect the corporate image through association. These positive and negative effects might therefore cancel each other out. In addition, celebrities can cost companies a great deal of money and the return on their investment in terms of increased profits again might not exceed the initial cost.

The value of celebrity endorsers to corporate sponsors can not only vary between different endorsers, with some posing a greater potential risk than others, but can fluctuate also for the same endorser over time. We have already noted that when celebrities become embroiled in scandals, their public stock can fall. The extent to which this occurs can in turn depend upon the degree to which a celebrity is held personally responsible for events surrounding their negative publicity. There is an additional set of potentially important factors that can also fluctuate over time, especially for celebrity endorsers from sports fields. Their personal achievements and form can change over time. What happens to a celebrity's corporate capital, for example, every time they win a major tournament? At that time, their public profile can climb as the media focus on their success. Do these events also add to their value as endorsers?

Elberse and Verleun (2012) conducted an event analysis, which as well as replicating features of earlier analyses of this type, also investigated the question of celebrity success and its contribution to a celebrity's value to sponsors. They compiled a sample of celebrity endorsement contracts involving athletes that were signed in the United States between January 1990 and March 2008. Following searches of different media and online sources, they compiled a sample of 341 endorsement contracts involving 95 firms and 178 sports celebrity endorsers. As well as collecting data on corporate stock price movements, they also collated data on sales of corporate brands and major achievements of the sports endorsers. The sports achievements data focused on victories in Grand Slam tournaments (in golf and tennis), major racing events and finals of team sports competitions. They also included victories in some second-tier events for some sports. Because other factors could come into play in influencing outcomes such as sales, they also compiled further data on price promotions and advertising expenditure levels for specific endorsed brands, the endorser's brand strength as measured by their national or world rankings, and each sponsoring firm's overall market value at different points in time.

In this analysis more emphasis was placed on establishing the brand strength of both the corporate sponsor and the celebrity endorser. Previous evidence had shown that when two strong brands enter into partnership, they can feed off each other in mutually beneficial ways (Rao & Ruekert, 1994; Washburn, Till & Priluck, 2004). Hence, if celebrities and corporations that each have strong brands and join forces, the outcome can be profitable for both. A high profile endorser can enhance consumer confidence in the corporate brand. Any claims the corporate sponsor might make about the quality of its brands will carry more weight if a highly regarded celebrity endorser publicly supports them. Trusted brands can then capture more market share, pushing up corporate revenues and eventually its stock market value.

Elberse and Verleun found that celebrity endorsements could drive up sales and stock value. More significantly, they found that a celebrity could provide added corporate value during a sponsorship contract if they were also highly successful in their sport. Hiring a sports celebrity endorser generally had a positive effect on the corporate sponsor's core brand sales. Weekly sales could benefit, on average, to the tune of US$200,000 or US$10 million annually. This effect was confined to the sponsor's sales and did not spread across the product category. This meant that competitor's sales were not affected in this way.

When a celebrity sports endorser scored a major victory during the endorsement contract period, this could add another US$70,000 to the value of the sponsor's primary brands' weekly sales. Further major tournament wins could add further value to sales figures, though with gradually diminishing returns for each successive win. That is, each win did not add another US$70,000 to weekly sales, but impacted upon them at lower amounts.

Announcements of celebrity endorsements had a significant impact on short-term stock market valuation, though there was no direct long-term effect of this event. Sports celebrity endorsers' competition successes also had a further impact on corporate stock price. While smaller in absolute terms than the initial signing of an endorsement contract, this effect was statistically significant. It was essential however for sports stars to score major victories to secure this benefit for their sponsors; minor tournament wins had no financial market impact.

Another important finding was that celebrity endorsers produced larger benefits for already strong corporate brands as compared with weaker corporate brands. Brands that already enjoyed large market shares at the point of a celebrity endorsement being signed tended subsequently to gain more in sales than did brands that had relatively smaller market shares when celebrity endorsement partnerships were formed. Similarly the higher the standing of the sports endorsers, the greater was the benefit to a corporate sponsor. Champions brought better sales returns and stock valuations than high performers who did not win major tournaments.

Combating negative celebrity images

It is important for companies to know how to respond when celebrities with whom they are associated experience negative publicity. It is important to establish first of all whether the celebrity in question is blameless or blameworthy. In choosing celebrities to sponsor, it is advisable for companies to conduct a reputational audit of each celebrity they target. This should consider, in the case of a previous history of negative publicity, the extent to which the celebrity in each instance was found to be blameless or not. Where celebrities have become stigmatized because of past misdemeanours or indiscretions from which negative publicity has arisen and where they have publicly been held to account, it may be advisable for companies to distance themselves from those with high blame and restrict themselves to celebrities with low blame records. Hence, if a celebrity with a history of high blame, negative publicity suffers a blow to their image again while under sponsorship from a company, it is usually advantageous for that company to act swiftly and terminate their arrangements with that celebrity. In considering celebrities to sponsor, companies should avoid celebrities with colourful lives if they have a history of high blame (Louie & Obermiller, 2002).

Gupta (2009) explored how consumers make judgements about whether celebrities are to blame when their images take a tumble in the wake of negative publicity about them. He focused on the specific case of Michael Vick, quarterback for the Atlanta Falcons whose celebrity image was tarnished when a news story surfaced that he was involved with dog fighting. His corporate sponsors reacted swiftly by withdrawing from or terminating his endorsement deals. In this instance, corporate sponsors rapidly reached a conclusion that continued association with Vick would be bad for business because he had clearly been personally culpable. Gupta wanted to find out more about how consumers would reason their way in a case such as this and whether this process might reveal when celebrities are doomed in terms of their corporate capital when embroiled in negative stories about them.

What emerged from in-depth interviews that gave consumer participants the freedom to express their opinions openly and in their own words was that negative publicity per se might not necessarily completely undermine a celebrity's corporate capital. Judgements about the extent to which the celebrity could be deemed to be to blame for the events that had happened were critical here. If events were perceived to be outside the control of the celebrity, his or her positive public image could survive. In contrast, if the celebrity was clearly to blame for the negative publicity, public opinion about them would deteriorate along with their value to sponsors.

Another approach to investigating the potential damage of negative publicity to a celebrity's public image was adopted by Ulun Akturan of Galatasaray University in Turkey. In the internet era, a great deal of online chatter exists about celebrities that for high profile public figures might get refreshed everyday. This repository of electronically transcribed speech provides a rich source of ongoing opinion about celebrities (see Akturan, 2010). Akturan measured public opinion about Tiger Woods as expressed in weblogs. Woods was the most successful sports star of all time in terms of the value of his corporate sponsorships. By 2009, financial monitoring organization Forbes reported that he had become the first sports star to earn 1 billion dollars in his career. His personal worth was calculated to be around $600 million (Badenhausen, 2009).

In November 2009, however, Woods' fortunes changed when media publicity emerged about multiple infidelities during his marriage that culminated in his separation from his wife. In December 2009, Woods announced he would take a break from golf to concentrate on his private life. In less than six months, however, he had returned to the professional golf circuit when in April 2010 he contended the US Masters golf tournament. In the aftermath of the scandal surrounding his private life, many of Woods' sponsors announced terminating their sponsorship deals with him. One of his major sponsors, Nike, in contrast, confirmed that it would continue to work with him. After his return to competition, Nike produced a new television advertisement that featured Woods. In this commercial, he is seen questioned by his late father Earl (who had died in 2006), who questions him about his conduct.

Given what is known about the potential impact on a celebrity's corporate capital of negative publicity that might damage their image, Nike clearly took a risk in launching this campaign. Akturan wanted to find out about the climate of public opinion about Tiger Woods during this period and turned to comments made about him across a random sample of more than 50 weblogs that were selected from a larger pool of nearly 11,000 websites identified from a web search using the keywords 'Tiger Woods Nike ad'. The selected sites yielded 451 posts that contained public comment. A technique called discourse analysis was used to identify the nature of the language used to describe Tiger Woods and the Nike campaign. The language used in these posts was classified in terms of the sentiments expressed (positive, negative or neutral) about the Nike advertisements, about Tiger Woods and about Nike. These narratives were also assessed in terms of whether they contained any references to blog posters' likelihood of purchasing Nike items being advertised.

The emergent evidence did not make comfortable reading for Nike or for Woods in terms of the opinions being expressed at the time. More than three times as many posts contained negative comments about the Nike advertisement as positive comments (46% vs 14%). While there were far fewer posts that contained opinions about Nike, where these did occur, again more than three times as many were negative in sentiment as positive (23% vs 7%). The gap was much narrower for opinions about Woods, but again, negative opinions outnumber positive opinions (36% vs 28%). Effects, if any, of negative publicity about Woods or negative sentiments about him or about Nike on likelihood of purchasing Nike items appeared to be small. An overwhelming majority of the blog posts (93%) made no mention of this. Where future purchase intentions were mentioned, an intention to boycott Nike merchandise (6%) outweighed an intention to buy it (1%).

What emerged from this research was a warning to Nike that public feelings were still raw enough to question the judgement of the company in putting out the advertisement. Although there no direct evidence was available from this study to confirm whether public rejection of the advertisement was linked to its contents or to its timing (or both), some of the blog posts revealed that consumers felt that the nature of the campaign was inappropriate.

What the blog comments also revealed was that Nike and not Woods was held accountable for this campaign and this may in turn have contributed to the weight of negative sentiments that were attached to the corporate brand. To some extent, despite his self-confessed culpability in the scandal that surrounded him, Woods attracted some degree of public understanding and even forgiveness. According to one post, '. . .Tiger is human and a fool so what else is new. Politicians do it everyday'. Another posted: 'Why so hard on this guy? He is a man. Give me 10 men and I will show you 8 of them if not all that have cheated on their wife. Who cares? Their business. Just thank God he is not your husband' (see Akturan, 2010, p. 11). Other comments underlined the need to separate the public Tiger from the private one. 'Pathetic! Leave his private life to him and his family. Just have him play golf. He's good at that' (p. 12).

The morality codes of the posters who produced these comments could be debated, but what is more important in the marketing context is that Woods' value as an endorser had not been seriously undermined as far as some consumers were concerned. What we cannot judge from these data is the extent to which these views could be taken as representative of broader public opinion about him. This study did reveal the complexity and diversity of consumers' reactions to celebrities gone bad. A combination of factors can come into play in these contexts that include the perceived seriousness of any offence, the pre-existing level of admiration for the celebrity and the degree of personal blame that could attach to the celebrity for what had happened.

The need for sponsors to ensure that any research-based decisions about whether to drop or persevere with a celebrity whose star has fallen derives from research with consumers samples that represent the general population is underlined by findings that some people can be less forgiving of celebrity indiscretions than are others. In particular, there can be a pronounced gender difference in the way consumers react to celebrity endorsers who have acquired negative publicity.

Research among Australian students found that male celebrity sports stars with positive and negative personal images attracted different ratings and had different potential effects on purchase decisions, with such differences being more pronounced among women than among men (Murray & Price, 2012). Two male sports star personalities, Roger Federer (tennis) and Tiger Woods (golf) were used in different versions of advertisements for a sports-relevant product (sports drink) and a sport-irrelevant product (a mobile phone). A sample of university students aged between 18 and 39 years was randomly allocated across 4 conditions defined by the sports star and the product type. Immediately after viewing the printed advertisement, they completed a number of rating scales in which they expressed their opinions about the sports star, their familiarity with him, their attitudes towards the product and their intentions to purchase it. They were also asked to evaluate the degree of involvement with the sport played by the celebrity. In terms of their personal reputations, both Federer and Woods had been highly regarded as exceptional performers in their respective sports – seen by many as the greatest exponents of their sports ever seen. Federer had also led a spotless and scandal-free private life. Woods in contrast had been embroiled in controversy when a story surfaced that he had repeatedly been unfaithful to his wife.

The use of a sports star had greater positive impact on opinions about the sports-relevant product than on the other product, but made little difference to purchase intentions. There was a difference between the influence of the sports star with the positive image and the one with the negative image, with the former promoting stronger positive attitudes and inclination to purchase the product. The level of involvement with each sport further mediated the impact of the celebrities with a positive or negative image, magnifying the image effect. What this meant was that the students who expressed greater involvement in tennis, held Roger Federer in even higher regard and were even more likely to be influenced by his endorsement of products. For those with greater involvement in golf, however, opinions about Tiger Woods were lower than average and weakened his ability to influence their attitudes towards products he endorsed or their likelihood of purchasing those products. Women expressed even lower opinions of Woods than did men and were therefore even less likely to be influenced by him in their orientations towards products he endorsed.

Summary

Celebrities can produce genuine financial yields for companies via direct and indirect corporate links. Hollywood stars can add box office value to films and this in turn can contribute to the profitability of the companies that produce them. Celebrities who become sponsored by companies and who lend their names to corporate brands likewise can add to sales figures for commercial operations, increase their profits and in turn their stock market values. Hence, the corporate capital of celebrities can become manifest in very real financial returns for their sponsors.

As with their consumer capital, however, a positive return is not always guaranteed. When producers or sponsors make the wrong celebrity choices, they can become expensive failures that can cause significant financial damage to companies. If celebrities suffer damage to their own images because of events in their professional or private lives, there can be serious consequences for their employers or sponsors as well. A celebrity whose reputation becomes tarnished can attract public criticism, a loss of fan support and become labelled as liabilities by financial market analysts with more serious knock-on financial impact upon the market values of companies that have sponsored those celebrities. A celebrity scandal does not invariably spell the end of a celebrity's economic value to a corporate sponsor. A lot can depend upon the celebrity's prior public standing, the nature of the behaviour that caused damage to their reputation and whether people decide that the offence was not all that serious or simply not relevant to judging them in the context of their careers.

Key points

- Through their sponsorship of celebrities, large corporations can benefit their businesses through increased sales of their brands and an overall growth in the value of their companies.
- Celebrities can have significant economic value for their sponsors.
- Even the announcement of a new celebrity sponsorship deal can be enough to increase the share value of the sponsoring company.
- Celebrities often continue to have economic value after they have died.

- A sponsored celebrity can also damage a corporation's business and its own value in the marketplace if the celebrity suffers damage to their own public image.
- Celebrities that spread themselves across multiple sponsorships can also experience image value damage when consumers perceive them to be greedy.
- Celebrities that enjoy ongoing achievements, especially awards or competitions they win can enhance their overall corporate value. When their careers take a performance downturn, this can have a knock-on effect on the value of those businesses that sponsor them.
- The public will reach their own judgements about a celebrity's corporate capital after a scandal and can be forgiving depending on the nature of the event that called the celebrity's image into question.

Topics for reflection

- In what ways can celebrities have value for companies that sponsor them? Discuss with relevant evidence.
- Thinking about when a celebrity's image is tarnished by scandal, refer to specific case examples to advise sponsors on whether to distance themselves from a celebrity or not.
- Discuss the circumstances under which the public reject a sponsor-celebrity relationship.
- Can the public be forgiving of a celebrity whose image has taken a tumble? Discuss relevant case studies to produce an argument that answers this question.

Further readings

Agrawal, J., & Kamakura, W. A. (1995). The economic worth of celebrity endorsers: An event study analysis. *Journal of Marketing, 59*, 56–62.
Ding, H., Molchanev, A., & Stork, P. (2011). The value of celebrity endorsements: A stock market perspective. *Marketing Letters, 22*(2), 147–63.

Elberse, A., & Verleun, J. (2012). The economic value of celebrity endorsements. *Journal of Advertising, 52*(2), 149–65.

Wildschut, T., Sedeikes, C., Arndt, J., & Routledge, C. (2006). Nostalgia and consumption preferences: Some emerging patterns of consumer tastes. *Journal of Consumer Research, 20*(2), 975–93.

5

The Political Capital of Celebrity

The worlds of politics and celebrity have historically never been far apart. At one time, before the days of Hollywood and television, and multi-millionaire sports stars, politicians were *the* celebrities of their day (Grier & McLaughlin, 2003). We should probably not be too surprised that the two are closely linked. Politicians, like show business celebrities, need to be able to perform in front of large audiences and cope with fame and the intrusion that they can bring into their private lives. The close relationship between these two worlds has been further illustrated and manifest in the extent to which public figures have moved between the two. Politicians hang out with celebrities. Celebrities adopt political causes and endorse politicians. Celebrities have with, varying degrees of longevity and success, sought entry into elected political office.

In 1980, former movie star Ronald Reagan was elected President of the United States, having previously served as Governor of California. In October 2003 former Austrian world body-building champion turned movie star Arnold Schwarzenegger was elected Governor of California. He served a second term from 2007 to 2011. In 1986 move actor and director Clint Eastwood was elected Mayor of Carmel California. Celebrity and politics have been closely intertwined for a long time. It is not unknown either for elected politicians to leave public office to enter the world of entertainment. In the United States, Jerry Springer was Mayor of Cincinnati and in the United Kingdom, Robert Kilroy-Silk was a Member of Parliament before they both quit politics to become television chat show hosts. Sometimes, public figures move repeatedly in both directions. Thus, the American actor, Fred Thompson, moved from acting into politics, then back into acting again before once more seeking political office. Some political observers have concluded that Washington and Hollywood have become so closely intermeshed at different levels that they are barely separable any more (Cannon, 2003).

During the final two decades of the twentieth century, politics and celebrity came increasingly into close contact. This development might be seen as part of a wider push on the part of politics, political parties and politicians towards the use of commercial marketing techniques to reach electorates during major election campaigns. Given that celebrities, as we have seen already, have been widely used to endorse commercial products, it would seem to be a natural extension of this process to use them in a political marketing context. This is not the only factor though. Many celebrities have become politically active independent of party politics by taking on causes usually associated with poverty and man-made or natural disasters.

There are several aspects to this trend in relation to party politics. One has been a transformation of political messages that concentrate on style rather than substance. Formally dull election broadcasts within the United Kingdom, for instance, were transformed over two decades from 1980 as political parties sought the help of advertising agencies and television producers to construct promotional campaigns centred on the use of television (Gunter, Saltzis & Campbell, 2013). The mixing of politics with celebrity culture represents an extension of the growth of marketing approaches to party politics and of the wider personalization of politics, whereby politicians focus on selling their personalities rather than their policies (see Couldry & Markham, 2007). This persistent trend in using personality to gain political capital also coincides and has undoubtedly been driven by declining party identification and membership and weakening ties to specific political ideologies (Langer, 2007, 2009). The adoption of celebrity-cultivating strategies by politicians is a further extension of personalization with the belief that by gaining celebrity status a politician can gain yet further political capital in societies permeated by celebrity-obsessed populations (Couldry & Markham, 2007).

To make political broadcasts more convincing rather than always using politicians to speak to camera – a skill that many did not possess – professional actors or presenters have increasingly been instead. In the United States such techniques had been used for a long time, and have become increasingly important over time. Coupled with this change, political parties and politicians courted celebrities to offer their endorsements during election campaigns not just by appearing in political advertisements or broadcasts but also by turning up to live political events and going on mainstream television shows.

At the same time, politicians themselves have sought formal media training to enhance their own performances when appearing on television, radio and in other media settings. In becoming more skilled as performers, their televised appearances diversified and these evolved from short interviews on mainstream news broadcasts to more lengthy appearances in entertainment shows where they frequently sat alongside established celebrities. In so doing, some celebrity status began to rub off on politicians as well.

Despite the high profile attained by celebrity activists and endorsers in recent times, celebrity political activism has a longer history (West & Orman, 2003). Before the days of movie stars, well-known artists, musicians and writers spoke out on important political issues of their times. Some writers such as Ernest Hemingway even fought in overseas conflicts. One early movie activist was Marlon Brando who, in the 1960s, worked on behalf of UNESCO to raise money for child poverty. French movie star Brigitte Bardot meanwhile campaigned to control the killing of baby seals (West, 2008; West & Orman, 2003).

Former journalist turned rock star, Bob Geldof, has been perhaps the highest profile musician activist with the 1985 Live Aid concert instigating a quarter of century of lobbying for an end to poverty and famine in Africa. Long before Geldof's entry into activism, Beatle George Harrison teamed up with other major pop music artists in 1971 to hold a concert at Madison Square Garden in New York to raise money for the United Nations Children's Fund for Relief to Refugee Children in Bangladesh (West, 2008). Other celebrity campaigners who have worked on behalf of movements designed to tackle poverty, starvation and disease around the world have included actresses Mia Farrow and Angelina Jolie and rock star and lead singer of U2, Bono. Jolie has also campaigned on behalf of women subjected to sexual violence in war zones around the world (Sands, 2013).

Celebrities have also got involved in domestic politics as vocal and public endorsers of specific political candidates in general elections. Celebrities in the United States have aligned themselves with or against specific presidential candidates and incumbents during the 1960s and 1970s, with John Wayne and Sammy Davis Jr supporting Richard Nixon in 1972 and Warren Beatty speaking up for Nixon's rival George McGovern. During this period, Oscar-winning actress Jane Fonda was vocally opposed to American involvement in the Vietnam War and almost risked her career over her political views.

Some celebrities got involved in debates about nuclear armament with well-known recording artists such as Linda Ronstadt and James Taylor playing at concerts to raise money in support of anti-nuclear lobby groups. Others, such as Stevie Wonder, got involved in racial discrimination issues both in the United States and South Africa.

Some celebrities have embarked on campaigns to raise public awareness and understanding of matters by which they have been personally touched or directly affected. Actor Michael J. Fox has worked tirelessly to support research that can find a cure for Parkinson's disease, from which he suffers. Some celebrities have created their own lobbying organizations. Member of one of the most successful pop bands of all time, Bono, established DATA (Debt, AIDS, Trade, Africa) with support from the US administration to tackle debt in poor countries (see West, 2008).

Whether the intersection of celebrity and politics is a good thing or not is a matter that is open to debate. In the context of determining the value of 'celebrity' the core question is: Does celebrity have political capital? The answer to this question is not straightforward. There is little doubt that politicians prefer to use mass media such as television to reach electorates over attending lots of live meetings. Political meetings and gatherings still take place, but no longer have the significance they once did. They tend to be carefully orchestrated and are often televised. The political capital of celebrity in politics also depends upon the precise nature of the link between the two. Celebrity politics can take different forms (Marsh, 't Hart & Tindall, 2010). In each case, a different formula may be needed to establish whether celebrity has political capital.

The political capital of celebrity might also depend upon the political system in which it is used. The use of celebrities to endorse political contenders has been commonplace in countries such as the United States for some decades, whereas it has a shorter history in countries such as the United Kingdom. The two countries differ in the length of time over which commercial marketing techniques have infiltrated politics. The politically interested in the United Kingdom have traditionally relied upon political party information released by political sources and have therefore been less attuned to reception of political endorsements from celebrities (Schuessler, 2000).

West and Orman (2003) identified a number of celebrity politics types. There are politicians skilled at dealing with the media and who get a lot of coverage because of this. This coverage in turn enhances their public profile. There are then other non-elected political figures who work with or alongside politicians and also have media profiles in their own right. There are elected politicians who were formerly famous outside politics and carry that celebrity with them into the political arena. There are also spokespersons for non-political organizations that nevertheless get involved in politics to lobby for their employers.

According to Marsh et al. (2010) these authors identified six celebrity political types: 'celebrity actors (Leonardo DiCaprio), celebrity politicians (Arnold Schwarzeneggar), celebrity athletes/sports figures (David James, an England footballer), celebrity businesspeople (Richard Branson), celebrity musicians (Alanis Morrisette), and celebrity public intellectuals (George Monbiot), a UK writer and journalist)'.

Street (2004) distinguished between a celebrity politician who is a standard politician with a public profile and one who is by profession a celebrity but who talks about political issues or causes. Despite criticisms that have been levelled against politicians who court publicity through activities designed to accumulate some kind of celebrity status, such actions can serve useful democratic purposes provided the political figure utilizes fame for justifiable political communication reasons rather than as a pure self-indulgence. Mukherjee (2004) made further distinctions between celebrity endorsers of politicians (Oprah Winfrey) and celebrities who become politicians (Jesse Ventura/Ronald Reagan). 't Hart and Tindall (2009) offered the following typology: celebrity advocates, celebrity endorsers, celebrity politicians, politician turned celebrity.

Pulling these various lists of public figures types together, the following principal celebrity/political types emerge. The Celebrity Advocate is a high profile celebrity figure who tries to raise public awareness of specific policies. The Celebrity Activist is a high profile celebrity from outside mainstream politics who speaks out on behalf of good causes. The Celebrity Politician is a celebrity, possibly from the world of film, television or sport, who seeks political office. The Politician Celebrity is a professional politician who acquires quasi celebrity status by associating with celebrities. Then, there is the Politician who uses Others' Celebrity, and this is a professional politician who receives an endorsement from a celebrity. In so doing, he or she also becomes connected to celebrities and may acquire some celebrity status themselves through association. We shall now take a closer look at each of these types.

Celebrity advocates

Celebrities often become involved in politics as advocates of specific causes as well as endorsers of politicians. Celebrities such as Angelina Jolie, Bono and

Bob Geldof represent prime examples of celebrity figures who have spoken out on behalf of international political issues. Often these celebrity political figures do not disclose their own 'politics' in terms of how they might vote, but use their public profiles to speak out on behalf of causes that often require action on the part of all politicians regardless of their specific political orientations. Other celebrities pin their colours to the masts of specific politicians – much as Oprah Winfrey did in the 2008 US presidential election in supporting Barack Obama.

Celebrities may have many different reasons for becoming supporters of political issues or causes. For some, it may be a first step towards a career switch into politics. More often however it does not mean this. Instead, celebrities may feel drawn to specific issues as a result of events in their own lives that have raised their awareness of specific social problems. Because they have wealth and fame through their professional lives, this means they have access to media platforms to speak out on issues. Their public profile means that people may listen to what they have to say (Dunscombe, 2007). Sometimes they may even use their personal wealth to fund the causes they support so as to directly intervene to bring about change.

The political capital of celebrity endorsers can depend upon the specific celebrity and their own standing as celebrities. The type of celebrity they are and the ways they obtained their status can be critical factors underpinning their political capital with the general public. A celebrity who achieved that status because of their talent, hard work – in other words they earned it, celebrities whose status is linked to a high status activity, celebrities whose longevity, and celebrities with a broader demographic appeal all potentially have greater political capital ('t Hart & Tindall, 2009). Examples here include Ronald Reagan and Arnold Schwarzeneggar. The political capital of celebrities is a phenomenon not restricted to West democracies. There are other examples that can be found in Eastern countries such as India and Indonesia (Hughes-Freeland, 2007; Mukherjee, 2004).

The idea behind using celebrities to promote politics and politicians derives from the perceived effectiveness of using celebrities to endorse commercial products and services. As we have already seen, advertisers love to use celebrities and often take it on faith that a celebrity's endorsement of their brands will enhance the brands' public image and ultimately volume of sales. Using celebrities to 'sell' politics is based on a premise that politics can be treated as a commercial commodity and made more appealing to people when popular celebrities speak out of its behalf. Sometimes celebrities emerge simultaneously promoting commercial products and political issues. This happened with film actress Virginia Madsen who at the same time promoted anti-ageing cream and combined with that commercial brand to back a campaign for the American League of Women Voters designed to get women more engaged with politics. While acknowledging that it was important for women to look good and feel good about themselves, the campaign also encouraged them to become more intellectually active by thinking about important issues of day in the context of deciding how to vote in political elections.

Another hook-up between celebrities and politics occurred in the United States in the Declare Yourself campaign that encouraged people to become involved in civic activities and voting in elections. The primary target was young people and young celebrities such as America Ferrera, Zac Efron and Jessica Alba were deployed to try to promote the youth vote (Stanley, 2006).

Whether celebrities have any significant political impact has been widely debated. Certainly, many members of the public have been found to dismiss such celebrity influences. A survey by CNN/USA Today/Gallup found that very few Americans surveyed (3%) believed that celebrities can be effective in influencing the political process in relation to causes and issues on which they speak out. Most people (64%) believed that celebrities were not too effective or effective at all. When asked more directly whether entertainment celebrities could influence their personal position on a specific issue, making them feel more positive about it, an overwhelming majority (87%) rejected any celebrity influence, while only around one in ten (11%) said that a celebrity might influence them. Equally, most people (78%) claimed that a celebrity's political activism made no difference to their interest in that celebrity's professional work. Although among those individuals who acknowledged that they had been politically influenced by a celebrity, half claimed that the celebrity's activism had made them more interested in his or her professional work as an entertainer (Gillespie, 2003).

Another American survey found that just over half of people questioned (51%) claimed that celebrities had little or no positive influence on the causes they promoted. Older people tended to be more sceptical than younger people on this matter. Around 1 in 2 people aged up to 43 years believed that celebrities could make a difference to the causes they supported, compared with 4 in 10 people aged 44 and older (Public Relations Society of America, 2008). Of course, this sort of public opinion about celebrities' political influences does not constitute evidence of celebrity effects on people awareness of political issues or their feelings about political candidates.

Celebrity activists

Celebrity activists are defined by their adoption of causes that they speak out about, raise money for and actively become engaged through the launch of initiatives. There are many celebrities, especially from the fields of music and movies, that become politically engaged in this way. In some instances, their political (with a small 'p') status becomes formalized when political organizations other than political parties adopt them to operate as ambassadors to represent their political sponsors in spheres such as fighting disease, poverty and political suppression. Two of the best examples here are film stars Angelina Jolie and George Clooney. Celebrities who are serious about gaining real political capital take a leaf out of the book of professional politicians and hire political consultants to advise them in terms of how to lobby effectively (Smillie, 1998). There have even been celebrities, such as rock star, Bono, that have established their own lobbying organizations.

According to some commentators, political debate has become simplified to a point where politics has become closely entwined with entertainment (Corner & Pels, 2003). There is no doubt that politicians and celebrities can enjoy a symbiotic relationship that brings them each valuable benefits. Celebrities have fame but may not be taken seriously in the sphere of politics. Politicians may have political credibility and seek to raise their profile (Smillie, 1998).

Political parties and social movements that engage in political lobbying can adopt celebrity spokespersons to increase their popularity. This means not just utilizing a celebrity to raise public awareness of the policies or issues on which they stand or campaign, but also to increase the degree to which they are liked (Street, 2002).

Bang (2007) has documented the rise of the so-called cartel party that embraces a range of political hues. Such parties can articulate a diverse range of political standpoints without being accused of hypocrisy or indecision. Whether such parties represent a more robust position in respect of obtaining or retaining political office is less clear. In a climate in which the public hold a general distrust of all politicians, the failure of politicians to display consistent policies only confirms their unreliability. What has emerged, according to Bang, is a new phenomenon of the expert-celebrity party. This is a response to an increasingly complex political landscape in which ordinary citizens have been empowered through their use of digital technologies. Fighting on the basis of policies may be less successful than demonstrating one's fitness to govern. This approach places emphasis of personality politics in which the person seeking office is the brand being sold. New media tools such as blogs, micro-blogs and social networking sites are used alongside mainstream entertainment to reach out to ordinary people using platforms to which they can relate.

These observations have been contested and certainly more empirical evidence is needed to verify Bang's model. Nonetheless, one fact that cannot be disputed is that politics is a world built upon networking. The world of celebrity works in a similar fashion. Engaging with one celebrity can result in others joining in. If a political cause attracts support from a number of celebrities – each with their own fan bases, which may also comprise different demographics – a critical mass of support can emerge that has significant political capital (Street, 2002).

The value of celebrity support of political movements has been confirmed by opinion polls that have investigated the political capital associated with celebrity. Jackson (2005) found that young people in Canada were more likely to agree with specific political statements when they were apparently endorsed by well-known celebrities from the worlds of music and sports. Even relatively unpopular political positions were rendered somewhat more acceptable when endorsed by celebrities.

Frizzell (2011) used an interventionist study to investigate celebrity effects on people's political opinions. In this case, the people who took part were presented with a statement made by rock star Bono regarding a fictional foreign policy issue. Support for a specific political position was stronger when it was promoted by Bono than when its endorsement apparently derived from a more traditional political party source.

The potential downside for political movements in adopting celebrities is that there is a risk that closer integration of politics with the world of entertainment could be regarded as trivializing political debate. There have already been concerns voiced about a 'dumbing down' of politics with political parties increasingly adopting commercial marketing techniques to promote their policies and their candidates, the relentless rise of personality politics, and politicians' increased use of negative campaigning that focuses on the incompetency of political rivals rather than informing electorates about the changes they will make if elected to office. Some writers, however, have argued that 'dumbing down' may be a good thing if it takes the form of a less elitist type of political news reporting that engages more people (Temple, 2006).

A more positive use of celebrity in politics has taken the form of celebrities engaging in campaigns to encourage people to take part in the democratic process. Thus, rather than pinning their colours to a specific political mast, celebrities promote politically neutral campaigns that aim to get people to take an interest in politics and to participate in elections, regardless of whichever party they might vote for. Such non-partisan celebrity activity was illustrated by the 'Rock the Vote' campaign in the United States in which music TV channel, MTV, recruited celebrities such as Public Enemy's Chuck D to encourage young Americas aged between 18 and 24 to vote in the 2004 and 2008 US Presidential elections. A similar campaign ran in parallel to this in 2004, titled 'Vote or Die', with Sean 'P Diddy' Combs actively involved (Media Vest, 2004). What is not clear so far is what impact these campaign eventually had on voter turnout (Payne, Hanlon & Tworney, 2007).

Celebrity politician

Celebrities sometimes go beyond simply taking up good causes and lobbying on their behalf and seek to take political office. One of the best examples of this 'celebrity politician' is Ronald Reagan, a one-time 1940s and 1950s B-movie star who formally entered the political arena through his trade union work within the film industry and eventually became a two-term Governor of California, America's richest state and ultimately a two-term President of the United States. Following in his footsteps some decades later as Governor of California was ex-champion body builder and movie star Arnold Schwarzeneggar.

Celebrities who turn to politics to serve in political office must be popular, but be popular for the right reasons. They must display a genuine commitment to wanting to serve rather than seeking high office simply to add a further dimension to their existing celebrity status. They must be able to demonstrate to the people that they are seeking office for the right reasons and that they have the authority, commitment and know-how to do the job.

Some writers ('t Hart & Tindall, 2009) have also noted that there are other factors that will play an important part in determining whether a celebrity will seek to become a politician. The more the political system is controlled by political parties, the less often celebrities will put themselves forward. The extension of a party's brand through association with a famous celebrity may be attractive to the party, but have less appeal to the celebrity.

Another factor that might come into play and enhance a celebrity's chances of gaining capital with the public is when the existing political system and politicians in general are held in low regard. Finally, a celebrity who turns to professional politics must be able to show how their past life can be framed within the expectations and requirements of their new political life. If a celebrity's past life involved incidents or remarks that might call their character into question, some damage limitation will be needed to sweep the slate clean. A celebrity-linked financial or sexual scandals, or who engaged in immoral or illegal practices, might be regarded as problematic for responsible public office. Equally, even if a celebrity led a respectable, blame-free life, if they espoused social or political values at odds with the political party they have become aligned with, these inconsistencies must be addressed directly and honestly.

Even if celebrities are successful in being elected to political office, there is evidence to show that not only their tenures but also their wider involvement in politics tends to be temporary. Celebrities-turned politicians tend to remain in politics for shorter time periods than non-celebrity political entrants ('t Hart & Tindall, 2009).

Political celebrity

Celebrity can enter politics through another route. In this particular instance, a politician seeks to gain celebrity status by engaging in activities that underpin celebrity-dom for other celebrities. A politician's own attractiveness and charisma can sometimes be sufficient to win them this status. If they attract sufficient media attention and if that attention does not simply promote them for their political activities but also enables the public to become familiar with them in other ways, celebrity status will follow. For this to work, however, a politician must possess qualities that make them interesting in their own right. Such qualities might distinguish them by their intellectual brilliance or sometimes in terms of their quirkiness or stupidity.

Usually, positive qualities such as speaking their mind, being amusing, or perhaps being normal will deliver longer-lasting celebrity status, while pulling stunts such as appearing on a reality show, will more often attract short-term celebrity profile only. Thus, when UK Member of Parliament for Bethnall Green and Bow, George Galloway, appeared on the Channel 4 reality show *Celebrity Big Brother* in January 2006, he attracted considerable criticism from the public and Parliament for what was seen as a publicity stunt. Although he lost this parliamentary seat in 2010, he won a different one (Bradford West) in 2012. In 2012, British politician, Nadine Dorries, who was Member of Parliament (MP) for Mid-Bedfordshire entered as a contestant in the ITV1 reality show *I'm a Celebrity, Get Me Out of Here*, and claimed she did so to create a platform to communicate political issues to the public, she was criticized by the press and Parliament for failing to be available for a month for her constituents while being paid as an MP, and was then the first contestant voted off the show (Batty, 2012).

Is celebrity politics good for society and good for democracy? The answer depends upon the nature of the political celebrity and the way celebrity is used in politics. A well-known and well-liked celebrity might be capable of brightening up a dull political landscape and stimulating the interest of electorates that have become alienated from political culture. A trusted celebrity could bring public confidence in political institutions. In contrast if political parties misuse celebrity entrants and the celebrities themselves allow this to happen, and the public perceive that a celebrity-turned politician is no different from other politicians, the celebrity can quickly lose his or her political capital. Any disingenuous tendency on the part of professional politicians to court and cultivate a celebrity status for themselves can also trigger negative responses from the public. A politician who appears on a high profile television chat show will do themselves no good if their appearance only serves to underline how far removed and out of tough they are with everyday public interests and concerns.

Bang (2004) referred to 'everyday makers' to describe citizens who feel driven to enter politics or speak out on political matters publicly. These individuals are often not politically aligned and so it can be difficult for political parties successfully to co-opt the opinions of such people as part of their own policy portfolio. Bang (2009) further described how the 'everyday maker' phenomenon came to prominence during the 2008 US presidential election to the benefit of Barack Obama. What also surfaced here was the way that second generation web technology, and in particular interactive websites used by politicians facilitated the involvement or ordinary citizens in the political process. Obama's website MyBO had 2 million active users and was a site from which 200,000 events were organized. Obama's own rapidly evolving celebrity status at the time, driven largely by his charisma when interviewed by the media and when speaking at rallies undoubtedly helped to attract online interest in his campaign.

His opponent John McCain lacked this celebrity status. Acknowledgement of this led his campaign team to recruit little-known Alaska governor, Sarah Palin, as his vice-presidential running mate. Palin was regarded, initially, as a good public performer who would appeal to women. Unfortunately, her inexperience at the highest political level and apparent lack of knowledge about many domestic and world political affairs meant that she was out of her depth intellectually. Despite her homespun appeal that resonated well with voters across much of Middle America, she was no match for tough media interrogators and attracted ridicule from late night television satirists. This was a clear example of celebrity status thrust upon someone who had not yet earned it.

Politicians using the capital of other celebrities

We have already seen that politicians can benefit from celebrity capital that is provided by celebrity endorsers. In those cases, it is established celebrities who were in the driving seat. In other words, the celebrities unilaterally elected to endorse a political contender because they agreed with their policies or admired their personal qualities (or both). There are increasingly occasions when politicians themselves seek out celebrities to be seen with in the hope that this will pull in political support from those celebrities' fan bases. Do celebrities therefore have democratic value?

Celebrity and democratic value

The democratic capital of celebrity emerges when celebrities can exert a positive impact on the political engagement of members of the public. This might be measured in terms of people's open acknowledgement that a celebrity has ignited in them a greater interest in or deeper involvement with politics. It might also be manifest in terms of more widespread public discourses about politics linked to celebrity discourses.

The big question here is whether people who previously had little interest in politics or civic affairs can become more enthusiastic about it because a celebrity whom they admire has spoken out about political issues. In one investigation of this issue, Couldry and Markham (2007) combined a national survey with a smaller qualitative exercise in which 37 people agreed to maintain diaries for

3 months in which they recorded in their own words their reflections on different current political issues and involvement with celebrity issues.

For many diarists, keeping up with the lives of celebrities was a regular feature of their own lives. For some, keeping up with celebrity gossip was far more important that keeping up with political developments. On a much wider scale, when clustered on the basis of their relative levels of interest in a wide range of different political, economic, and cultural topics, only a minority (14%) exhibited interests dominated only by celebrity matters. Many more (41%) were interested in a range of current affairs issues while many others (30%) were interested predominantly in just one major issue (though not the same issue for everybody). For celebrity enthusiasts, their interests were dominated by realty television and celebrity gossip. They were also health and fashion conscious. They had relatively little interest in the economy, environment, crime, or Europe. Many of them were interested in the war with Iraq which was a major event at the time of this research. What this research revealed was that there are people whose lives appear to be preoccupied with celebrity culture, but they were by no means a majority of the population.

Another interesting approach has been to find out whether online political discourses are more prominent on websites operated by politically vocal celebrities as compared with celebrities more generally. Pedelty and Keefe (2010) applied a computer-assisted analysis of the linguistic contents of fan blogs of top-selling popular music stars and of similar sites run by popular music stars with a reputation for being politically vocal. They identified ten weblogs of each type. For the mainstream pop stars they began by selecting the top-selling artists during a period spanning 1960 to 2005. Their final list comprised the Beatles, Bruce Springsteen, Elton John, 50 cent, Hootie and the Blowfish, Janet Jackson, Kingston Trio, Pink Floyd, Paul Simon and N' Sync.

For the 'political musicians' blog sample, they narrowed the field down to four themes – environment, human rights, peace and labour. They then consulted activists who specialized in each area to identify which musical artists were recognized as having been most active in respect of each theme. The resultant ten artists were Bob Dylan, Rage Against the Machine, Pete Seeger, John Lennon, Phil Ochs, Woodie Guthrie, Bob Marley, Neil Young, Joan Baez and U2. Ten fan blogs were located for each of these music artists yielding 2 samples of 100 blogs for each type of musician.

They devised a political lexicon to underpin analysis of the texts of these weblogs. This was used to measure the amount of political talk that occurred on each site. They also compiled a further control sample of independent blogs that were known to specialize in discussion of music and politics. Their findings showed that the blogs of 'political musicians' contained significantly more political talk than did those of the best-selling artists. Nevertheless when compared with blogs that specialized in the discussion and music and politics together, even the political musicians' weblogs generated a fairly low level of political chatter. This study was unable to show whether popular music artists triggered political involvement among their fans, but it was apparent that artists known for their political views and activism did attract visitors to their websites with a greater willingness to engage in political discussion.

Keane (2009) asks whether celebrity enhances democracy or impedes it. Celebrities can draw attention to politicians but also draw significant attention to themselves. There is a risk that the presence of celebrities can trivialize politics (Meyer & Gamson, 1995). There is a further concern that reliance on celebrities leads to a style of personality politics that lowers the quality of political debate. In consequence, politics becomes dumbed down (Van Zoonen, 2006). Because celebrities' voices can be so prominent, they can drown out the voices of those more experienced debaters (Klein, 2007). Experts may be co-opted by celebrity activists to provide policies that acquire more political capital because a high profile public figure is articulating them. This can result not only in more attention from the public but also from governments.

According to Cowen (2000), politics has been changed by the rise of entertainment culture and market forces. Despite concerns about an apparently growing public ignorance of politics, the reality is that citizens live in a world in which power is linked to fame and wealth. Celebrity power and influence are fuelled as much by effective public relations as by pure talent and performance. It is not surprising therefore to see politics – which is ultimately about power – adopting celebrity tactics.

West and Orman (2003) argued that celebrity endorsement of political issues or of politicians does not have to be seen as detrimental to democracy. Carefully used, celebrities can prove useful in drawing in public attention to issues that might otherwise have been ignored. At the same time, they can operate in a socially and democratically constructive way in making endorsements of politicians by again catalysing public attention to political policy messages. Debates that are led by celebrities can inform and edify electorates because celebrities command public attention. Political messages can only begin to get through to people if they at first attract sufficient attention. The trick here is to ensure that the celebrity's fame and appeal do not overshadow the political endorsee or the issues being considered. The democratizing effects of celebrity politics therefore operates by breaking down the predominance of political elites in determining the ways in which serious political issues are discussed. Celebrities can open up even complex political issues and make them accessible to ordinary people.

The benefits of celebrity involvement in politics can only fully be felt however if the issues upon which political debates take place are comprehensively examined and made understandable to the people. Fame alone is not enough to ensure a more open democracy. There must be a wider consideration and debate of issues that is not dominated by elite professional politicians who have their own agendas. Even if this occurs, there remains a risk that politics underpinned by celebrity – whether manifest in the form of celebrities becoming politically engaged or politicians adopting celebrity personas and tactics – results in weak leaders whose pronouncements and decisions are driven by the need to attract positive media coverage and to maintain a positive public profile (Cowen, 2000).

How influential is celebrity endorsement in politics?

We known that celebrities have played prominent parts in political elections and that celebrity involvement in political events in this way has become highly fashionable (Maurstad, 2004). But ultimately do they make a difference? Can celebrity influence be measured? To answer the last question, we do need to consider the different forms that celebrity influence might take. Celebrities have been influential in several prominent ways. The first of these has been to offer their support to politicians seeking election (or re-election). The second way is that celebrities can operate as activists who speak out about specific causes. Finally, celebrities might have a broader and less acutely defined role in raising the profile of politics more generally among electorates that are often not intrinsically interested in politics or impressed by professional politicians. What evidence exists on each of these types of celebrity political influence?

It is increasingly common these days to see political candidates standing alongside celebrities or to witness through camera cutaways from politicians' speeches celebrities in the audience listening intently. In the 2012 US Presidential primaries, republican candidate Mitt Romney was able to call upon the support of Donald Trump, Kid Rock and Cindy Crawford. When UK Labour Party leader Ed Milliband gave his keynote address to his party's annual conference in October 2012, the cameras showed actor and comedian Eddy Izzard looking on intently. Whether celebrity endorsement, whether explicit or implicit, is used as part of a politician's armoury, does it make a difference? Does it make the audience more interested in the political event? Does it lend more credibility to a politician's credibility or authority? Ultimately does it make people more likely to support the politician in question?

Commentators have presented mixed opinions about whether celebrities can make a difference in terms of the way people vote in elections. Some have observed that celebrities have little effect on people's voting decisions (Grimes, 2004; Maurstad, 2004). Occasionally celebrities shoot themselves in the foot by lobbying for people to behave one way, while behaving differently themselves. One illustration of this point was the case of the film actor Ben Affleck, who supported Democratic candidate Al Gore in the 2000 US presidential election and emphasized the need for young people to get out and vote. Affleck was then subsequently exposed for failing to vote himself in that election (The Smoking Gun, 2003).

In the end, we need hard empirical evidence to establish whether celebrity endorsers can influence political outcomes rather than opinion based on the personal observations of political commentators. One study conducted in the United States on the 2004 presidential election concluded that celebrities can make a difference (Media Vest, 2004). There was particularly strong interest in young, first-time voters in 2004, because a significant increase had been observed compared with 2000 in the proportion of 18 to 24s saying they intended to vote.

Media Vest's poll of 1,000 people found that 4 in 10 (40%) of those aged 18 to 24 were reportedly influenced by celebrity endorsers (compared to 15% of all adults). In contrast to this finding, another poll carried out around the same time reported that two-thirds of members of the electorate (65%) stated a preference for candidates who did not associate themselves with celebrity endorsers (The Front Runner, 2004).

Media Vest also reported that two celebrity-backed campaigns to promote participation in the election had begun to gain currency among voters. Two months before the Media Vest poll was conducted, rapper P Diddy launched the *Citizen Change* campaign and this was found to be known to more than one in five (22%) of their respondents. Another campaign, backed by MTV and a range of popular music artists, called *Rock the Vote*, was known to twice as many respondents (45%), with more than 7 in 10 (71%) of 18 to 24s having heard about it. The last result had no doubt been driven by the concentration of this campaign on college campuses and music concerts attended predominantly by young people.

Media Vest (2004) also reported that acknowledgement of a celebrity effect on personal voting decisions was more widespread among Democrats than among Republicans. A clear majority of Republican supporters (69%) strongly disagreed that they had been influenced by the two celebrity campaigns. This finding was confirmed by other research conducted during the 2004 US presidential campaign, which we will examine later in this chapter (Wood & Herbst, 2007). One explanation for the Democrat-Republican difference was that most celebrity endorsers during this election campaign were aligned with Democrat contenders.

Craig Garthwaite of the Kellogg School of Management, Northwestern University and Timothy Moore of the University of Maryland observed that celebrities have the ability to influence the opinions of their fans, but how and to what extent this can translate into transferred influence to a political figure who is endorsed by a celebrity is more difficult to measure. Garthwaite asked: 'If [celebrity] endorsements affect all kinds of behaviour, why would we think that they couldn't affect voting behaviour?' (Kellogg Insight, 2012).

During the Democratic primary campaign of 2008, Oprah Winfrey openly endorsed Barack Obama. A number of political researchers including Garthwaite and Moore explored whether her endorsement of Obama when he sought his party's nomination made a difference to his political fortunes.

Oprah Winfrey is extremely famous not just in the United States but also all around the world. While her influence stemmed in the first instance from her highly popular television talk show, it reaches out through other important channels. Her book club and monthly magazine represent two vehicles through which the influence of Oprah can be measured with specific metrics – her influence on book sales and the numbers of readers she can attract. In 2008, when she endorsed Obama, she has been ranked by Forbes as the most powerful celebrity in the world.

Garthwaite and Moore audited the number of subscribers to *O – the Oprah Magazine* and looked at their geographical distribution around the United States. They then related the number of subscribers in each region with Obama's electoral performance in the same regions. This simple analysis revealed that Obama performed better in those areas with the most subscribers to Oprah's magazine. As a further check on the veracity of this evidence, Garthwaite and Moore also looked back at Obama's performance in the 2004 primary race for the Senate and found no relationship between the areas in which he performed best and *O* subscribership. In fact, they estimated that Oprah's endorsement of Obama had been worth about 1 million votes to him. Given that Obama beat Hilary Clinton by fewer than 280,000 votes. One might argue that without Oprah's assistance, the outcome of the Democratic primaries could have been much different (Garthwaite & Moore, 2008).

Other evidence emerged that she might also be able to affect the political opinions of her audiences as well as the reading habits. A poll commissioned by *Forbes Magazine* found that 14 per cent of likely US voters and 26 per cent of those aged 18 to 24 years said that they might be influenced by Oprah's endorsement of a political candidate. A poll by the Pew Research Institute in 2008 followed up on this and reported that 14 per cent of people they asked said that Oprah's endorsement made it more likely that they would vote for Obama. A similar proportion said that her endorsement would make it less likely they would vote for him. Most people in the United States however (69%) stated that celebrity endorsement of Obama did not influence them in any way. Although not acknowledging personal influence of Oprah's endorsement of Obama, many people surveyed by Pew (60%) felt that others might be influenced. Out of a list of potential celebrity endorsers, Oprah Winfrey was seen more often than any other has having the potential to influence their vote. Bill Gates was in second place, with 13 per cent saying they would be more likely to vote Obama with his endorsement. Angelina Jolie, Tiger Woods and Jay Leno (6%) trailed much further behind (see www.people-press.prg/2007/09/20/the-oprah-factor-and-campaign-2008). Women (17%) were more likely to listen to Oprah than men (13%). Blacks (28%) were much more likely to listen to her than whites (12%). Oprah also resonated strongly with young adults aged 18 to 29 (26%) (O'Regan, 2012).

Another study reported that the 'Oprah effect' was influential in specific ways. Her endorsement of Obama did not invariably result in people liking him more, but it did influence the extent to which they thought he was a viable candidate. Among those people who were tested, the ones who knew about Winfrey's endorsement of Obama were more likely than those unaware of this endorsement to believe he could win the Democratic nomination (Pease & Brewer, 2008).

Another analysis by Jennifer Brubaker of the University of North Carolina investigated the role of celebrity endorsers during the 2004 and 2008 US Presidential campaigns (Brubaker, 2011). She was particularly interested in voters' perceptions of celebrity endorsement effects on which candidates were supported and their beliefs in the extent to which they felt they had been influenced themselves by celebrity endorsers and that others had been similarly influenced. Public opinion research had previously revealed that these two sets of perceptions often tend to differ. People may attribute stronger media effects to others than to themselves or to people very similar to themselves (Davison, 1983; Perloff, 1996). This phenomenon has been termed the 'third person effect'. When Oprah Winfrey endorsed Barack Obama's presidential candidacy in the 2008 election, most American voters denied that this would influence their own voting choice, but most also felt that the endorsement would benefit Obama, meaning by implication that many other people would be influenced by her endorsement of him (Pew Research Centre, 2007).

Brubaker collected data in 2004 and 2008 from samples of undergraduate students. At the time of interview, she asked them who they would vote for if there was an election that day, whether they were Democrats or Republicans, and how interested they were in the campaign. Participants were then told of various celerity endorsements of the candidates in each campaign. For instance, in 2004, George W. Bush received celebrity endorsements from the film actor Bruce Willis, singer Jessica Simpson and comedian Dennis Miller. His Democratic rival had been endorsed by actors Ben Affleck and Martin Sheen and singer Bruce Springsteen. In 2008, John McCain was supported by Arnold Schwarzeneggar and Sylvester Stallone and Barack Obama had been endorsed by George Clooney, Robert DeNiro and, of course, Oprah Winfrey (Brubaker, 2011).

After being given this celebrity-related information, the participants were invited to evaluate their liking for each candidate, their impression of him, the extent to which the celebrity endorsements had influenced their decision to vote for him and their estimates of the extent to which other people might be influenced by these celebrity endorsements. Little evidence emerged of first-person effects here whereby participants admitted that they would be strongly influenced themselves in their voting decisions by celebrity endorsers.

The findings showed that in general, participants did not believe that celebrity endorsers would have a greater impact on their own voting choices that on the voting choices of other people. The one exception to this result occurred in 2004 when George W. Bush supporters believed that celebrity endorsers would have a stronger influence on their decision to vote for him than they would have on other people. The third-person effect was supported elsewhere. Participants who identified themselves as Democrats believed that celebrity endorsements of Republican candidates would have greater influences over the voting decisions of Republican supporters than over any decisions of their own or of Democrat supporters to vote for the Republican candidate. These outcomes were mirrored among participants who identified themselves as Republican supporters when making judgements about the impact of celebrity endorsements of the Democratic candidates on Democrat supporters compared with their own decision to vote (or not) and that of other Republican supporters in relation to the Democratic candidates.

According to Brubaker (2011), these results meant that 'people distanced themselves from undesirable messages' (p. 18). They also indicated that people felt that celebrity endorsements of political candidates would usually have stronger effects on people politically dissimilar from themselves than on people similar to themselves. The results question the political capital of celebrity endorsements in general elections at times when political beliefs and convictions are polarized. What this means is that most people tend to have their minds made up about the candidate they will vote for before campaigning is very far advanced. With only a few floating voters, there may be little scope for celebrity endorsements to influence voters' positions.

Celebrities and good causes

Celebrities like to back causes. Trevor Thrall of the University of Michigan and colleagues confirmed this observation when they examined a sample of 147 celebrities identified by website Celepedia and found their ranking by Forbes before searching the celebrities' own websites and a news database for links between the celebrity's name and specific words such as 'advocacy', 'politics' and 'charity' (Thrall, Lollio-Fakhreddine, Berent, Donnelly, Herrin, Paquette, et al., 2008). Number of hits on Google and number of stories about the celebrity in the news database were used as key metrics to generate a star power rating for each celebrity. They found that over six in ten (63%) of their sample of celebrities had been involved in some type of political campaigning, and those who also featured in the Forbes top 100 list tended to be the more politically active (90% engaged in advocacy).

The same authors conducted a follow-up analysis with a different sample of 165 celebrities linked to 53 environmental groups. Once again, celebrities with the highest star power rating were the most politically active. Although celebrities seem to be increasingly politically active as their own power rating rises, does this necessarily make them more influential? Thrall and his colleagues found that over a period spanning 1981 to 2007, celebrities were actively involved in debating and speaking out about global warming but there was no indication that celebrity involvement in such issues was associated with more news coverage. Celebrities may make regular media appearances but often these are fleeting and have little influence on public debate. Celebrities might have star power and this can help to raise the public profile of lobbying organizations but does not also impact upon the news agenda or indeed public awareness of causes (Brockington, 2014; Brokcington & Henson, 2014).

Further evidence emerged from research into the role of celebrity engagement with the make Poverty History Campaign. This was also known as the 'One' campaign. A number of music concerts – the Live 8 concerts – were held a few days before the G8 Summit at Gleneagles in Scotland in July 2005. The presence of certain celebrities did influence the agenda of the campaign which became focused on poverty in Africa despite the initial pronouncements from the concerts organizers about an agenda to draw international governments' attention to worldwide poverty (Sireau & Davis, 2007).

A follow-up report (DATA report) about the G8 summit indicated that the group had delivered on many of its poverty-reduction promises and that celebrity influence had played a part in shaping this outcome. Further closer examination of G8 countries' aid commitments found that while it had increased, it had failed to reach earlier targets for increased investment. There was no evidence where investment had been made that the size and location of this aid had been influenced by pressure from celebrities. An analysis of 'One' TV advertisements found that their narratives were suffused with Western values and rhetoric endorsing materialism and individualism rather than humanitarianism and collectivism (Fain, 2008). In many ways the celebrities had moved towards the agenda of G8 governments rather than setting their own independent agenda for change (Monbiot, 2005).

Celebrities' political views and their influence on young people

Evidence has emerged that young people can have their political beliefs and opinions influenced by celebrities. Celebrities who speak out on behalf of political issues can draw people's attention to these issues. Among young people, there is evidence that celebrities can encourage young people to become more interested and engaged in political matters (Austin, Van de Vord, Pinkleton & Epstein, 2008). Whether this increased attention to politics translates into whether young people choose to vote in elections and which candidates they will vote for is much less certain (Austin et al., 2008; Wood & Herbst, 2007).

The challenge of getting young people interested in politics is important because as first-time voters they may lack the knowledge they feel they need to have to take the right decision or to place a vote that makes a difference. In lacking the knowledge of politics, young people can also lack the confidence to cast a vote. An interest in politics can also drive its perceived importance. When the political process is regarded as important, then people will be more strongly motivated to take part in it (Rothschild, 1978). People who do not feel involved in politics and who also lack much knowledge about political matters can create an environment of instability for political candidates. Those ignorant of politics are also likely to lack any degree of familiarity with political candidates and may therefore not know who they should vote for (Burton & Netemeyer, 1992).

This political and candidate ignorance means that first-time voters or others who feel politically uninvolved are susceptible to outside influences over the way they vote. It is not surprising therefore that political marketing activities and the use of celebrity endorsers are regarded as important vehicles for attracting these voters. Citizens who are not confident in their own knowledge and political judgement may turn to opinion of leaders for guidance in forming their own political positions and allegiances. One theory of persuasion has argued that behaviour is usually driven by the attitudes we hold and can also be shaped by perceived social norms that are relevant to the behaviour being considered (Ajzen, 1991). In relation to voting behaviour therefore the way our family members and close friends vote can be highly influential in determining the way we choose to vote. In fact, for voters who generally exhibit low involvement in politics, it may be perfectly acceptable to vote in the same way as immediate family members to retain consistency with those closest to us. Under these circumstances, celebrity endorsers are likely to have little impact because maintaining political conformity with our immediate social network is most significant.

Another set of factors can come into play however that can be a game changer in terms of how voting decisions are influenced. If a politically naïve or uninvolved voter adopts the opinion that his or her vote does not really matter in the greater scheme of things, they may become further withdrawn from the political process. This situation can arise if the individual wishes to vote for one political party knowing that it stands no chance of winning the election within the constituency in which the vote will be cast because of the overriding dominance of a rival party. In this instance, celebrities can be utilized to draw attention to the need to vote and to give reasons why a specific candidate should be supported (Howell, 1986). Celebrities can be especially useful here when targeting young voters because they often represent an important point of social reference for individuals whose psychological identity is still developing (Crouch, 2004; Kamins, 1990).

The potential of celebrities to promote politics among young people might also depend upon whether the existing political system has customarily adopted celebrity as an integral part of the political process. In the United Kingdom, for example, political marketing techniques were used sparingly before the 1990s, but have been adopted more vigorously in more recent times (Gunter et al., 2013). The use of celebrity in politics has been regarded as one method for effectively re-engaging a politically alienated youth. In practice, celebrities have experienced mixed success in terms of their political capital with young people. A movement called 'Red Wedge', led by musician Paul Weller in the United Kingdom in the 1980s enjoyed little success in encouraging young people to vote for the Labour party (Heard, 2004). The relevance of celebrity to politics however may depend upon the degree to which it has traditionally formed an integral part of political campaigning processes.

Jackson and Darrow (2005) carried out a study of college students in Canada. They found that celebrities could influence the political attitudes of these young people. Where a celebrity endorsed an opinion already held by a student, that opinion became even more strongly held. More significantly, opinions initially found to be unpopular among these students, became less so if a well-liked celebrity was found to hold them. In a further study along similar lines with American students, he found once again that when a celebrity endorsed a specific political opinion, it became more accepted among students (Jackson, 2007).

One of the problems with this type of research has been that the 'celebrities' are chosen by the researchers. The students who took part were presented with so-called celebrities and then invited to indicate their political attitudes on specific issues before and after finding out that these celebrities held these attitudes. What we don't know here is whether these 'celebrities' were regarded as having true celerity status by the students who took part in the studies.

Wood and Herbst (2007) conducted research with first-time voters from the 2004 US presidential election to find out whether celebrity endorsers influenced voting decisions. They also made comparisons in this respect between Democrats and Republicans. They reasoned that celebrities would potentially have greater impact on young voters with low involvement in politics. This expectation was based on the findings of previous research that confirmed that when people's political interest and involvement are at a low level, they will be more likely to turn to external sources for advice about how to vote (Burton & Netemeyer, 1992). They also expected to find differences in susceptibility to celebrity endorser influences between democrats and republican supporters. This difference was anticipated because most celebrity endorsers at that time supported Democrat candidates. Republicans could therefore be expected to reject these endorsements.

Wood and Herbst surveyed more than 500 undergraduate students online. Respondents declared which political party they supported and the extent to which different sources – family and friends, celebrity advertising campaigns, celebrity-attended events – helped them with their voting decisions, that is whether to vote at all and which candidate to vote for. Respondents were also asked to recall the names of any celebrities to whom they could attribute specific voting decision effects.

Overall, family and friends emerged as the most influential sources over voting decision identified by these first-time voters. The two least influential sources were community events arranged or attended by celebrities and political advertisements that featured celebrities. As anticipated, political advertisements were more widely endorsed as sources of influence by Democrat supporters than by Republican supporters. In fact, celebrity endorsers were regarded more often by Democrats than by Republicans as influential in encouraging first-time voters to vote and in deciding which candidate to vote for. Around half of the respondents could recall the name of one celebrity who they could single out as an influence telling them to vote, one in three could recall two celebrities and one in six could recall three celebrities. In total, the respondents named 74 public figures including actors, entertainers, and other media figures, and also some politicians.

According to this evidence therefore celebrity endorsers were perceived by a few young, first-time voters as having some part to play in helping them decide to vote and who to vote for. More importantly, though, perceived celebrity influence was weak compared to family and friends. For many first-time voters, celebrities were not regarded as credible sources of advice about political decision making. From some of the quotes provided by these respondents, young voters could be quite scathing about celebrity endorsers. According to one respondent here, 'Ben Affleck has no idea what he is talking about'. Another remarked, 'I find it funny that a rapper (P Diddy) was telling people to vote' (Wood & Herbst, 2007, p. 154). Yet another was even more dismissive: 'If you need a celebrity to help you to vote, then you should not be voting' (Wood & Herbst, 2007, p. 153).

Another approach has been to try to manipulate political outcomes through controlled celebrity exposure. This method was used by Usry and Cobb (2010) who conducted an experiment to investigate whether celebrities could influence American college students' choice of presidential candidate. Before they did anything else however these researchers carried out initial ground work to establish the 'celebrity status' of a number of public figures. On this occasion, however, the endorsement of a celebrity did not help the candidate. In fact, celebrity support worsened the candidate's position among the students.

Using a different approach, Inthorn and Street (2011) carried out 13 focus groups and 26 in-depth interviews with young people in the United Kingdom. These young people, who were in their teens, were willing to accept that celebrities could play a part in drawing public attention to political issues but felt that some celebrities were better suited to this than others. A celebrity needed to be more than famous to serve as an effective and credible advocate on a political cause. There were gender stereotypes in play when the teenagers were invited to judge the credibility of male and female celebrities in political contexts. On a show such as *The X-Factor*, for instance, the judge and founder of the show, Simon Cowell was seen as the dominant figure for reasons linked to his apparent masculinity. Female judges on the British version of this talent contest, such as British pop singer Cheryl Cole and Australia actress and singer, Danii Minogue, were subtly denigrated in terms of their political maturity through references to them as 'girls'. The teenagers' awareness of the political involvement of favourite celebrities did not result in a feeling of political empowerment on their part. The political influence of celebrities – which attached mostly to specific public figures who were differentiated by their wealth and power within their profession from other celebrities who were simply 'well-known' to the public – was regarded as contained within a specific community of which the teenagers did not see themselves as a part.

Veer, Becirovic and Martin (2010) conducted another experimental study with adult participants of voting age recruited from Bath and Bristol in the south-west of England. Data were collected from a variety of locations including public libraries, medical centres and on trains. Pre-tests were used to select a small number of celebrities from a larger pool who satisfied a criterion of being likely to appear in political advertising. A further criterion was that the celebrity was recognizable at all. Three female celebrities (Helen Mirren, Kate Winslet and Lily Allen) and three male celebrities (David Beckham, Anthony Hopkins and James Blunt) were chosen. Photographs of these six celebrities were obtained and presented with the slogan 'I vote Conservative, do you?' The main sample of participants provided further ratings of each celebrity in terms of their familiarity, attractiveness, trustworthiness and persuasiveness. In the end, Kate Winslet emerged as the highest regarded celebrity of all those evaluated.

In a further pre-test two articles were drafted that were each allocated to ten participants – an experimental group and a control group. The article given to the experimental group talked about the importance of voting in the election and about poor voter turnout in the 2001 election. The control article discussed the history of Bath city. Two further sets of scales were given to the participants to provide measures of their own political engagement and involvement to pre-test the power of the articles to create political salience in readers, that is, to raise their awareness of the importance of taking part in the democratic process by voting in elections.

In the main study, participants recruited from different public locations were randomly allocated one of the two articles. After presentation of one of the articles, the participants received one of two version of the vote Conservative advertisement. One version featured a celebrity endorser (Kate Winslet) and the other featured a non-celebrity endorser. Finally, the participants completed further questions and scales that included measures of their degrees of interest and involvement in politics, attitudes towards the political advertisements and the endorser, and their voting intentions. The researchers were completely blind to which condition the participants had been assigned to.

Further checks confirmed that Kate Winslet was familiar to the participants and far more so than was the non-celebrity endorser. While exposure to a celebrity endorser resulted in the advertisement being more favourably regarded, it had no impact on voting intention. A further analysis revealed however that the effect of celebrity endorser on voting intention did occur among participants who had indicated a relatively low level of involvement with politics. In this case, the celebrity endorser increased the strength of their voting intention. Among participants for whom politics and involvement in political processes were important, exposure to a celebrity endorser made no difference to their voting intentions.

The researchers concluded from this analysis that celebrity endorsers can have political capital. This is most likely to be felt among people who customarily are not deeply involved with politics. Celebrities can draw in their attention, produce more positive attitudes towards political messages and encourage them to think more seriously about voting.

Nownes (2012) conducted a controlled experiment with pre-tests and post-tests during which 500 participants were exposed to factual information about different celebrities' support for political parties. He randomly allocated a sample of over 500 American college students to conditions in which one group was presented with a description detailing how actress Jennifer Aniston had supported and given money to the Democratic Party and more specifically to Barack Obama's presidential campaign, a second group received a similar description concerning quarterback Peyton Manning's support of the Republican Party and candidate John McCain's campaign, and a third, control group received no such descriptions. All groups were tested twice, once before and once after this intervention about their own political allegiances and attitudes. Nownes found that celebrities can influence the public's views of political parties and at the same time celebrities' own political activities with parties can affect public opinion about them. The mere presence of a celebrity endorser is not sufficient to guarantee a positive result for the associated politician. In fact, when a celebrity is disliked, this negative image can transfer also to people's perceptions of the political party being endorsed. Equally, among those people who already dislike a political party, their liking for a celebrity who publicly supports that party can take a tumble.

Summary

As we have seen in this chapter, the political capital of celebrities can be measured in a number of ways. Celebrities have engaged in political activism to draw public and government attention to important political issues or to speak out about political events. They have also engaged in events to raise money for political campaigns or the outcomes of political actions – especially in relation to the outcomes of armed conflicts, natural disasters and poverty. Celebrities have endorsed politicians during elections campaigns. They have also stood for election and sometimes served in political office themselves. Celebrities can effectively use their public profiles to draw attention to political issues, to raise funds and support professional politicians who are seeking election to high office.

As with other forms of celebrity capital, however, the successful impact of celebrities in the political sphere cannot always be guaranteed (Brockington, 2014). The reputation of the celebrity in question is an important factor as well as the perceived goodness of fit between the celebrity and the nature of the political campaigning in which they had become involved. There have been instances when celebrity endorsers have boosted the election performance of politicians – with the most talked about example of this being Oprah Winfrey's backing of Barack Obama in the 2008 US Presidential election. Politicians should be advised though always to observe caution before courting celebrities or being seen by the public to do so, particularly if the purpose is transparently designed to persuade people that they have greater political credibility because they have the support of famous public figures. The political capital of celebrities is a moving target that does not simply exude from a celebrity because of their public fame, but is to a great extent negotiated by people in their role as citizens on the basis of the relevance of celebrity involvement in each political instance.

Key points

- The worlds of celebrity and politics have historically often been inter-mixed.
- Politicians have used celebrities to enhance their standing with the public in an attempt to win votes during election campaigns.

- Celebrities have got involved in politics through political activism or even by becoming professional politicians. A number of well-known film and popular music stars have spoken out on political issues or engaged in events designed to raise money or other forms of support for communities in need.
- Research has shown that celebrities can trigger greater public interest in specific political issues.
- There is less clear evidence that celebrities have sufficient political capital to influence the outcome of political elections.
- Professional politicians can achieve celebrity status in their own right if they have charisma and demonstrate that they have the ability to step outside politics and still do or say things that impress the public.
- Scholars have debated whether celebrities' involvement in politics has been good or bad for democracy. For critics there is a risk that celebrity can cheapen politics through a process of 'dumbing down'. For other observers, if celebrities can draw people's attention to important political issues and motivate them to get more involved, this must be seen as a good thing for democracy.
- Whether a celebrity can have a significant impact on the political opinions or behaviours of people depends upon the standing of the celebrity and whether in a political context the celebrity is perceived to be a genuine and credible spokesperson.

Topics for reflection

- Are citizens more likely to vote for a politician endorsed by a celebrity or not. Discuss with examples.
- Celebrities can be effective in raising the public's interest in political matters at home and abroad. Present an argument for this premise with relevant evidence.
- Celebrities make better politicians than politicians made celebrities. Is this true?
- Celebrities can be effective at getting young people interested in political matters. Examine the evidence to support this claim.

Further readings

Bang, H. (Ed.) (2003). *Governance as social and political communication.* Manchester, UK: Manchester University Press.

Brockington, D. (2014). *Celebrity advocacy and international development.* London, UK: Routledge.

Brubaker, J. (2011). It doesn't affect my vote: Third-person effects of celebrity endorsements on college voters in the 2004 and 2008 Presidential elections. *American Communication Journal, 13*(2), 4–22.

Couldry, N., & Markham, T. (2007). Celebrity culture and public connection: Bridge or chasm? *International Journal of Cultural Studies, 10*(4), 403–21.

Mukherjee, J. (2004). Celebrity, media and politics: An Indian perspective. *Parliamentary Affairs, 57*(1), 80–92.

Nownes, A. J. (2012). An experimental investigation of the effects of celebrity support for political parties in the United States. *American Politics Research, 40*(3), 476–500.

6

The Health Capital of Celebrity

In September 2012, film actress Gwyneth Paltrow and a number of other A-list celebrities publicly endorsed the 'Stand Up to Cancer' campaign that aimed to raise money for cancer research. Major American TV networks offered their support by donating an hour of peak-time to cover a related fund-raising event. Paltrow subsequently promoted the same campaign in the United Kingdom, where she continued to spend much of her time (Time, 2012). For Paltrow, this was a cause close to her heart and a serious commitment. In terms of outcomes, however, how much influence can a celebrity like Paltrow have on enhancing public awareness or raising funds?

In November 2012, rock star manager, reality TV show star, and talent show judge Sharon Osbourne announced that she underwent a double mastectomy as a preventive measure against getting breast cancer, a decade after recovering from colon cancer. She said she took the decision to have both breasts removed when she discovered she had a faulty gene that increased her chances of getting breast cancer. In one report, Mrs Osbourne was quoted as saying: 'As soon as I found out I had the breast cancer gene, I thought: "The odds are not in my favour".' It was further reported that she had spent £300,000 on cosmetic surgery to her face, stomach and legs (Harding, 2012).

On 14 May 2013, the news media around the world reported that film actress Angelina Jolie had announced she had undergone a double mastectomy as a preventative measure against breast cancer after her doctors had told her that owing to her family history she had an 87 per cent chance of getting the disease. Her own mother had died from cancer at the age of 56 and Ms Jolie said she wished to give assurances to her children that the same disease would not carry her away prematurely (BBC News, 2013).

Linking a famous and familiar face to a health campaign might succeed in drawing attention to it, but does it have any more profound and lasting effects? Can celebrities help people remember the issues better? Can they help to shift public attitudes and beliefs? Can they render campaigns more effective at influencing public health behaviour? Does celebrity have health capital? When celebrities personally experience serious illness or as in Sharon Osbourne's and Angelina Jolie's cases also take extreme preventive measures, do they have additional health capital because they are more closely connected to the health issue being considered? How many women might think after reading her story that they ought to get genetically screened and take similar preventative action if diagnosed as being in an 'at risk' category?

Celebrities' involvement in health issues tend to occur for one of two reasons. The first is through a personal experience of suffering from a particular chronic or potentially life-threatening health condition themselves or knowing someone close to them who has. The second is that they have been recruited to endorse a health issue for payment. While the health capital of high profile celebrities has been widely acknowledged, medial experts have disagreed on whether celebrities have a socially and medically useful role to play in promoting public health.

In one debate about this matter between medical experts conducted in the British Medical Journal, that subsequently received widespread media attention, Geoff Rayner, former Chair of the UK's Public Health Association and an Honorary Research Fellow at City University argued that celebrities can be effective at drawing in short-term public attention to health campaigns, but that they have less useful capital in terms of shifting health beliefs or behaviours (Raynor, 2012).

In the opposite corner, Professor Simon Chapman of the University of Sydney countered that celebrities could have many positive benefits in relation to the promotion of health-enhancing practices on the part of the public. Celebrities might not be medical experts, but often they have had personal experiences that make them qualified to advise ordinary people, in lay terms, to take action to protect themselves or those they care about in relation to health matters. Chapman acknowledged that celebrities who got involved in health campaigns did sometimes receive a bad press, and were occasionally personally culpable, but that more often, they added significant value in terms of raising the profile of health issues and doing so in a way that ordinary people could identify with (Chapman, 2012).

According to Chapman, 'Those concerned about celebrities in health campaigns invariably point to examples that have gone badly wrong or that fail to change the world for ever. They hone in on celebrity endorsement of flaky complementary medicine or quack diets, ridicule incidents where celebrities have wandered off message or blundered, or point out cases where celebrity "effects" are not sustained. But they are silent about the many examples of celebrity engagement that have massively amplified becalmed news coverage about important neglected problems or celebrity involvement in advocacy campaigns to promote evidence based health policy reform' (Chapman, 2012, p. e6364).

A number of extremely well-known celebrities of their day have engaged in widely publicized battles of their own with serious illnesses and were believed anecdotally to have played important roles in raising public awareness and understanding of specific health conditions. Singer, Olivia Newton-John was treated for breast cancer, actor, Michael J. Fox developed Parkinson's disease and cyclist Lance Armstrong recovered from testicular cancer to continue competing successfully at the highest level in his sport. Armstrong was later discredited and stripped of his Tour de France titles when disclosures emerged that he had taken performance-enhancing drugs and other treatments banned by the sport (Quigley, 2012).

When celebrities do lend their names to health causes, they often attract disdain from media commentators who question their motives. There could indeed be a valuable initial benefit to a health campaign of adopting a celebrity endorser. The longer-term effects can be less certain. It is not simply a question of whether celebrities can have any long-term effects at all on how the public engage with major health issues, but also whether their influence is positive or negative. The public can be selective in whether they take celebrities' health messages to heart. This applies even to young people who are often identified as the ones most at risk from celebrity influence.

A prime example of selective rejection of celebrities has been evidenced in the United Kingdom, where growing numbers of people aged under 25 have cut back on their consumption of alcohol, often citing the excessive behaviour of celebrities as the reason why. In a climate dominated by social media in which their own drunken antics might be captured via mobile cameras and uploaded onto the internet to be seen by employers, many young people have sought to avoid doing embarrassing things in public. Rather than emulating celebrities pictured in the media falling drunkenly out of night clubs, young people are rejecting these role models (Dowling, 2012).

In contrast, cases in which well-known celebrities get seriously ill can have a major impact on public awareness and action associated with specific health issues. This impact can also be especially pronounced among at-risk groups in the general population who are the same age or gender as the celebrity. When Australian actress and pop singer Kylie Minogue had breast cancer, her high profile, especially among the young, drew attention to the disease. Anecdotal evidence surfaced that there had been a 'Kylie effect' here. The publicity she attracted about her condition and treatment led to more women in the target age range seeking to have mammography. The downside of this effect was that many women at low risk of breast cancer sought mammograms unnecessarily and some subjected themselves to radiation exposure even though they had no symptoms (Debnath, 2012; Tucker, 2012).

In another case, again from Australia, of cricketer Shane Warne was seen in public smoking again after taking part in a well-paid advertising campaign in which he had endorsed nicotine replacement therapy. Critics in the press challenged his motives for taking part in the advertising campaign, when a more serious health message to emerge from this incident was the risk to relapse even when taking this therapy. What are these risks and what can be done about them (Tucker, 2012)?

Another sphere is which 'celebrity' has been identified as having a potential impact upon public health has been in regard to people's eating habits and how these might be shaped by celebrity chefs. Since the earliest years of television broadcasting, there have been professional cooks that have presented cookery programmes and usually spin-off recipe books or recipe articles in popular magazines (Dawes, 2009). The cooking genre has grown dramatically on television during the twenty-first century driven by cooking magazine programmes, and most of all by reality competition shows with culinary themes. Some of these performers are chefs – often world renowned – with their own award winning restaurants and others are home cooks or food writers. There is no doubt that the most popular TV chefs and cooks accrues significant celebrity capital as measured by the sales figures of their recipe books, which tend often to top best-sellers lists.

In the United Kingdom, professional chefs/cooks such as Heston Blumenthal, Nigella Lawson, Jamie Oliver, Gordon Ramsay and Delia Smith have international fan bases. It has been claimed that these individuals have shaped cooking habits and diets through their signature menus and publications (Rohrer, 2009). Public polls have found that people claim that celebrity chefs had influenced decisions they had taken about their eating habits (Magee, 2011). More formal analyses of celebrity chefs' recipes, however, have discovered that many dishes contain excessive amounts of fat, salt, and sugar and have nutritional values that fall below healthy benchmarks set by health authorities (Jones, Freeth, Hennessy-Priest & Costa, 2013). As yet, no controlled tests of specific celebrity chef effects on the way people eat or prepare food have been published.

We have seen already that there is evidence that celebrity endorsers can have consumer capital, corporate capital and political capital. Can they also have health capital? Can celebrities serve as effective spokespersons for health issues and as effective endorsers of health campaigns? As with political endorsements by celebrities, in the health context, celebrities can get involved in specific campaigns or become involved more generally in raising the public profile of specified health conditions. In both instances, the ultimate objectives are to make the public more aware, to change public beliefs and behaviours, and to raise money for research and treatment. The potential health capital of celebrities can derive from healthy celebrities as well as from celebrities who have personally suffered from specific illness or ill-health conditions.

Media coverage, celebrities and health capital

Celebrities depend upon the media to maintain their own public profile and when they get involved in endorsing good causes. Whether or not celebrity has its full impact is therefore dependent upon the nature of media coverage it receives. This observation is true in respect of the realization of celebrity health capital. A celebrity may offer the potential to promote a health condition and to raise public awareness in ways that might benefit public health. Whether relevant health messages get through to people however will depend upon whether health issues are foregrounded or whether the celebrity's personal profile overshadows the health lessons. This outcome has been observed in relation to celebrities' endorsements of commercial products and has been referred to as the 'Vampire effect'.

One example of where media coverage of a celebrity's health-related behaviour presented a distorted message that failed to take advantage of an opportunity to present a more positive one comes from Australia. The Australian cricketer, Shane

Warne, was regarded as one of the greatest exponents of his sport ever and at his peak was one of the country's biggest sports celebrities. Warne was a smoker. In November 1998, Pharmacia Upjohn, a large pharmaceutical company announced a deal with Warne to promote Nicorette gum and patches. This product was designed to help smokers ease themselves off the habit of smoking. As part of the publicity surrounding this advertising campaign, Warne undertook to quit smoking with Pharmacia Upjohn, according to many Australian press reports, allegedly offering him a $200,000 incentive to stop smoking for four months. It was not very surprising that the press subsequently engaged in a campaign on monitoring him to ensure he did not relapse. Just a few days short of the four months deadline, he was photographed smoking. Much critical media coverage followed. About a year later, he was spotted smoking again while on a cricket tour in New Zealand.

Chapman and Leask (2001) examined news coverage of Warne's involvement in this campaign in Australia in newspapers and on radio and television. They classified this coverage in terms of whether it had been positive or negative towards Warne or treated him a neutral fashion. Was he regarded by the news media as setting a good example to others seeking to give up smoking? Or was the fact that he was paid to give up smoking a cynical commercial ploy on his part wrapped up in a package that purported to be doing good?

Much of the initial coverage after the announcement of his sponsored campaign to stop smoking focused on whether Warne would be successful or not. It also comprised numerous alleged sightings of him still smoking. Radio commentators were particularly critical of the fact that Warne had taken money to quit smoking. In doing so, it confirmed for many media commentators that he was prepared to capitalize on his celebrity status as much as possible. For Chapman and Leask, however, more attention could have been paid to the difficulties of quitting smoking. This was illustrated well by Warne who clearly experienced great difficulty giving up despite the financial incentive given to him to do so and despite being under the watchful and critical eye of the Australian media. For Warne's sponsor, the publicity surrounding this campaign was beneficial and the company experienced significantly increased sales of their product.

The loss of an opportunity to use a celebrity to promote important health messages was reported in relation to the death from cervical cancer of British reality TV celebrity, Jade Goody. She dies of cervical cancer on 22 March 2009 aged just 27. Her illness had attracted widespread media coverage and coincided with the introduction in the United Kingdom in September 2008 of the Human

Papillomavirus (HPV) vaccination programme that targeted girls and young women. The Goody story therefore provided an opportunity to generate publicity for cervical cancer and more importantly for the preventative treatment that was being made available to those most at risk. Claims were made, including by the British Prime Minister of the time, that Goody's illness had improved public awareness of cervical cancer.

The seriousness of this disease should not be underestimated. In Britain alone, it was the second most prevalent cancer in women and killed 950 women each year. A number of risk factors have been confirmed in relation to the disease that include early onset of sexual intercourse, number of sexual partners, smoking and family history of cervical cancer. The HPV is very common and the great majority of sexually active women will become infected with it at some point in their lives. Awareness of the virus and the risk factors could be much higher than it is. The importance of screening cannot be understated and again more women need to be aware of this. Hence it might have been hoped that Jade Goody's story and the media coverage she received would have provided the information needed to promote wider public awareness of cervical cancer and the need to be screened for HPV.

Evidence has been reported however that the British press coverage of Jade Goody's illness paid considerable attention to her personal circumstances and events in her personal life but presented relatively little coverage concerning risk factors associated with this cancer. Goody got married after being diagnosed with cancer. More than one in five articles about her during the period between her initial diagnosis and her death concerned her wedding. More than one in ten press reports dealt with christenings of her children and a similar proportion covered her funeral. Only about 2 to 3 per cent of news stories mentioned any of the risk factors associated with cervical cancer or described the signs and symptoms of this cancer. As such, Goody's story represented a missed opportunity on the part of the British press to spread the word about HPV and cervical cancer (Hilton & Hunt, 2010).

Analyses of the way the media have covered health issues can reveal insights into the potential message effects of celebrities who speak out on health issues or who suffer from them, but do not measure these effects in any direct way. What evidence is there that celebrities can effectively change the public's awareness of specific health issues or encourage people to take appropriate action for purposes of prevention, early diagnosis or treatment of specific illnesses? There are four types of research evidence we can turn to for further analysis of this question. The first of these consists of instances when a celebrity experiences a health problem which receives a lot of media attention. The second is when a celebrity speaks out on a health issue perhaps because someone close to them has become ill or died. The third is when a celebrity promotes a specific product or treatment because they have been paid to do so. The fourth type of evidence concerns the lifestyle choices of celebrities who engage in behaviour that can place their health at risk.

There has been plenty of commentary and research about the role that the media can play in raising the public's health awareness. It can also encourage people to engage in preventative behaviours and to be vigilant in terms of responding quickly to any problematic or unusual symptoms they might experience. Key messages here are that it is better, if possible, to prevent than to cure where some illnesses are concerned and that where prevention is not always possible, early diagnosis improves chances of making a full recovery.

The media can play their part in drawing attention to health issues, health risks and actions to take. Public health messages can be conveyed via media news coverage as well as through fictional drama stories. What has become clear, however, is that the news media can often give disproportionate attention to specific health issues, while ignoring others. For example, cancers such as melanoma and cervical cancer have been found to receive a little over a quarter of the news coverage of breast cancer. There is further evidence that celebrity involvement in stories about cancer appears to enhance their perceived newsworthiness and increases their chances of receiving coverage (Hilton, Hunt, Langan, Bedford & Petticrew, 2010). The advantage that accrued from celebrity involvement is that in the event that a celebrity was diagnosed with a form of cancer that normally would receive little coverage, it could have its profile boosted, at least temporarily (MacKenzie, Chapman, Johnson, McGeechan & Holding, 2008).

Fictional storylines that involve popular characters in long-running televised soap operas can draw people's attention to serious health issues. When *Coronation Street's* Alma Baldwin died of cervical cancer in 2001, a 22 per cent increase was registered in the numbers of women taking smear tests (Richardson, Owen-Smith & Howe, 2002). TV drama storylines have been identified as serving a helpful health consciousness raising purpose that is more subtle than formal educational campaigns (Collins, Elliott, Berry, Kanouse & Hunter, 2003; Verma, Adams & White, 2007). Nonetheless, there is also a view that more could be done to emphasize the full range of at-risk groups for certain diseases, while also changing the ways in which others are dramatically treated to ensure that the most relevant health messages are being conveyed. Mortality rates and the primary causes of death among characters in televised soap operas depart significantly from what happens in real life. Causes such as ill-health in the form of cancer and heart disease that represent prevalent killers in everyday life tend to appear rarely in the world of soaps (Crawford, Hooper & Evans, 1997).

Celebrity illness and celebrity health capital

From time to time, well-known public figures get seriously ill with life-threatening health conditions. Some recover and others do not. These cases can attract a lot of media attention and through this the story about the celebrity's health problems can reach a wide audience. As we have already seen, news media might focus on particular aspects of a celebrity's illness while ignoring broader issues about it that would be of greater educational value to the public. Nevertheless, if a celebrity has a very high profile and has previously apparently enjoyed good health, the fact that even those who are rich and famous have become seriously unwell might convey the message to others that a particular health condition is something that could happen to anyone. Two health issues where celebrities have been most prominently involved are sexually transmitted diseases and cancer.

Acquired immunodeficiency syndrome (AIDS) is caused by infection with the human immunodeficiency virus (HIV). This syndrome first attracted public attention in the mid-1980s. HIV can be contracted via the exchange of bodily fluids that in most cases takes place during sexual activity. It can also be acquired through transfusions of infected blood. When it initially received wide media attention, in developed countries HIV infection was associated most prominently with homosexual activities. This message distracted from the fact that the disease can be transmitted just as readily through heterosexual intercourse. Despite extensive media coverage – some of it driven by high profile celebrity cases such as those of Hollywood actor Rock Hudson and rock star Freddie Mercury – for many years public sensitivities to personal risk did not reflect the scale of the epidemic that emerged across the 1980s and into the 1990s (Aruffo, Coverdale & Vallbona, 1991; DiClemente, Boyer & Morales, 1988; Kappel, Vogt, Brozicevic & Kutzko, 1989).

Research evidence has emerged however that indicated that people are responsive to disclosures of celebrities being infected by HIV. One particularly high profile case occurred when American basketball star, Earvin 'Magic' Johnson revealed at a press conference on 7 November 1991 that he was HIV positive. One follow-up investigation led by Seth Kalichman of the Medical College of Wisconsin surveyed Chicago men as they waited for their trains to work. In all, 361 men took part who were on average aged 29 years. Most were single and over half had had at least two sexual partners in the previous year. One in five had had homosexual contact and nearly one in three had previously contract a sexually transmitted disease. Nearly one in four had been with a prostitute. Some of these men were interviewed before Magic Johnson's HIV disclosure and others were questioned between three and ten days afterwards.

Kalichman and his colleague Tricia Hunter reported that there was greater concern about personal risk from HIV infection among those men interviewed *after* Johnson's disclosure than among those interviewed before it. Many more of those interviewed after the disclosure compared with those interviewed before it said they were interested in getting more information about AIDS. All the men surveyed afterwards said they had heard about Magic Johnson's disclosure. Most of them (86%) said they had talked to others about it three days after his press conference, while by ten days after his disclosure all the men interviewed said they had spoken to others about it. Another interesting finding was that Caucasian respondents were far less concerned about AIDS than were African-American respondents in the post-disclosure interviews.

This investigation did not provide conclusive causal evidence of an effect of a celebrity disclosure about their infection with a potentially life-threatening disease, but its findings were indicative that it could have had this impact. The increase in concern about HIV/AIDS among an at risk male sample most of whom had openly acknowledged not only knowing about Johnson's disclosure but also to talking about it provides evidence that it had impacted upon their conscious awareness of risk. What the study failed to do was control for other possible factors that could have influenced risk perception here and also to find out whether perceived risk was eventually translated into safer sexual practices (Kalichman & Hunter, 1992).

A further investigation followed through with the idea that 'Magic' Johnson's announcement that he had tested positive for HIV had a public health impact and considered also whether the strength of this influence depended upon what people thought about Johnson before this disclosure had been made. Brown and Basil (1995) hypothesized that the health impact of this announcement would be more profound among people who had already established an emotional involvement with Johnson – that is among people who held him in high regard as a basketball star and looked up to him as a role model.

As we have seen before, this type of emotional attachment to a celebrity arises from what psychologists have termed a 'parasocial relationship'. Fans can forge strong emotional bonds with their favourite celebrities from afar that can seem every bit as real as relationship they form with people with whom they interact more directly.

Brown and Basil's research found that this emotional bond was a critical factor underpinning any potential effects 'Magic' Johnson's personal health circumstances might have on the subsequent reactions of people who had heard the news. Young men who had forged a vicarious emotional bond with the basketball star were more likely than those who had not to show increased concern about AIDS, concern about their own risk of AIDS and increased intention to reduce any of their own high-risk sexual practices. Others who knew about 'Magic' Johnson but who had not entered into any kind of parasocial interaction with him were far less likely to exhibit changed perceptions or intentions linked to HIV/AIDS.

Celebrity capital has been measured in relation to cancer awareness and preventive action. There have been a number of high profile cases of celebrities who have succumbed to cancer. Some have recovered fully, and some have not. The death of a celebrity from serious illness can trigger a significant public response in terms of more people proactively getting themselves checked out. The death of Linda McCartney from breast cancer on 19 April 1998 produced an unprecedented level of enquiry about breast screening in the United Kingdom. In the 12 months leading up to April 1998, the telephone information service CancerBACUP answered 160 telephone calls on average each day. In the week after Mrs McCartney's death, daily calls that were answered averaged 204, a 28 per cent increase. The number of calls recorded on answer machines that week doubled from normal levels. Other public announcements about cancer that occurred during 1998 had nothing like this level of impact of public enquiries about the disease (Boudioni, Mossman, Jones, Leydon & McPherson, 1998).

Further evidence has emerged from the United States and from Australia about the impact of celebrities who suffered from cancer on public awareness of different forms of the disease and prevention and treatment measures associated with them, and of the power of celebrity capital in this context to motivate people to get their own health checked out.

In July 1985, a story surfaced in the United States that President Ronald Reagan had developed colon cancer. An analysis of records of telephone calls to the cancer Information Service of the National Cancer Institute about colorectal cancer found that public interest in this disease had been heightened with increased phone calls being made about it and a corresponding increase in numbers of people taking early detection tests. Despite the spike in enquiries about colon cancer, after the President's diagnosis had been made public, they returned to normal levels after a few weeks (Brown & Potosky, 1990).

In October 1987, the American First Lady, Nancy Reagan was diagnosed with breast cancer. She chose to have a mastectomy rather than a lumpectomy and had her left breast removed that same month. Mrs Reagan's choice of procedure in this case led to questions about the influence it might have on other breast cancer sufferers' treatment choices. Evidence surfaced initially that American women aged 50 and older exhibited greater awareness of breast cancer risks after announcements of Nancy Reagan's cancer than beforehand. In one survey of middle-aged women living in Long Island, New York, a small proportion of women (8%) who were surveyed also stated that they had been influenced by her case to contact a health professional with a few (2%) had their first mammogram as a result of Mrs Reagan's breast cancer (Lane, Polednak & Burg, 1989).

Subsequent, larger scale research was carried out to investigate the impact of the Nancy Reagan case among women in America utilizing large health databases from the Surveillance, Epidemiology and End Results tumour registry (SEER) and Medicare. The SEER repository drew its data from cancer patients across nine states and other areas in the United States, including Connecticut, Hawaii, Iowa, New Mexico, Utah, Atlanta Georgia, Detroit Michigan, San Francisco-Oakland California, and Seattle-Puget Sound Washington State. SEER data were analysed for over 82,000 women aged 30 and over from 1983 to 1990. Medicare data were nationwide and comprised over 80,000 women aged 65 to 79 years who received cancer inpatient surgery for breast cancer in 1987 and 1988 (Nattinger, Hoffman, Howell-Pelz and Goodwin, 1998).

Data from the SEER registry indicated that there had been a steady increase in the percentage of patients who chose conservation surgery or radiation therapy from 14 per cent in 1983 to 35 per cent by 1990. There was small drop in breast conservation therapy from 28 per cent to 22 per cent from the 3-month period before Nancy Reagan's cancer diagnosis was made public to the 3 months after it. There was evidence that women who perhaps most strongly identified with

Mrs Reagan were the most influenced by her treatment choice. The decrease in breast conservation treatment was most pronounced in women aged 65 to 79 years – Mrs Reagan's own age group. It was also almost entirely restricted to white American women with little apparent influence on the treatment choices of African-American women. The Medicare data also for women aged 65 to 79 years confirmed the SEER data. This shift in personal treatment choices was sustained for some women, but was temporary among better educated women from higher income groups who exhibited a gradual return to less invasive treatments in the case of early diagnosis where treatment options are more varied (Nattinger et al., 1998).

One of the highest profile cases for which follow-up scientific enquiry is available is that of Australian actress and singer Kylie Minogue's breast cancer. It was on 17 May 2005 that a public announcement was made about Miss Minogue's cancer. The story was carried in major newspapers in Australia and the United Kingdom, as well as in other parts of the world. Professor Simon Chapman and his colleagues at the University of Sydney had already launched a research project examining the way the news media in Australia cover health issues and the implications of such coverage for the public's health awareness just a few weeks before Kylie Minogue's diagnosis was made public. They took the opportunity to combine with this study a supplementary investigation of the impact of this announcement (Chapman, Holding, McLeod & Wakefield, 2005).

In the seven days following this story breaking, the amount of coverage given to Kylie Minogue in television news broadcasts multiplied twentyfold compared with the 13 days beforehand. Analysis of the nature of this coverage revealed that there was a lot of comment about her chances of making a full recovery and the importance of her own health and fitness (18% of coverage), and more prominently the support of her family and friends (61% of coverage) and of the public (51%) at this time.

Despite the fact that she was a major celebrity, journalists conveyed the image of her as an ordinary person like the rest of us and also commented on the tragedy of being diagnosed with an illness such as this when she was still so young (36 years old). Other celebrities and public figures spoke out offering her words of support. The coverage repeatedly maintained an upbeat tone and reminded everyone that the prospects of a full recovery were enhanced by the early diagnosis of the disease. Integrated with this coverage were other messages aimed at the public encouraging women to get themselves checked out if they discover any symptoms and for those over 40 years old to take advantage of free mammograms that were available in Australia.

Chapman and his colleagues conducted further analyses on bookings data for mammograms at four state-based BreastScreen programmes over nineteen weeks before Miss Minogue's illness being announced, during the two weeks at the height of the publicity about it, and then for six further weeks. During the 2 weeks of peak publicity a 40 per cent increase was registered in average weekly breast screening bookings. The bookings during this period for women seeking screenings for the first time doubled. Bookings continued to occur at a much increased level for a further six weeks of monitoring and this effect was especially pronounced among women who sought screenings for the first time. The 'Kylie effect' was clear enough and had been more substantial than previous and quite extensive government-backed health campaigns about breast cancer. This effect was subsequently detected among women seeking breast cancer referrals and radiographic investigations in Britain during the month following Kylie Minogue's breast cancer diagnosis (Twine, Barthelmes & Gateley, 2000).

There was a downside to the surge in breast cancer screenings and referrals that were found to occur in Australia and Britain as a result of the 'Kylie effect'. Clinics, health centres and hospitals were overwhelmed and diagnosis times lengthened. There was further evidence that the Minogue story had also encouraged many low-risk women to come forward for breast screenings and this reduced the capacity of health services to deal with high risk patients (Kelaher, Cawson, Miller, Kavanagh, Dunt & Studdert, 2008; Williamson, Jones & Hocken, 2010). In Australia for instance there was a 20 per cent increase in breast imaging in the 6 months that followed the publicity about Kylie Minogue's breast cancer (Kelaher et al., 2008).

We looked earlier at the case of Jade Goody, a British reality TV celebrity who died of cervical cancer in 2009. Extensive news coverage was given to her illness and untimely death. Relatively little attention was given to using the story as a platform to provide wider health messages to the public about this form of cancer (Hilton & Hunt, 2010). Is there any evidence that the media attention she received had any actual impact on public awareness of cervical cancer or on screenings for it?

Lancucki, Sasieni, Patrick, Day and Vessy (2012) analysed cervical screening data for women in England between 2004 and 2010. The researchers wanted to know whether the publicity surrounding Jade Goody's illness changed the rates at which women sought cervical cancer tests. Women aged between 25 and 49 years are invited to take screening tests every 3 years and women aged between 50 and 64 years are invited to have screenings every 5 years. Screening rates can vary with time of the year. This meant that normal seasonal effects had to be smoothed out statistically in order to show whether there was a distinctive 'Goody effect'.

Celebrity endorsers of preventive health practices

One area in which celebrities have played a prominent part is in the promotion of cancer screening. We have examined evidence that has shown the health capital of celebrities who have been diagnosed with cancer in relation to motivating members of the public to get screened. What about celebrities who speak out on health issues who are not sufferers? Celebrity involvement has usually arisen because the celebrity either knew someone close to them who had cancer or had been diagnosed with cancer themselves. In determining whether celebrities can affect cancer awareness among the public researchers have a number of methods available to them in their research tool boxes. One approach is to find out how many people exhibit any self-reported awareness of celebrities talking about cancer issues. Another approach is to find out whether there are behaviour changes that occurred contingent upon celebrity-endorsed campaigns receiving widespread media attention.

When surveyed, people have been found to report some awareness of celebrities endorsing health screening or treatment practices. Telephone interviews with adults in the United States have revealed that those of screening age without a history of cancer said they could recall seeing and hearing celebrity endorsements of screening for breast, prostate and bowel cancers. After initially telephoning a sample of 4,000 households, interviews were carried out with 360 women aged 40 years and over and with 140 men aged 50 and over.

Survey respondents were initially asked, 'Have you ever seen or heard celebrities like Rosie O'Donnell and Nancy Reagan talk about getting mammograms?' Nearly three out of four of the women (73%) said they had heard celebrities talk about mammography and more than six in ten (63%) of the men could recall celebrities talk about screening tests for prostate cancer. Following a similar question, more than half of all these adult respondents (52%) said they had seen or heard celebrities such as TV news anchor, Katie Couric, talking about sigmoidoscopy or colonoscopy. Of those who had been aware of celebrities talking about these issues, one in four (25%) said that this had made them more likely to undergo mammography, three in ten (31%) a prostate test, and well over one-third (37%) a sigmoidoscopy or colonoscopy (Larson, Woloshin, Schwartz & Welch, 2005).

It is one thing for people interviewed in a survey to say they can remember seeing or hearing a celebrity talking about health issues and quite another to determine whether this represents 'health capital' on the part of celebrities. Even when claiming that celebrity endorsements of health checks made them think about getting checked out themselves, such self-attributed celebrity effects fail to pin down exactly the extent of the celebrity influence. Some celebrities may carry more weight than others in terms of attracting the public's attention or in shaping their beliefs or behaviours. Moreover, as research into the value of celebrities as commercial brand endorsers has shown, a celebrity must be seen as a credible information source. In the context of health, capital is most likely to be influenced by credibility defined mainly in terms of expertise. Does the celebrity possess relevant expertise or experience that renders them a credible source when they recommend that members of the public should seek different kinds of health screening or treatment?

Expertise in this context will derive not from questions about whether a celebrity possessed relevant medical qualifications to talk about health issues, but whether they have relevant personal experience of a health condition. This type of personal expertise may be important if healthy celebrities are to be taken seriously as public health spokespersons. Celebrities who have fallen ill or who have recovered from serious illness will be taken seriously because everyone can see where they are coming from. Do celebrities in good health who elect to speak out on specific health issues about which they feel strongly have sufficient health capital to produce real changes in health behaviour?

One particularly prominent case example involved the TV news anchor Katie Couric whose husband Jay Monahan died from colon cancer when aged only 42. To help promote the disease and more especially the importance of early screening for it, Ms Couric underwent a live colonoscopy on air on the *Today Show*. This examination formed part of a week-long campaign designed to raise public awareness of colon cancer. The campaign attracted substantial media attention. Did it have any impact?

An epidemiological assessment of colon cancer screening rates found that this campaign and the accompanying 'Couric effect' did seem to have generated important results. Extracting relevant data from physicians involved in these screenings revealed that colonoscopy rates across 22 states in the United States increased in March 2000 compared with before from 14.6 colonoscopies per physician per month to 18.6 procedures. Data were examined for 20 months before this TV campaign with 9 months following it. Patient data for a Midwestern region confirmed that the average number of procedures per 1,000 patients increased each month after Katie Couric's on-air cancer screening compared with beforehand (Cram et al., 2003).

The researchers who produced these findings concluded that the changes they observed in colonoscopy rates were linked specifically to the Couric campaign and could not be explained by wider cancer awareness events. The effects observed were also more prevalent among younger women (up to middle age) which also matched the dominant demographic for the *Today Show* in which she appeared.

These findings showed that celebrities can have health capital even when they do not themselves suffer from the disease on which they are campaigning. What is important is that the celebrity must have credibility in the health promotion context and this must derive from having some perceived professional expertise or personal experience of relevance. In Katie Couric's case, the authenticity of her commitment to the health cause she was championing stemmed from her personal bereavement and also from the fact that she was prepared herself to undergo an invasive medical analysis live on air.

Celebrities and commercial endorsement of health

Celebrities' involvement in health promotion can often occur in a commercial rather than a purely public service setting. In these cases, a celebrity is commissioned by a sponsor to provide an endorsement to a health product or service that is being made commercially available. As with other forms of celebrity-endorsed advertising, celebrities are paid for their services. For the sponsor, a celebrity's value here resides in their ability to raise the profile of the health brand and also to make the brand seem more appealing because of its association with a celebrity. The credibility of a celebrity is critical in this context. The celebrity must be liked, but must also be seen as someone with relevant expertise and the right reasons for lending his or her name to the health brand. In a health context, consumers want to know whether the product or treatment being promoted is relevant for them and safe. A highly regarded and trusted celebrity could lend then the reassurances they seek. Are consumers always swayed by celebrity endorsers, however, when it comes to their health-related purchases?

Some professional commentators have issued words of caution about the role of celebrity endorsers as endorsers of commercially sold health brands. It is always important for consumers to take care about self-prescribing drugs or treatments. It is essential to recognize that where these promotions have been funded by commercial drugs companies, sales and not public well-being can be the primary driver. This point was illustrated by a campaign for magnetic therapy products run by a company called Lifes2good in the Republic of Ireland. The company's brochure featured athlete Eamonn Coghlan on its front page quoted as saying that the therapy had benefited him. Inside the brochure, Coghlan was joined by the Irish professional golfer, Christ O'Connor who also spoke positively about these products. Yet, according to Paul O'Donoghue, a clinical psychologist and member of the Irish Sceptics Society, the medical evidence that magnetic therapy works as a cure for various ailments is scant. There is little or no scientific backing for claims that magnets can be used to treat conditions, such as rheumatism and arthritis or cancer (O'Donohue, 2012).

Celebrities and rejection of anti-health practices

We saw earlier that celebrities can provide important role models to members of the public. Children and teenagers can be especially susceptible to role model influences as they pass through stages of their psychological development in which they seek to define their personal identities as social beings. Members of media audiences, young and old, can develop strong psychological attachments to celebrities. By engaging in what psychologists have called 'parasocial relationships' with celebrities, their fans perceive them as a real part of their own lives. They can develop genuine and sometimes strong emotional feelings for their favourite celebrities. In extreme cases, fans become obsessed with their idols, follow their lives closely, collect items with their names on, model their appearance and behaviours of them and seek to have direct contact with them.

Celebrities therefore have the power, potentially, to exert considerable influences over people who admire them. This influence can be positive or negative depending upon the behaviour of the celebrity. Where celebrities indulge in behaviours that are damaging to their health, they might in turn encourage others to follow suit. Equally, if celebrities use their capital with their fans to encourage health-promoting behaviour, they could do a lot of good. In turning to the fourth type of evidence about potential celebrity effects on public health, are there general lifestyle choices or specific behavioural actions linked to a celebrity's general state of mind that have capital – in this negative capital – in the form of providing a bad influence to others?

One potentially important area of influence of celebrities in terms of health matters is drug use. Celebrities have a long history of getting involved with drugs. This might range from excessive consumption of alcohol, through reliance on prescription drugs, to addiction to illegal substances. Alcoholism and drug taking has been closely linked to Hollywood movies stars, rock stars and also sports stars. In the latter case, drugs are often taken to enhance sports performance. While there can be considerable negative currency in media coverage of celebrities who develop addictions, celebrities can also provide catalysts that enhance campaigns designed to combat drug abuse.

As his career waned, the Argentinean soccer star Diego Maradona battled with drug abuse for a number of years. His role model status with young people around the world meant that his behaviour provoked considerable concern. At the same time, the deterioration in his physical condition within just a few years after retirement from top-flight football also served as a warning to those who considered taking hard drugs. It provided a very real case study in the damage that taking hard drugs can wreak on abusers, from which even supremely fit and talented athletes such as Maradona are not immune.

A study of the 'Maradona effect' found that young people who had a stronger parasocial relationship with Maradona displayed an increased awareness of drug abuse. More importantly, these individuals exhibited greater concern about drug abuse, abstained from it and were more strongly supportive of drug abuse prevention programmes (Brown & de Matviuk, 2010).

Further evidence of how people's parasocial relations with celebrities can mediate the influences of those celebrities on awareness of issues related to well-being derived from the case of Mark McGuire, the baseball star. When he broke the home run record in September 1998, McGuire was declared an American hero and a great role model for young people. He subsequently attracted media attention for his use of a muscle-building dietary supplement called Androstenedione. Accompanying this story was further coverage of McGuire's efforts to raise awareness of child abuse. The complexity of this case stems from the mixed messages – some positive and others negative – that this sports celebrity received. In fact, for those people who felt a social affinity with him, he represented a celebrity role model with the potential to encourage both health risk behaviour – taking of muscle-enhancing substances – and public concern for child abuse (Brown, Basil & Bocarnea, 2003).

Summary

Celebrities can have value in the public health field. They can champion health issues both formally through their involvement in campaigns and informally through their personal experience of or involvement with specific health conditions. As with consumer and political endorsements, health-related activism on the part of celebrities is most likely to be effective when the celebrities are perceived to have credibility in the campaign context in which they become engaged.

When a celebrity falls ill or dies of a specific health condition, public attention can be drawn to it. Furthermore, the realization that even those individuals who seem to have everything can have their lives suddenly terminated by ill-health, especially when they have not become ill because of old age, can raise the risk awareness among the public. The message is simple, even celebrities are human. They need to take care of their health and so too does everyone else.

The health capital of celebrities can be enhanced when they can demonstrate more than just a peripheral attachment to a health issue. Where their own lives have been touched by illness either directly or through someone close to them becoming ill, there is perceived to be an emotional connection to the issue which makes anything they have to say about it more meaningful for people in general.

Key points

- When celebrities get ill or speak out on a health matter, they can draw the public's attention to specific health problems.
- Public attitudes to health do not invariably change because a celebrity has made their opinions known.

- High profile celebrities who get cancer or some other serious health condition can accumulate sufficient 'health capital' to encourage members of the public to engage in preventative behaviours.
- The fame of a celebrity is one factor that can mediate his or her influence on public health attitudes and behaviours. Celebrities that are well-liked will attract more attention. They must also be seen as having had relevant experience – either first-hand or second-hand to enhance their credibility as health advisors.
- Celebrities have credibility when they have suffered from a specific illness themselves. Their influence can be acute when the illness is a source of embarrassment for its sufferers.
- Celebrities can get involved in behaviours that pose a health risk and their effects can be either to encourage such behaviour among others or to discourage it depending upon the outcome of the high risk behaviour for them.

Topics for reflection

- Can public awareness of health issues be enhanced by the illness of a celebrity? Examine with examples.
- Investigate the factors that enhance or impede a celebrity's credibility as a health spokesperson.
- Is the 'Kylie effect' celebrity specific or can it be applied to other celebrities? Examine the evidence and consider the lessons that might be learned in terms of understanding the role that celebrities might play as promoters of good health practice.
- Discuss, with reference to relevant research evidence and case examples, how celebrities can have a negative effect on health behaviour.

Further readings

Chapman, S., Holding, S., McLeod, K., & Wakefield, M. (2005). Impact of news of celebrity illness on breast cancer screening: Kylie Minogue's breast cancer diagnosis. *Medical Journal of Australia*, 183(5), 247–50.

Dowling, K. (2012, 4 November). Boozy stars drive young onto wagon. *The Sunday Times*, p. 4.

Hilton, S., Hunt, K., Langan, M., Bedford, H., & Petticrew, M. (2010). Newsprint media representations of the introduction of the HPV vaccination programme for cervical cancer prevention in the UK (2005, 2008). *Social Science and Medicine, 70*(6), 942–50.

Kalichman, S. C., & Hunter, T. L. (1992). The disclosure of celebrity HIV infection: Its effects on public attitudes. *American Journal of Public Health, 82*(10), 1374–6.

7

The Evolving Capital of Celebrity

This book has examined the concept of celebrity capital. We have seen that celebrities now abound in many walks of life where they are seen by others to add value. This value can be financial and political, and it can impact upon the social, psychological and physical well-being of ordinary people. The diversity of celebrity has also increased over time. There are many more different kinds of celebrity today than in the past. The terms and conditions under which an unknown individual can rise to public prominence and in the process gain the accolade of 'celebrity' have also changed. While celebrities still emerge on the basis of special achievements and through association with others whose achievements have led to them gaining public prominence, earned success in the form of talent, skill, hard work and other related factors has been joined by success and prominence for which no special abilities and achievements were demonstrated other than an ability to be in the public eye. Hence, the concept arose of people who are 'famous for being famous' (Rojek, 2001).

Although many celebrities derive from traditional sources such as acting, entertainment, journalism and writing, music, politics, and sports, the celebrity community has grown in the digital era courtesy of the facilitating effects of new communications technologies that have opened many new routes to fame. At the same time, celebrities have expanded the range of activities in which they get involved and sought to extend their capital beyond their specialist fields to other domains. The general public's preoccupation with all things to do with 'celebrity' has continued to grow in the twenty-first century. The market expansion of mass media such as television and magazines and the rapid evolution of digital online media have played a part in this phenomenon.

Growing attention to celebrity and fame is manifest in rapid expansion of the readership markets for celebrity gossip magazines. In the United States, for instance, during the first half of the first decade in the new millennium, the circulations of major current affairs magazines such as *Newsweek, Time* and *New Yorker* increased by 2 per cent, but those of celebrity news publications such as *Entertainment Weekly, InStyle, People,* and *Us* expanded by nearly 19 per cent (Halpern, 2008).

In part, the continued growth of interest in and preoccupation with the celebrity phenomenon can be attributed to communications technology developments that have altered both the shape and demands of media landscapes, in turn opening up new platforms and opportunities for celebrity creation. Another factor has been the actions of some celebrities in terms of the different ways they have attempted to capitalize on their primary celebrity appeal by extending themselves into new fields where they may have no relevant qualifications or expertise.

One feature that has surfaced that underpins celebrity status and any value that attaches directly to it is the notion of a celebrity as a 'brand'. It is not sufficient that a celebrity becomes aligned with brands as a signal to the value of fame in their specific case. They must operate as a 'brand' in their own right. Their intrinsic value as a commodity is a key variable that determines how much distinctive 'capital' they possess as a celebrity which in turn determines their potential capital value to other brands that might seek to be associated with them (Pringle, 2004). Celebrities such as soccer player David Beckham who establish a personal brand that extends far beyond their original field of expertise and their continued media profile provides a self-sustaining feedback loop that maintains their celebrity capital (Harris & Clayton, 2007; Vincent et al., 2009).

The brand concept as it attaches directly to a celebrity as both a reflection of their public profile and a measure of their reputation and the public regard they command is also important to their longevity as a 'celebrity'. Although the pathways to a social profile position at which point the general public would wish to 'celebrate' an individual's image because of the level of fame they have achieved have grown in the digital era, this has created an environment in which the attainment of celebrity status can be fast-tracked, but an extended celebrity status is not guaranteed. This can mean that instant celebrities can quickly fall back into being non-entities again. The key to survival of celebrity status is the nature, strength and credibility of the 'brand' that is established around the individual's fame profile (Pringle, 2004). In the case of celebrity gained through hard work, talent, and earned achievement, continued high-level performance is the critical brand reinforcing variable. For that gained through fast-track media coverage for doing nothing in particular, it may be sustained by continuing to be seen at the right events in the right places (Currid-Halkett, 2010).

Over extensions of celebrity brands

Much of the concept of celebrity 'capital' or the value that associating or identifying with the 'famous' has for the lives of 'ordinary' people, the promotion of commodities, the wealth of businesses, the success of politicians, the awareness of political issues and the adoption of healthy behaviours has centred on a presumption that there is some specific and measurable effect that occurs in each context. In other words, there is a direct outcome of celebrity which is manifest in a capital gain for individuals, organizations, institutions and societies. An alternative view that has surfaced is that celebrity impact can be less direct and quite subtle.

Dutch researchers Siegwart Lindenberg, Janneke Joly and Diedrik Stapel have argued that celebrities can influence people through their effect on social norms. These researchers conducted a series of experiments with university students to demonstrate this celebrity effect. In one experiment, a male sports star and a female television personality endorsed a campaign against littering. Exposure to this campaign resulted in students exhibiting stronger acknowledgement of the need to look after the environment and the endorsement of standards of behaviour that reflected not only littering but other related issues.

The celebrity's impact here was enhanced if they had received positive media publicity which raised their personal status. Exposure to publicity that was critical of the celebrity and left their personal image tarnished, however, reduced and even reversed their influence on students' responses to the campaign on which the celebrity spoke out. This research demonstrated the potential campaigning capital of celebrity and how it could quickly be undermined by loss of popularity cultivated by negative media coverage (Lindenberg, Joly & Stapel, 2011). There are occasions, however, when celebrities who are well-respected in their own fields for perfectly legitimate reasons can over-extend themselves – even though they may have the best of intentions.

We have already examined the social, political and other issue (in relation to health) capital that some celebrities possess that can be applied to endorse or exemplify social scripts and issues linked to politics and personal well-being. In this vein, however, some celebrities have not just spoken out on important issues but sought to get directly involved in major intra- and international conflicts by make sweeping public pronouncements or even by offering to negotiate directly with conflicting parties.

One example of this phenomenon concerns the American film actor, Richard Gere who broadcast a televised message to voters during the Palestinian presidential elections in 2005. In a videocast published on the website of The Electronic Intifada and sponsored by Israeli-Palestinian peace lobby, One Voice, Gere was filmed saying: 'Hi, I'm Richard Gere and I'm speaking for the entire world . . . We're with you during this election time. It's really important. Get out and vote' (The Electronic Intifada, 2005). There are two kinds of naïve behaviour on display here. The first is the unqualified presumption on the part of Gere that he represented a legitimate spokesperson for 'the entire world', which he did not. The second is that his video appeal was backed by an organization with its own political agenda and this was not acknowledged.

Another example is the case of the British actor Jude Law who attempted, unsuccessfully, to negotiate a temporary ceasefire with the Taliban in Afghanistan. Law travelled to Kabul on 1 September 2008 where he gave a press conference in which he lobbied for all militant parties in Afghanistan to observe the United Nations Global peace Day on 21 September. As with an earlier Peace Day in 2007, the temporary cessation of hostilities would be used to allow health workers to enter conflict torn areas to vaccinate children. He said: 'What we hope to do . . . is to remind all parties that it is happening and see then what happens through negotiations' (contactmusic.com, 2008).

It is difficult often to know whether such celebrity interventions make a difference to those they are purporting to help, but it does seem that some celebrities have become increasingly aware of the capital they possess with mass publics beyond those domains from which they first obtained their celebrity status. A more cynical interpretation of these celebrity interventions, however, might be that they are driven by a more selfish need on the part of the famous to extend and enhance their own brand through the media publicity they can attract from such activities.

New forms of celebrity

The nature of celebrity has shifted not only in terms of the extent to which celebrities themselves believe they can make a difference politically and socially, but also in terms of the ways celebrities are now created. The rapid technological developments that have underpinned the emergence of digital broadcasting and online media have played a critical role in all of this. The development in the television market with digitization that has substantially increased the volume of broadcasts that is beamed out to people has also created a demand for more cheaply made programming to fill enormously expanded amounts of airtime. This void has created a market for reality genres that use inexpensive production techniques and actors. While some reality formats seek out fresh talent, many others do not. The actors here are a key component and often comprise ordinary people with no special talents who agree to have the spotlight thrown on their lives by cameras and beamed out for everyone to see (Bignell, 2005; Heller, 2007; Hill, 2005).

Some reality programmes have created celebrities from talent bases that had previously not managed to get a break. Hence, television talent contests that have sought to find new recording artists or general entertainers such as the *Got Talent*, *Popstars*, *Pop Idol*, *X-Factor* franchises have achieved worldwide attention and been adopted by many different nations. Although many of the contestants do not make the big-time, a few do. Others manage to develop respectable careers in which they can earn a decent living doing something they like to do (e.g. entertain people) rather than something they do not like. In this sense, such programmes might be deemed to serve a useful social purpose, not only of providing entertainment but also of finding some people new jobs and careers. On the surface there is a risk that such shows can give false hope by making the attainment of celebrity status seeming to be easy – when it is not – but the final lesson usually learned from such shows is that celebrity in the entertainment field comes on the back of genuine talent and hard work. Then there are other shows that have provided opportunities for celebrity-seeking that demand no special talents of participants (Holmes, 2004).

Fly-on-the-wall coverage of the everyday lives of individuals has captured a great deal of public attention and spawned a new breed of celebrity. American series such as *Jersey Shores* and *The Hills* and UK equivalents such as *The Only Way Is Essex* and *Made in Chelsea* are prime examples. Often these 'celebrities' are paid a pittance by the producers but enjoy the trappings of celebrity lifestyle because of their public profile – often enhanced by the attention they receive in entertainment magazines – with spin-off financial benefits that accrue from public appearances and merchandizing. 'Celebrity' here arises out of simply being observed – in this case on television – and does not call upon much in the way of talent. The intrigue for the audience stems from the voyeuristic experience of being able to peer unseen into the 'real lives' of those being filmed. Whether such programming is genuine 'reality' can be debated as television producers usually seek to follow the conventions of the medium in creating a narrative that will engage the audience (Kilborn, 1994, 2005).

For many of these 'celebrities' their celebrity status or capital can be short-lived. Nonetheless, an inherent attraction of these individuals and a powerful pull towards emulation on the part of others who seek to copy their experiences is that apparent wealth they can rapidly accumulate for not apparently having to do very much. The cheapening of celebrity capital in this way can often give false hope in terms of young people's career aspirations, in turn misdirecting them from thinking about more realistic career paths, but it also dilutes the traditional value of celebrity capital when it is borne out of real talent and striving.

The ultimate appeal of celebrity is sustained on a mass level through the performance of 'star performers' whose talents are extraordinary or unusual. They are primarily responsible for the status of genuine 'celebrity' and set targets for celebrity 'wannabes'. Over time, the growth of entertainment media has created a demand for a larger pool of performers and generated financial challenges for producers in terms of costs of employment and whether the expected returns of investment will always be achieved. The reality genre opened up a different perspective on entertainment that enabled a focus to be placed on the ordinary in the shape of everyday 'reality' as a source of entertainment rather than the extraordinary. This shift in orientation of entertainment sourcing was underpinned by financial imperatives in that with television in particular the expansion of airtime to fill created a need for cheaper programming solutions (Raphael, 2004). An episode of the situation comedy *Friends* for example cost five times as much to produce per hour as did an episode of the reality, adventure and survival series 'Survivor' (Magder, 2004). The cost of employing the talent was a major contributory factor to this differential.

Self-made celebrity online

The emergence of the internet has also been a contributory factor in the evolution of new strands of celebrity. The internet has captured the imaginations of younger generations in particular and fed their growing desire for fame. The rapid penetration and adoption of the internet around the world has produced a global communications system to which ordinary people have access not just as receivers of content but also as producers. Ordinary citizens are no longer restricted in their access to mass audiences by elite media operators. Anyone with some minimal level of computer literacy can access audiences of millions and attract global attention within a matter of moments. By uploading messages, speeches, pictures and performances any of us can gain global online celebrity status, at least on a temporary basis. For some observers, the realization that fame can be found only a few clicks away has magnified public interest in and the quest for celebrity (Choi & Berger, 2010; Hyde, 2009). Anyone who has a pet hobby on which they might claim some specialist knowledge can establish a website, upload videos of themselves and become a worldwide expert on any subject (Chossat & Gergaud, 2003).

Evolutionary psychologists have shown that it is a special quality of humans that they can observe and copy complex sequences of behaviour and internalize these patterns as cognitive schemas. In so doing, our species has developed a capacity to identify and remember those behavioural scripts that serve us best in terms of facilitating our end-goal achievements, whatever they might be. Individuals who acquire a degree of expertise in specific fields of activity that are important to the species acquired special capital or value. Accompanying this capital went social status or prestige (Neuberg, Kendrick & Schaller, 2010).

In due course, so-called prestige hierarchies developed with those individuals possessing the highest valued skills being placed at the top of the social hierarchy. Such individuals stood out from the rest of the community and acquired a localized fame or celebrity status. The emergence of the mass media facilitated the creation of communities of shared experiences (or behavioural scripts) that went beyond local communities defined by direct interpersonal interactions. Instead, communities could emerge that comprised members who were dispersed over wide geographical areas and were defined as communities only by their shared mediated experiences rather than by the fact they knew one another. Within these media communities, the most skilled exponents of specific patterns of behaviour (acting, performing, delivering expert advice and so on) rose to the top of the social order in terms of their prestige status. Media celebrities were born. Access to such celebrity status was still restricted to a relative few however.

The emergence of the digital communications era has enabled many more people to demonstrate idiosyncratic abilities to extended communities. Assuming the talent being displayed is genuine and has some relevant capital for those people who are looking on many more of us can now seek to rise to the top of different prestige hierarchies. Returning to the concept of 'celebrity as brand' the rise of the 'reality' production that features initially unknown individuals has created a new form of commodified celebrity. Reality television has become a vehicle through which commercials brands can obtain public exposure and experience news forms of brand extension through association with the emergent celebrity brands in this genre (Deery, 2004).

There is clearly no shortage of aspirant celebrities today. A survey conducted by the *Washington Post* and Harvard University among American teenagers in 2005 found that nearly one-third believed they would become famous one day (Carter, 2006). When asked to choose attributes they most wished could define them in the future, many more American youngsters chose 'fame' over 'intelligence' or even 'wealth' (Choi & Berger, 2010).

As already noted, the mainstream media have also accommodated the growing thirst for celebrity 'wannabes' with the rapid growth of reality programmes that eschew the use of professional performers and instead focus on the everyday lives of 'ordinary people' or take established celebrities and place them in circumstances where they play themselves. Whether the people who volunteer and are selected to take part in shows such as *Big Brother, Survivor, Jersey Shore* or *The Only Way Is Essex* can be classed as 'ordinary' is debatable. Many seek fame and see these shows as a fast-track to celebrity without needing to possess or demonstrate any relevant 'prestige hierarchy' skill set. Indeed, exposure on these shows generally fuels further media exposure, usually through celebrity news magazines, where these 'reality stars' sit directly alongside more traditional celebrities from the worlds of show business and sport.

The world of show business still beckons for many young people, but very often they seek easy entry through association with it than by demonstrating genuine prestige hierarchy abilities or expertise. A survey of middle-school students in the state of New York found that over four in ten chose being 'the personal assistant to a very famous singer or movie star' as their ideal job (Warren & Halpern-Manners, 2007). The difficulties and challenges of becoming genuine celebrity based on talent and performance were not lost on these youngsters, it seems, but for many of them, they sought the glamour of the celebrity world through a backdoor as preferable to another career where they might have to work equally hard to achieve success and status.

The digital era has created a form of celebrity status that is not grounded in real ability, talent and hard work. The origins of 'celebrity' derive from the prestige acquired by individuals in their communities because they were the best at what they did and because what they did was highly prized by their communities. In a mass mediated world, the everyday skills associated with everyday living have been usurped by the need to be entertained. This is doubtless connected to the fact that for most people in developed societies the service of their basic needs is secured leading them to switch their attention to higher-level social needs (see Maslow, 1954). Even with traditional mass entertainers, however, those who attained highest status were skilled exponents of specific crafts for which they had had to train long and hard. The digital era has created an environment in which fame can be won without that kind of investment of effort. Lasting celebrity still requires genuine ability and effort, but temporary celebrity can be taken without either. Reality television shows that provide pathways to fame create their own distinctive notions of 'stardom' that, in the context of 'real fame' need their own 'reality check' particularly when adopted by reality TV participants (Hill, 2007; Holmes, 2004).

At the same time, the digital era has created platforms for genuinely skilled celebrities to extend their cultural capital into consumer, corporate spheres and then beyond and more readily into social and political arenas (Choi & Berger, 2010). Such extensions of their celebrity capital can sometimes bring real benefits to others who operate in other spheres. The capital value of celebrity can bring real and substantial financial benefits to brands, the companies behind them, to national economies and to global trade. Local celebrities can oil the wheels of local events ensuring they attract more funding or social support. National and international celebrities can help to build corporate value, public awareness of important issues, and even psychological succour to the lonely and socially disenfranchised.

The emergence of online social media and the 'reality' genre on television have together opened up new routes to stardom. The appeal of these new formats for discovery of talent lies in the illusion that they appear to put 'celebrity' or 'stardom' within the grasp of everyone. The usual pathways to fame and fortune that require entrants to negotiate a more winding road to success and have to negotiate the value of their talents with professional gatekeepers who act as sole arbiters and judges can be circumvented (Andrejevic, 2003).

For many, however, the road to fame and fortune is not always paved with gold. The only 'reality' that ultimately counts is the one that sets the terms of conditions for a lasting successful career. The value of celebrity for those who seek it through fast-track routes lies in the apparent ease with which it can be grasped. Once a breakthrough has been made via the reality route, however, lasting celebrity eventually requires some degree of conformity with traditional forms of celebrity management and publicity. A reality show performer who graduates to become a *bone fide* 'celebrity' performer will acquire the usual trappings of this status including agents and managers, appearance stylists and performance coaches, and so on. Their celebrity capital will need to grow beyond its initial reliance on 'being known' for a particular series of reality genre appearances. For most of those who tread this pathway to fame, it leads nowhere beyond a fleeting appearance in the public spotlight. Even for those who reach the final stages courtesy of the audience vote, their celebrity capital is temporary and limited to feeding the distinctive news and entertainment appetites of tabloid newspapers and glossy magazines (Murray & Ouellette, 2004).

If we accept these observations, it becomes apparent that 'celebrity capital' can be differentiated not only by the metrics used to measure it or by the field in which a celebrity operates, but also more hierarchically within these spheres. Hence, there are celebrity A-lists, B-lists, C-lists and so on (Holmes, 2004). There are celebrities that command genuine public affection and respect on a large scale and over time. There are others that command public interest only among some communities or 'niches' and then only for temporary periods. Real stars today must perform in the same way as their historical counterparts. They have been joined however by a much expanded community of 'celebrities' that operate at lower levels and that come and go. Debates have ensued them about whether all these types of publicly visible individuals qualify for the title of 'celebrity' or whether they might be classified differently as 'personalities' (Collins, 2008).

Celebrity creation by the media can generate aspiration scripts for realizing personal potential, hope for the future and specific career opportunities. There are risks associated with the rapid expansion of the 'celebrity' community in that making it too all-embracing, giving the impression that it is not founded upon special talent and effort, and linking it too closely to the everyday realities of ordinary people might dilute its capital because it no longer has special cache. At the same time, celebrities that do command high capital value for their special abilities or achievements must not then allow their success to encourage personal brand extensions to realms where they are no more than ordinary. When celebrities presume to have expertise they do not possess and extend themselves too far, they run the risk of damage not only to their own capital but also to that of celebrity.

Summary

The community of celebrities has grown steadily over time and the diversity of sources from which these public figures emerge has diversified. Many celebrities still emerge from traditional sources such as acting, entertainment, journalism and writing, music, politics, and sports. The digital media era has spawned many other new supply chains. The ubiquity of so-called reality programmes on television has enabled individuals with specific talents as well as those with no particular talent at all to gain a platform for self-publicity. If media attention is sustained these individuals can accrue celebrity capital that can be used to benefit their personal career and financial fortunes and adopted by others to obtain some spin-off value. More often than not, however, this new breed of 'instant' celebrity can see their celebrity status fall away as quickly as it emerged. We have entered an era of throwaway celebrities that come and go. A few manage to achieve celebrity longevity, but often these are ones with talent and who have served their apprenticeships over many years before the door to fame was opened.

The breadth and numerical growth of the celebrity community has served a further purpose of providing fodder for burgeoning and content hungry media outlets. The media – whether we are talking about television, radio, newspapers, magazines or content published on other platforms – need a steady supply of celebrity fuel. Their own market status can depend upon it. Hence, they play along as willing partners in the creation and subsequent destruction of celebrities and through a process of celebrity 'quantitative easing' inject media marketplaces with more liquid celebrity currency of their own creation.

Celebrities can also invent themselves quite independently of the mainstream media, although in the end fame can only be scaled up to a truly lucrative level with the cooperation of the media. Digital online technologies have spawned platforms for self-publication that can command huge audiences and raise an individual performer's public profile far beyond the reach of localized performances. YouTube can act as a catalyst for instant fame and audiences that can rival in scale those of mainstream television where appearances must first be negotiated with and are often denied by choosy gatekeepers.

Despite the expansion of the pathways to celebrity, lasting celebrity capital remains for the most party the preserve of the genuinely talented and hard working. It can also depend upon celebrities not stepping outside the parameters of public expectations in terms of the settings and contexts where they have genuine capital contributions to make. Celebrities that overstep that particular mark can lose credibility and lose capital value. This loss of celebrity capital might be localized and apply to an out of the ordinary setting into which a celebrity has positioned themselves (that is making expert pronouncements on issues or topics where they lack expertise) or could if repeated become more generic.

Key points

- The digital media era has witnessed an extension of types of celebrity.
- Celebrities still emerge through the traditional routes of talent and achievement, but fame can also be captured simply by being in the right place at the right time to get media attention.
- Celebrities have capital value that can be assessed in terms of how much they are able to command public attention, raise public awareness of issues and change public attitudes and behaviours.
- Celebrities also have brand value in their own right. Ensuring that an appropriate and credible celebrity 'brand' has been produced can be the secret to longevity otherwise celebrity can be taken away as quickly as it can be obtained.
- Reality television and online media have opened up new channels for the creation of celebrities, but whether celebrity status can be retained still depends upon having a brand that signifies some value that other people attach to a celebrity's fame.

Topics for reflection

- Celebrity is more easily gained today than in the past, but can be more easily lost. Discuss with examples.
- New forms of celebrity have emerged in the digital media era. Discuss how these differ from more traditional forms of celebrity.
- Why must a celebrity also become a 'brand'? Critique this question and make an evidence-based case that provides an answer.

Further readings

Bignell, J. (2005). *Big Brother: Reality TV in the twenty-first century*. Basingstoke, UK: Palgrave Macmillan.

Deery, J. (2004). Reality TV as advertainment. *Popular Communication, 2*(1), 1–20.

Hill, A. (2005). *Reality TV: Audiences and popular factual television*. London, NY: Routledge.

Holmes, S. (2004). 'Reality goes pop!': Reality TV, popular music, and narratives of stardom in Pop Idol. *Television and New Media, 5*(2), 147–72.

Kilborn, R. (1994). How real can you get?: Recent developments in 'reality' television. *European Journal of Communication, 9*(4), 421–39.

— (2005). Reality TV: The work of being watched. *Media, Culture and Society, 27*(4), 624–6.

Neuberg, S. L., Kendrick, D. T., & Schaller, M. (2010). Evolutionary social psychology. In S. T. Fiske, D. T. Gilbert & G. Lindzey (Eds), *Handbook of social psychology* (5th. ed., Vol. 2, pp. 761–96). New York, NY: John Wiley & Sons.

References

Adorno, T. W., & Horkheimer, M. (1944/1972). *Dialectic of Enlightenment*. [Trans. John Cumming]. New York: Herder and Herder.

Agrawal, J., & Kamakura, W. A. (1995). The economic worth of celebrity endorsers: An event study analysis. *Journal of Marketing, 59*, 56–62.

Ainslie, A., Dreze, X., & Zufryden, F. (2005). Modelling movie lifecycles and market share. *Marketing Science, 24*, 508–17. Accessed 8 October 2012.

Ajzen, I. (1991). The theory of planned behaviour. *Organizational Behavior and Human Decision Processes, 50*, 179–211.

Akturan, U. (2010). Celebrity advertising in the case of negative association: Disclosure analysis of weblogs. Proceedings of the 13th International Conference of the American Society of Business and Behavioral Sciences. Available at: http://www. asbbs.org. Accessed 6 August 2012.

Albert, S. (1998). Movie stars and the distribution of financially successful films in the motion picture industry. *Journal of Cultural Economics, 22*, 249–70.

Allen, K., & Mendick, H. (2012). Keeping it real? Social class, young people, and 'authenticity' in reality TV. *Sociology, 47*(3), 460–73.

Amos, C., Holmes, G., & Strutton, D. (2008). Exploring the relationship between celebrity endorser effects and advertising effectiveness: A quantitative synthesis of effect size. *International Journal of Advertising, 27*(2), 209–34

Andrejevic, M. (2003). *Reality TV: The work of being watched. Critical media studies.* Lanham, MD: Rowman & Littlefield Publishers.

Aruffo, J., Coverdale, J., & Vallbona, C. (1991). AIDS knowledge in low-income and minority populations. *Public Health Reports, 106*, 115–19.

Ashe, D. D., Maltby, J., & McCutcheon, L. E. (2005). Are celebrity-worshippers more prone to narcissism? A brief report. *North American Journal of Psychology, 7*, 239–46.

Aubrey, J. S. (2007). The impact of sexually objectifying media exposure on negative body emotions and sexual self-perceptions: Investigating the mediating role of body self-consciousness. *Mass Communication & Society, 10*, 1–23.

Aubrey, J. S., Henson, J., Hopper, K. M., & Smith, S. (2009). A picture is worth twenty words (about the self): Testing the priming influence of visual sexual objectification on women's self-objectification. *Communication Research Reports, 26*, 271–84.

Austin, E. W., Van de Vord, R., Pinkleton, B. E., & Epstein, E. (2008). Celebrity endorsements and their potential to motivate young voters. *Mass Communication and Society, 11*, 420–36.

Badenhausen, K. (2009). Woods is sports' first billion-dollar man. Forbes, Yahoo! Available at: http://sports.yahoo.com/golf/pga/news?slug=ys-forbestiger. Accessed 30 October 2012.

Bailey, A. A. (2007). Public information and consumer scepticism effects on celebrity endorsements: Studies among young consumers. *Journal of Marketing Communication*, *13*(2), 85–107.

Bang, H. (Ed.) (2003). *Governance as social and political communication*. Manchester, UK: Manchester University Press.

Bang, H. (2004). Culture governance: Governing self reflexive politics. *Public Administration*, *82*(1), 157–90.

— (2005). Among everyday makers and expert citizens. In J. Newman (Ed.), *Remaking governance: Peoples, politics, and the public sphere* (pp. 159–79). Bristol, UK: The Polity Press.

— (2007). Parties in the swing: Between democratic representation and communicative management. Mimeo, Department of Political Science, University of Copenhagen.

— (2009). 'Yes we can': Identity politics and project politics for the late modern world. *Urban Research and Practice*, *2*(2), 1–21.

Barich, H., & Kotler, P. (1991). A framework for marketing image management. *Sloan Management Review*, *32*(2), 94–104.

Basil, M. (1987). Identification as a mediator in celebrity effects. *Journal of Broadcasting and Electronic Media*, *4*(4), 478–96.

Batra, R., & Homer, P. M. (2004). The situational impact of brand image beliefs. *Journal of Consumer Psychology*, 14(3), 318–30.

Batty, D. (2012, 22 November). Nadine Dorries voted off I'm A Celebrity . . . Get Me Out of Here. *The Guardian*. Available at: www.guardian.co.uk/politics/2012/Nov/nadine-dorries-voted-off-celebrity. Accessed 18 February 2013.

Baumeister, R. F., Zhang, L., & Vohs, K. D. (2004). Gossip as cultural learning. *Review of General Psychology*, *8*, 111–21.

BBC News (2013, 14 May), Angelina Jolie has double mastectomy due to cancer gene. Available at: www.bbc.co.uk/news/world-us-canada-22520720. Retrieved 26 October 2013.

Belch, G. E., & Belch, M. A. (1998), *Advertising and promotion: An integrated marketing communications perspective*. Boston: McGraw-Hill.

Belk, R. W., & Bryce, W. J. (1986). Materialism and individualism in US and Japanese print and television advertising. *Advances in Consumer Research*, *13*, 568–72.

Bell, S., & Hindmoor, A. (2000). *Rethinking governance: The centrality of the state in modern society*, Port Melbourne: Cambridge University Press.

Bhonslay, M. (1997). Gender gap. *Sporting Goods Business*, 10 February.

Bignell, J. (2005). *Big Brother: Reality TV in the twenty-first century*. Basingstoke, UK: Palgrave Macmillan.

Biswas, S., Hussain, M., & O'Donnell, K. (2009). Celebrity endorsements in advertisements and consumer perceptions: A cross-cultural study. *Journal of Global Marketing*, 22(2), 121–37.

Boden, S. (2006). Dedicated followers of fashion? The influence of popular culture on children's social identities. *Media, Culture & Society, 28*(2), 289–98.

Bollen, K. A., & Phillipps, D. P. (1982). Imitative suicides: A national study of the effects of television news stories. *American Sociological Review, 47*, 802–9.

Boon, S. D., & Lomore, C. D. (2001). Admirer-celebrity relationships among young adults: Explaining perceptions of celerity influence on identity. *Human Communication Research, 27*, 432–65.

Boorstin, D. (1962). *The image: A guide to pseudo events in America*. New York, NY: Vintage.

Botta, R. A. (1999). Television images and adolescent girls' body image disturbance. *Journal of Communication, 49*, 22–41.

— (2000). The mirror of television: A comparison of black and white adolescents' body image. *Journal of Communication, 50*(3), 144–59.

Boudioni, M., Mossman, J., Jones, A. L., Leydon, G., & McPherson, K. (1998). Celebrity's death from cancer resulted in increased calls to CancerBACUP. *British Medical Journal, 317*(7164), 1016.

Braudy, L. (1986). *The frenzy of renown: Fame and its history*. New York, NY: Oxford University Press.

Braunstein, J. R., & Zhang, J. J. (2005a). Dimensions of athletic star power associated with generation Y sport consumption. *International Journal of Sports Marketing and Sponsorship, 6*, 242–67.

— (2005b). Dimensions of athletic star power: The consumer perspective. *Sport Marketing Quarterly, 14*, A81.

Braunstein-Minkova, J. R., Zhang, J. J., & Trail, G. T. (2011). Athlete endorser effectiveness, model development and analysis. *Sport, Business and Management: An International Journal, 1*(1), 93–114.

Brockes, E. (2010, 17 April). I want to be famous. *The Guardian*. Available at: http://www.guardian.co/uk/lifeandstyle/2010/apr/17. Accessed on 27 October 2012.

Brockington, D. (2014). *Celebrity advocacy and international development*, London, UK: Routledge.

Brockington, D., & Henson, S. (2014). Signifying the public: Celebrity advocacy and post-democratic politics. *International Journal of Cultural Studies, 17*. Available at: www.ics.sagepub.com/content/early/2014/04/25/1367877914528532.

Brooks, C. M., & Harris, K. K. (1998). Celebrity athlete endorsements: An overview of the key theoretical issues. *Sports Marketing Quarterly, 7*(2), 34–44.

Brown, M. L., & Potosky, A. L. (1990). The Presidential effect: The public health response to media coverage about Ronald Reagan's colon cancer episode. *Public Opinion Quarterly, 54*(33), 317–29.

Brown, W. J., & Basil, M. D. (1995). Media celebrities and public health: Responses to 'Magic' Johnson's HIV disclosure and its impact on AIDS risk and high-risk behaviours. *Health Communication, 7*(4), 345–70.

Brown, W. J., & de Matviuk, M. A. (2010). Sports celebrities and public health: Diego Maradona's influence on drug use prevention. *Journal of Health Communication, 15*(4), 358–73.

Brown, W. J., Basil, M. D., & Bocarnea, M. C. (2003). The influence of famous athletes on health beliefs and practices: Mark McGuire, child abuse prevention androstenedione. *Journal of Health Communication, 8*, 41–57.

Brubaker, J. (2011). It doesn't affect my vote: Third-person effects of celebrity endorsements on college voters in the 2004 and 2008 Presidential elections. *American Communication Journal, 13*(2), 4–22.

Burton, R., Farrelly, F. J., & Quester, P. (2001). Exploring the curious demand for athletes with controversial image: A review of anti-hero product endorsement advertising. *Sports Marketing Quarterly, 2*(1), 315–29.

Burton, S., & Netemeyer, R. G. (1992). The effect of enduring, situational and response involvement on preference stability in the context of voting behaviour. *Psychology & Marketing, 9*(2), 143–57.

Bush, A. J., Martin, C. A., & Bush, V. D. (2004). Sports celebrity influence on the behavioural intentions of Generation Y. *Journal of Advertising Research, 44*, 108–18.

Butler, L. T., & Berry, D. C. (2002). The influence of affective statements on performance on implicit and explicit memory tasks. *Applied Cognitive Psychology, 16*, 829–43.

Callcoat, M. F., & Phillips, B. J. (1996). Observations: Elves make good cookies. *Journal of Advertising Research, 36*, 73–9.

Cannon, A. (2003). The showbiz connection. *U.S. News & World Report, 135*, 22–3.

Capon, N., Farley, J. U., & Hoening, S. (1990). Determinants of financial performance: A meta-analysis. *Management Science, 36*, 1143–59.

Carter, B. (2006). Why hold the superlatives? American idol is ascendant. *New York Times*, 30 Janaury, p. 3.

Cashmore, E. (2002). *Beckham*. Cambridge, UK: Polity Press.

— (2006). *Celebrity/Culture*. New York, NY: Routledge.

Cashmore, E., & Parker, A. (2003). One David Beckham. . .? Celebrity, masculinity and the soccerati. *Sociology of Sport Journal, 20*(3), 214–32.

Caughey, S. (1982). *Imaginary social worlds*. Lincoln: University of Nebraska Press.

Chaiken, S. (1979). Communicator physical attractiveness and persuasion. *Journal of Personality and Social Psychology, 137*, 1387–97.

Chan, K. (2008). Use of celebrity in television commercials of youth products. Working paper, Hong Kong Baptist University.

Chan, K. W., Hung, K., Tse, C. H., & Tse, D. K. (2008). Understanding celebrity endorser effects in China: A consumer-celebrity relational perspective. *Journal of Advertising Research, 51*(4), 608–23.

Chaney, P. K., DeVinney, T. M., & Winer, R. (1991). The impact of new product introduction on the market value of firms. *Journal of Business, 64*(4), 573–610.

Chapman, M. (2011, 8 June). Celebrities moving product? Not so much. Consumers just say no to names aligned with brands. Available at: www.adweek.com/news/advertising-branding/celebrities-moving-product-not-so-much. Accessed 20 February 2013.

— (2012). Does celebrity involvement in public health campaigns deliver long term benefit? Yes. *British Medical Journal, 345*, e6364.

Chapman, S., & Leask, J.-A. (2001). Paid celebrity endorsement in health promotion: A case study from Australia. *Health Promotion International, 16*(4), 333–8.

Chapman, S., Holding, S., McLeod, K., & Wakefield, M. (2005). Impact of news of celebrity illness on breast cancer screening: Kylie Minogue's breast cancer diagnosis. *Medical Journal of Australia, 183*(5), 247–50.

Charbonneau, J., & Garland, R. (2005). Talent, looks or brains? New Zealand advertising practitioners' views on celebrity and athlete endorsers. *Marketing Bulletin, 16*, 1–10.

Cheng, A. T., Hawton, K., Lee, C. T., & Chen, T. H. (2007). The influence of media reporting of the suicide of a celebrity on suicide rates: A population-based study. *International Journal of Epidemiology, 36*(6), 1229–34.

Cheng, A. T., Hawton, K., Chen, T. H., Yen, A. M., Chen, C. Y., Chen, L. C., & Teng, P. R. (2007). The influence of media coverage of a celebrity suicide on subsequent suicide attempts. *Journal of Clinical Psychiatry, 68*(6), 862–6.

Cheng, A. T., Hawton, K., Chen, T. H., Yen, A. M., Chang, J. C., Chong, M. Y., . . . Chen, L. C. (2007). The influence of media reporting of a celebrity suicide on suicidal behaviour in patients with a history of depressive disorder. *Journal of Affective Disorders, 103*(1–3), 69–75

Chia, S. C., & Poo, Y. L. (2009). Media, celebrities and fans: An examination of adolescents' media usage and involvement with entertainment celebrities. *Journalism & Mass Communication Quarterly, 86*(1), 23–35.

Chitttenden, M., & McAviney, V. (2011, 11 November). Cool Charlie is first to win 1m YouTube fans. *The Sunday Times*, p. 3.

Choi, C. J., & Berger, R. (2010). Ethics of celebrities and their increasing influence in 21st century society. *Journal of Business Ethics, 91*(3), 313–18.

Choi, S. M., Lee, W., & Kim, H. (2005). A cross-cultural comparison of celebrity endorsement in advertising. *Journal of Advertising, 32*, 85–98.

Choi, S. M., Wei-Na, L., & Hee-Jung, K. (2005). Lessons from the rich and famous. *Journal of Advertising, 34*(2), 85–98.

Chossat, V., & Gergaud, O. (2003). Expert opinion and gastronomy: The recipe for success. *Journal of Cultural Economics, 27*, 127–41.

Chung, K., Derdenger, T., & Srinivasan, K. (2013). Economic value of celebrity endorsement: Tiger Woods' impact on sales of Nike golf balls. *Marketing Science, 32*(2), 271–93.

Collins, S. (2008). Making the most out of 15 minutes: Reality TV's dispensable celebrity. *Television & New Media, 9*(2), 87–110.

Collins, R. L., Elliott, M. N., Berry, S. H., Kanouse, D. E., & Hunter, S. B. (2003). Entertainment television as a healthy sex educator: The impact of condom-efficacy information on an episode of 'Friends'. *Pediatrics, 112*(5), 1115–21.

Contactmusic.com (2008, 1 September). Law calls for Afghan militants to recognise Peace Day. Available at: www.contactmusic.com/news/law-calls-for-afghan-militants-to-recognise-peace-day-1079043. Accessed 10 August 2012.

Cooper, M. (1984). Can celebrities really sell products? *Marketing and Media Decisions*, September, pp. 64–5, 120.

Copeland, R., Frisby, W., & McCarville, R. (1996). Understanding the sport sponsorship process from a corporate perspective. *Journal of Sport Management, 10*(1) 32–8.

Corner, J., & Pels, D. (Eds.) (2003). *Media and the restyling of politics: Consumerism, celebrity and cynicism.* London, UK: Sage.

Couldry, N., & Markham, T. (2007). Celebrity culture and public connection: Bridge or chasm? *International Journal of Cultural Studies, 10*(4), 403–21.

Coulter, R. A., Zaltman, G., & Coulter, K. S. (2001). Interpreting consumer perceptions of advertising: An application of the Zaltman Metaphor Elicitation Technique. *Journal of Advertising, 30*(4), 1–21.

Cowen, T. (2000). *What price fame.* Cambridge, MA: Harvard University Press.

Cram, P., Fendrick, M. A., Inadomi, J., Cowan, M. F., Carpenter, D., & Vijan, S. (2003). The impact of a celebrity promotional campaign on the use of colon cancer screening. *Archives of Internal Medicine, 163*, 1601–5.

Crawford, T., Hooper, R., & Evans, S. (1997). Death rates of characters in soap operas on British television: Is a government health warning required? *British Medical Journal, 315*, 1649.

Cresswell, J. (2008, 22 June). Nothing sells like celebrity. *The New York Times.* Available at: http://www.nytimes.com/2008/06/22/business/media/22celeb.html. Accessed 2 November 2012.

Cronley, M. L., Kardes, F. R., Goddard, P., & Houghton, D. C. (1999). Endorsing products for the money: The role of the correspondence bias in celebrity advertising. *Advances in Consumer Research, 26*(1), 627–31.

Crouch, C. (2004). *Post-Democracy.* Cambridge, UK: Polity.

Currid-Halkett, E. (2010). *Starstruck: The business of celebrity.* New York, NY: Faber and Faber.

Daneshary, R., & Schwer, R. K. (2000). The association endorsement and consumers' intention to purchase. *Journal of Consumer Marketing, 17*(3), 203–13.

Datamonitor (2006). A-list celebrity endorsements are failing to dazzle consumers. *MarketWatch:Global Round-Up, 5*(9), 29–30.

Davison, W. P. (1983). The third-person effect in communication. *Public Opinion Quarterly, 47*, 1–15.

Dawes, C. (2009, 25 February). The rise of the superchef. BBC Money Programme. Available at: www.bbc.co.uk/business/7908794. Accessed 16 February 2013.

Dean, D. H. & Biswas, A. (2001). Third party organization endorsement of products: An advertising cue affecting consumer pre-purchase evaluation of goods and services. *Journal of Advertising, 30*(4), 41–57.

De Backer, C., Nelissen, M., Vyncke, P., Braekman, J., & McAndrew, F. T. (2007). Celebrities; from teachers to friends. *Human Nature, 18*(4), 334–54.

Debevec, K., & Kernan, J. B. (1984). More evidence on the effects of a presenter's physical attractiveness: Some cognitive, affective and behavioural consequences. In T. C. Kinnear (Ed.), *Advances in consumer research*, Vol. 11, 127–32.

Debnath, B. (2012, 26 September). Can a celebrity promote public health? Available at: http://www.medindia.net/news/can-a-celebrity-promote-pulbic-health-107600–1. Accessed on 29 October 2012.

DeBord, G. (1995/1967). *The society of spectacle*. Translated by Donald Nicholson-Smith. New York, NY: Zone Books.

deCordova, R. (1990). *Picture personalities: The emergence of the star system in America*. Urbana, IL: University of Illinois Press.

Deery, J. (2004). Reality TV as advertainment. *Popular Communication, 2*(1), 1–20.

De Vany, A., & Walls, W. D. (1999). Uncertainty in the movie industry: Does star power reduce the terror of the box office? *Journal of Cultural Economics, 23*, 295–318.

Dickenson, N. (1996). Can celebrities ruin a launch. *Campaign*, 3 May, p. 24.

DiClemente, R., Boyer, C., & Morales, E. (1988). Minorities and AIDS: Knowledge, attitudes and misconceptions among Black and Latino adolescents. *American Journal of Public Health, 78*, 55–7.

Dietz, P. E., Matthews, D. B., Van Duyne, C., Martell, D. A., Parry, C. D., Stewart, T., Crowder, J. D. (1991). Threatening and otherwise inappropriate letters to Hollywood celebrities. *Journal of Forensic Sciences, 36*, 185–209.

Ding, H., Molchanev, A., & Stork, P. (2011). The value of celebrity endorsements: A stock market perspective. *Marketing Letters, 22*(2), 147–63.

Dittmar, H., Lloyd, B., Dugan, S., Halliwell, E., Jacobs, N., & Cramer, H. (2000). The 'body beautiful': English adolescents' images of ideal bodies. *Sex Roles, 42*, 887–913.

Dix, S. (2009). Sport celebrity influence on young adult consumers. ANZMAC.

Dix, S., Phau, I., & Pougnet, S. (2010). 'Bend it like Beckham': The influence of sports celebrities on young adult consumers. *Young Consumers: Insight and Ideas for Responsible Marketers, 11*(1), 36–46.

Dolce & Gabbana (2005). http://www.dolcegabbana.it Dolce & Gabban Homepage (2005) 'Dolce & Gabbana. Men's Spring/Summer Collection 2004, Available at: http://eng.dolcegabban.it. Accessed 10 August 2012.

Domjan, M., & Burkhard, B. (1986). *The principles of learning and behaviour*, Monterey, CA: Brooks/Cole.

Domzal, T. J., & Kerman, J. B. (1992). Reading advertising. *The Journal of Consumer Marketing, 9*(3), 48–53.

Doss, S. (2011). The transference of brand attitude: The effect on the celebrity endorser. *Journal of Management and Marketing Research*, 7. Available at: http://www.aabr. com/jmmr. Accessed 28 October 2012.

Dowling, K. (2012, 4 November). Boozy stars drive young onto wagon. *The Sunday Times*, p. 4.

Drake, P., & Miah, A. (2010). The cultural politics of celebrity. *Cultural Politics, 6*(1), 49–64.

Dunbar, R. I. M. (2004). Gossip in evolutionary perspective. *Review of General Psychology, 8*, 100–10.

Dunscombe, S. (2007, 29 October). Taking celebrity seriously. *The Nation*, pp. 22–4.

Duvak, S.-S. (2007). A star is made: News coverage of celebrity politics in the 2000 and 2004 US Presidential elections. Paper presented to the Political Studies Association Conference.

Duvall, S. (2007). A star is made: News coverage of celebrity politics in the 2000 and 2004 Presidential elections. Paper presented at the Political Science Association Conference, University of Bath, April.

Dyer, R. (1986). *Heavenly bodies: Film stars and society*. New York, NY: St Martin's Press.

— (1998). *Stars*. London, UK: British Film Institute.

Edwards, S. M., & La Ferle, C. (2009). Does gender impact the perception of negative information related to celebrity endorsers? *Journal of Promotion Management, 15*(1 and 2), 22–35.

Einerson, M. J. (1998). Fame, fortune and failure: Young girls' moral language surrounding popular culture. *Youth and Society, 30*, 241–57.

Eisend, M., & Langner, T. (2010). Immediate and delayed advertising effects of celebrity endorsers' attractiveness and expertise. *International Journal of Advertising, 29*(4), 527–46.

Ekelund, R. B., Jr, Ressler, R. W., & Watson, J. K. (2000). The 'death effect' in art prices: A demand-side exploration. *Journal of Cultural Economics, 24*, 283–300.

Elberse, A. (2007). The power of stars: Do star actors drive the success of movies? *Journal of Marketing, 71*(4), 102–20.

Elberse, A., & Verleun, J. (2012). The economic value of celebrity endorsements. *Journal of Advertising, 52*(2), 149–65.

Elliott, A. (2010). 'I want to look like that!': Cosmetic surgery and celebrity culture. *Culture Sociology, 5*(4), 463–77.

Elliott, R., & Leonard, C. (2004). Peer pressure and poverty: Exploring fashion brands and consumption symbolism among children of the British poor. *Journal of Consumer Behaviour, 3*(4), 347–59.

Engle, Y., & Kasser, T. (2005). Why do adolescent girls idolize male celebrities? *Journal of Adolescent Research, 20,* 263–83.

Erdogan, B. Z. (1999). Celebrity endorsement: A literature review. *Journal of Marketing Management, 15,* 291–314.

Erdogan, B. Z., & Baker, M. J. (1999). Celebrity endorsement: Advertising agency managers' perspective. *Cyber-Journal of Sport Marketing,* published online at: http://fulltext.ausport.gov.au/fulltext/1999/cjsm/v3n3/erdogan&baker33

Erdogan, B. Z., Baker, M. J., & Tagg, S. (2001a). Selecting celebrity endorser: The practitioner's perspective. *Journal of Advertising Research, 41*(3), 39–48.

— (2001b). Celebrity endorsement: A literature review. *Journal of Marketing Management, 15*(4), 291–314.

Evans, R. D. Jr, Hart, P. M., Cicala, J. E., & Sherrell, D. L. (2010). Elvis, Dear and lovin it – the influence of attraction, nostalgia and risk in dead celebrity attitude formation. *Journal of Management and Marketing Research,* 3. Available at: www.aabri.com/jmmr. Accessed 13 September 2012.

Ewen, S. (1988). *All consuming images: The politics of style in contemporary culture.* New York, NY: Basic Books.

Fain, S. (2008). Celebrities, poverty and the mediapolis: A case study of the One campaign. Paper delivered at the London School of Economics Media and Humanity Conference, September, London, UK.

Farrell, K. A., Karels, G. V., Montfort, K. W., & McClatchey, C. A. (2000). Celebrity performance and endorsement value: The case of Tiger Woods. *Managerial Finance, 26*(7), 1–15.

Ferris, K. O. (2001). Through a glass darkly: The dynamics of fan-celebrity encounters. *Symbolic Interaction, 24,* 25–47.

Fiel, J., McNeil, C. R., & Smaby, T. (2008). Athlete endorsement contracts: The impact of conventional stars. *International Advances in Economics Research,* May.

Fiske, J. (1989). *Reading the popular.* Boston, MA: Unwin Hyman.

Fizel, J., McNeil, C. R., & Smaby, T. (2008). Athlete endorsement contracts: The impact of conventional stars. *International Advances in Economics Research, 14*(2), 247–56.

Fletchner, M. E. (2004). *The Power of Endorsements.* Campaign & Elections, Inc, July, 2004. Available at: http://www.web.texts-lexis-nexis.com. Accessed 25 August 2012.

Folkes, V. S. (1988). The availability heuristic and perceived risk. *Journal of Consumer Research, 30,* 125–37.

Fombrun, C. (1996). *Reputation.* Boston, MA: Harvard Business School Press.

Fortini-Campbell, L. (1992). *Hitting the sweet spot.* Chicago, IL: The Copy Work Shop.

Fowles, J. (1996). *Advertising and popular culture.* London, UK: Sage Publications.

Fraser, B. P., & Brown, W. J. (2002). Media, celebrities and social influence: Identification with Elvis Presley. *Mass Communication & Society, 5*(2), 183–206.

Friedman, H. H., & Friedman, L. (1978). Does the celebrity endorser's image spill over the product. *Journal of the Academy of Marketing Science, 19,* 63–71.

— (1979). Endorser effectiveness by product type. *Journal of Advertising Research, 19,* 63–71.

Friedman, H. H., Santeramo, M. J., & Traina, A. (1978). Correlates of trustworthiness for celebrities. *Journal of the Academy for Marketing Science, 6,* 291–9.

Friedman, H. H., Termini, S., & Washington, R. (1976). The effectiveness of advertisements using four types of endorser. *Journal of Advertising, 6,* 22–4.

Frizzell, C. (2011). Public opinion and foreign policy: The effects of celebrity endorsements. *The Social Science Journal, 48*(2), 314–23.

Fu, K. W., & Yip, P. S. F. (2007). Long-term impact of celebrity suicide on suicidal ideation: Results from a population-based study. *Journal of Epidemiology and Community Health, 61*(6), 540–8.

— (2009). Estimating the risk for suicide following the suicide deaths of 3 Asian entertainment celebrities: A meta-analytic approach. *Journal of Clinical Psychiatry, 70*(6), 869–78.

Fujii, D. E. M., Ahmed, I., & Takeshita, J. (1999). Neuropsychologic implications in erotomania: Two case studies. *Neuropsychiatry, Neuropsychology and Behavioural Neurology, 12,* 110–16.

Gabler, N. (1998). *Life the movie: How entertainment conquered reality.* New York, NY: Alfred A. Knopf.

Gamson, J. (1994). *Claims to fame: Celebrity in contemporary America.* Berkeley, CA: University of California.

Garnham, N. (1990). *Capitalism and communication: Global culture and the economics of information.* Newbury Park, CA: Sage.

Garthwaite, C., & Moore, T. (2008). The role of celebrity endorsements in politics: Oprah, Obama and the 2008 Democratic Primary. Available at: http://www.econ. umd.edu/~garthwaite/celebrityendorsements/garthwaitemoore. Accessed 10 September 2012.

Giles, D. (2000). *Illusions of immortality: A psychology of fame and celebrity.* New York, NY: St Martin's Press.

— (2002). Parasocial interaction: A review of the literature and a model for future research. *Media Psychology, 4,* 279–302.

Giles, D., & Maltby, J. (2004). The role of media figures in adolescent development: Relations between autonomy, attachment and interest in celebrities. *Personality and Individual Differences, 36,* 613–22.

— (2006). Praying at the altar of the stars. *The Psychologist, 19*(2), 82–5.

Gillespie, M. (2003, 3 March). Celebrity protests have minimal impact on public opinion, Gallup News Service. www.gallup.com/poll/7930/celebrity-protests-minimal-impact-public-opinion. Accessed 1 October 2011.

Goldsmith, R. E., Lafferty, B. A., & Newell, S. J. (2000). The impact of corporate credibility and celebrity credibility on consumer reaction to advertisements and brands. *Journal of Advertising, 29*(3), 43–54.

Gould, M. (2001). Suicide and media. *Annals of the New York Academy of Science, 932*, 200–24.

Greene, A. L., & Adams-Price, C. (1990). Adolescents' secondary attachments to celebrity figures. *Sex Roles, 23*, 335–47.

Grier, P., & McLaughlin, A. (2003). Politics as another rung on celebrity ladder. *Christian Science Monitor, 95*(1), Available at: www.csmonitor.com/2003/0812/p01s01-upo.html. Accessed 12 November 2012.

Gu, F. F., Hung, K., & Tse, D. K. (2008). When does Guanxi matter: Issues of capitalization and its dark sides. *Journal of Marketing, 72*(4), 12–28.

Gunter, B. (2014, in press). *I want to change my life: Can reality TV competition shows trigger lasting career success.* Newcastle-upon-Tyne, UK: Cambridge Scholars Publishing.

Gunter, B., Saltzis, K., & Campbell, V. (2014, in press). The changing nature of party election broadcasts: The growing influence of political marketing, *Journal of Political Marketing.*

Gupta, S. (2009). How do consumers judge celebrities' irresponsible behaviour? An attribution theory perspective. *Journal of Applied Business and Economics, 10*(3), 1–14.

Halpern, J. (2008). *Fame junkies.* New York: Houghton Mifflin.

Han, S. P., & Shavitt, S. (1994). Persuasion and culture: Advertising appeals in individualistic and collectivistic societies. *Journal of Experimental Social Psychology, 30*(4), 326–50

Harding, E. (2012, 5 November). I couldn't bear to live in the shadow of cancer again, says Sharon. *Daily Mail*, p. 5.

Harlow, J. (2003). Blinded by the stars. *The Sunday Times,* 17 August, p. 14.

Harmsworth, A. (2012, 30 August). Celebrity role models can help inspire a generation. *Metro.* Available at: www.metro.co.uk/2012/08/30/celebrity-roles-models-can-help-inspire-a-ageneration-556844. Accessed 26 October 2013.

Harper, B., & Tiggeman, M. (2008). The effect of thin ideal media images on women's self-objectification, mood, and body image. *Sex Roles, 58*, 649–57.

Harris, J., & Clayton, B. (2007). David Beckham and the changing (re)presentation of English identity. *International Journal of Sport Management and Marketing, 2*(3), 208–21.

Harrison, K. (1997). Does interpersonal attraction to thin media personalities promote eating disorders? *Journal of Broadcasting & Electronic Media, 41*, 478–500.

— (2000). The body electric: Thin-ideal media and eating disorders in adolescents. *Journal of Communication, 50*, 119–43.

Hawton, K., & Williams, K. (2002). Influences of the media on suicide. *British Medical Journal, 325*(7377), 1374–5.

Hawton, K., Harriss, L., Simkin, S., Juszcak, E., Appleby, L., McDonnell, R., . . . Parrott, H. (2000). Effect of death of Diana, Princess of Wales on suicide and deliberate self-harm. *British Journal of Psychiatry, 177*, 463–6.

Hawton, K., Simkin, S., Deeks, J., O'Connor, S., Keen, A., Altman, D. et al. (1999). Effects of a drug overdose in a television drama on presentations to hospital for self poisoning: Time series and questionnaire study. *British Medical Journal, 318*, 972–7.

Heard, C. (2004). Rocking against Thatcher. BBC News. Available at: http://www.news.bbc.co.uk/1/hi/entertainment/music/3682281.stm. Accessed 22 September 2012.

Heath, T. B., McCarthy, M. S., & Mothersbaugh, D. L. (1994). Spokesperson fame and vividness effects in the context of issue relevant thinking: The moderating role of competitive setting. *Journal of Consumer Research, 30*, 520–34.

Heilman, E. E. (1998). The struggle for self: Power and identity in adolescent girls. *Youth and Society, 30*, 182–208.

Heinberg, L. J., & Thompson, J. K. (1992). The effects of figure size feedback (positive vs negative) and target comparison group (particularistic vs universalistic) on body image disturbance. *International Journal of Eating Disorders, 12*, 441–8.

Heller, D. (Ed.) (2007). *Makeover television: Realities remodelled.* London, UK]: I. B. Tauris.

Hesmondhalgh, D. (2002). *The cultural industries.* London, U]: Sage.

Hill, A. (2005). *Reality TV: Audiences and popular factual television.* London, NY: Routledge.

— (2007). *Restyling factual TV: Audiences and news, documentaries and reality genres.* Abingdon, UK: Routledge.

Hilton, S., & Hunt, K. (2010). Coverage of Jade Goody's cervical cancer in UK newspapers: A missed opportunity for health. *BMC Public Health, 10*, 368.

Hilton, S., Hunt, K., Langan, M., Bedford, H., & Petticrew, M. (2010). Newsprint media representations of the introduction of the HPV vaccination programme for cervical cancer prevention in the UK (2005, 2008). *Social Science and Medicine, 70*(6), 942–50.

Hofstede, G. H. (1984). *Culture's consequences: International differences in work-related values.* Beverly Hills, CA: Sage.

Holak, S. L., & Havlena, W. J. (1998). Feelings, fantasies and memories: An examination of the emotional components of nostalgia. *Journal of Business Research, 42*, 217–26.

Holmes, S. (2004). 'Reality goes pop!': Reality TV, popular music, and narratives of stardom in pop idol. *Television and New Media, 5*(2), 147–72.

Hopper, K. M., & Aubrey, J. S. (2011). Examining the impact of celebrity gossip magazine coverage of pregnant celebrities on pregnant women's self-objectification. *Communication Research, 15*, DOI: 10.11.77/0093650211422062.

Horsky, D., & Swyngedouw, P. (1987). Does it pay to change your company's name? A stock market perspective. *Marketing Science, 6*, 320–34.

Houran, J., Navik, S., & Zerrusen, K. (2005). Boundary functioning in celebrity worshippers. *Personality and Individual Differences, 38*, 237–48.

Hovland, C. I., & Weiss, W. (1951). The influence of source credibility on communication effectiveness. *Public Opinion Quarterly, 15*, 635–50.

Hovland, C. I., Janis, I. L., & Kelley, H. H. (1953). *Communication and persuasion.* New Haven, CT: Yale University Press.

Howard, A. (1979). More than just a passing fancy. *Advertising Age,* 50 (30 July) p. A-2.

Howell, S. E. (1986). Candidates and attitudes: Revisiting the question of causality. *Journal of Politics, 48*, 450–64.

Hsu, C.-K., & McDonald, D. (2002). An examination on multiple celebrity endorsers in advertising. *Journal of Product and Brand Management, 11*(1), 19–29.

Hughes-Freeland, F. (2007). Charisma and celebrity in Indonesian politics. *Anthropological Theory, 7*(2), 177–200.

Hung, K., & Li, S. Y. (2007). The influence of eWOM on virtual consumer communities: Social capital, consumer learning and behavioural outcomes. *Journal of Advertising Research, 47*, 485–95.

Hung, K., Gu, F. F., & Yim, C. K. (2007). A social institutional approach to identifying generation cohorts in China with a comparison to American consumers. *Journal of International Business Studies, 38*, 836–53.

Hung, K., Li, S. Y., & Belk, R. W. (2007). Glocal understandings: Female readers' perceptions of the new woman in Chinese advertising. *Journal of International Business Studies, 38*, 1034–51.

Hyde, M. (2009). *Celebrity: How entertainers took over the world and why we need an exit strategy.* London, UK: Harvill Secker.

Ilicic, J., & Webster, C. M. (2012, in press). Celebrity co-branding partners as irrelevant brand information in advertisements. *Journal of Business Research.* See also, www.anzmac.info/conference/2012/papers/089ANZMACFINAL. Accessed 19 August 2013.

Inglis, F. (2010). *A Brief history of celebrity.* Princeton, NJ: Princeton University Press.

Inthorn, S., & Street, J. (2011). Simon Cowell for prime minister? Young citizens' attitudes towards celebrity politics. *Media, Culture & Society, 33*(3), 1–11.

ITV (2012). Britain's got talent application. Available at: http://www.itv.com/Termsandconditions/Compertitionsandvotes/BritainsGotTalentapplication. Accessed 22 September 2012.

Jackson, D. J. (2007). Selling politics: The impact of celebrities' political beliefs on young Americans. *Journal of Political Marketing, 6*(4), 67–83.

Jackson, D. J., & Darrow, T. I. A. (2005). The influence of celebrity endorsements on young adults' political opinions. *Journal of Consumer Research, 11*, 954–61.

Jackson, T. I. A. (2005). The influence of celebrity endorsements on young adults' political opinions. *International Journal of Press/Politics, 10*(3), 80–98.

Jaffe, A. (2005). *Modernism and the culture of celebrity.* Cambridge, UK: Cambridge University Press.

Jarrell, G., & Peltzman, S. (1985). The impact of product recalls on the wealth of sellers. *Journal of Political Economy, 93*(3), 512–36.

Jonas, K. (1992). Modeling and suicide: A test of the Werther effect. *British Journal of Social Psychology, 31*, 295–306.

Jones, E. E., & Harris, V. A. (1967). The attribution of attributes. *Journal of Experimental Social Psychology, 3*, 1–24.

Jones, M., Freeth, E. C., Hennessy-Priest, K., & Costa, R. J. S. (2013), A systematic cross-sectional analysis of British based celebrity chef's recipes: Is there cause for public health concern? *Food and Public Health, 3*(2), 100–10.

Jones, M. J., & Schumann, D. W. (2000). The strategic use of celebrity athlete endorsers in Sports Illustrated: An historic perspective. *Sports Marketing Quarterly, 9*, 65–76.

Kahle, L. R., & Homer, P. M. (1985). Physical attractiveness of celebrity endorser: A social adaptation perspective. *Journal of Consumer Research, 14*, 954–61.

Kaikati, J. G. (1987). Celebrity advertising. *International Journal of Advertising, 6*(92), 93–105.

Kalichman, S. C. & Hunter, T. L. (1992). The disclosure of celebrity HIV infection: Its effects on public attitudes. *American Journal of Public Health, 82*(10), 1374–6.

Kambitsis, C., Harahousou, Y., Theodorakis, N., & Chatzibeis, G. (2002). Sports advertising in print media: The case of 2000 Olympic Games. *Corporate Communications: An International Journal, 7*(3), 155–61.

Kamins, M. A. (1989). Celebrity and non-celebrity advertising in a two-sided context. *Journal of Advertising Research, 29*(3), 34–42.

— (1990). An investigation into the 'match-up' hypothesis in celebrity advertising: When beauty may be only skin deep. *Journal of Advertising, 19*(1), 4–13.

Kamins, M. A., & Gupta, K. (1994). Congruence between spokesperson and product type: A matchup hypothesis perspective. *Psychology and Marketing, 11*(6), 569–86.

Kamins, M. A., Brand, M. J., Hoeke, S. A., & Moe, J. C. (1989). Two-sided versus one-sided celerity endorsements: The impact on advertising effectiveness and credibility. *Journal of Advertising, 18*(2), 4–10.

Kanazawa, S. (2002). Bowling with our imaginary friend. *Evolution and Human Behaviour, 23*, 167–71.

Kappel, S., Vogt, R., Brozicevic, M., & Kutsko, D. (1989). AIDS knowledge and attitudes among adults in Vermont. *Public Health Reports, 104*, 388–91.

Katz, D. (1994). *Just Do It: The Nike Spirit in the Corporate World.* New York: Random House.

Keane, J. (2009). *The Life and Death of Democracy.* New York, NY: W. W. Norton and Company.

Kelaher, M., Cawson, J., Miller, J., Kavanagh, A., Dunt, D., & Studdert, D. (2008). Use of breast cancer screening and treatment services by Australian women aged 25–44 years following Kylie Minogue's breast cancer diagnosis. *International Journal of Epidemiology, 37*(6), 1326–32.

Keller, K. L. (1993). Conceptualizing, measuring, and managing customer-based brand equity. *Journal of Marketing, 57*(1), 1–22.

— (2008). *Strategic brand management: Building, measuring and managing brand equity* (3rd ed.). Upper Saddle River, NJ: Prentice-Hall.

Kellogg Insight (2012, April). The Oprah effect: Celebrity endorsement of political candidates can make a difference at the polls. Available at: www.insight.kellogg. northwestern.edu/index.php/Kellogg/article/the_oprah_Effect. Accessed 22 September 2012.

Kemmelmeier, M. (2004). Separating the wheat from the chaff: Does discriminating between diagnostic and non diagnostic information eliminate the dilution effect? *Journal of Behavioural Decision Making, 17*, 231–43.

Kensinger, E. A., & Corkin, S. (2003). Effect of negative emotional content on working memory and long-term memory. *Emotion, 3*, 378–93.

Kessler, R., Downey, G., Milavsky, J. R., & Stipp, H. (1988). Clustering of teenage suicides after television news stories about suicide: A reconsideration. *American Journal of Psychiatry, 145*, 1379–83.

Kilborn, R. (1994). How real can you get?: Recent developments in 'reality' television. *European Journal of Communication, 9*(4), 421–39.

— (2005). Reality TV: The work of being watched. *Media, Culture and Society, 27*(4), 624–6.

Klein, S. B. (1991). *Learning: Principles and applications.* New York: McGraw-Hill.

Knittel, C. R., & Stango, V. (2012, 20 November). Celebrity endorsements, firm value, and reputation risk: Evidence from the Tiger Woods scandal. www.web.mit.edu/knittel/www/papers/tiger_latest. Accessed 18 August 2013.

Koernig, S. K., & Boyd, T. C. (2009). To catch a tiger or let him go: The match-up effect and athlete endorsers for sport and non-sport brands. *Sport Marketing Quarterly, 18*(1), 15–37.

Kozinets, R. V. (2001). Utopian enterprise: Articulating the meanings of Star Trek's culture of consumption. *Journal of Consumer Research, 28*, 76–88.

La Eeries, C., & Sejung, M. C. (2005). The importance of perceived endorser credibility in South Korean advertising. *Journal of Current Issues and Research in Advertising, 21*(2), 67–81.

Lafferty, B. A., & Goldsmith, R. E. (1999). Corporate credibility's role in consumers' attitudes and purchase intentions when a high versus low credibility endorser is used in the ad. *Journal of Business Research, 44*(2), 109–16.

Lafferty, B. A., Goldsmith, R. E., & Newell, S. J. (2002). The dual credibility model: The influence of corporate and endorser credibility on attitudes and purchase intentions. *Journal of Marketing Theory & Practice, 10*(3), 1–12.

Lancucki, L., Sasieni, P., Patrick, J., Day, T. J., & Vessy, M. P. (2012) The impact of Jade Goody's diagnosis and death on the NHS Cervical Screening Programme. *Journal of Medical Screening, 19*(2), 89–93.

Lane, D. S., Polednak, A. P., & Burg, M. A. (1989). The impact of media coverage of Nancy Reagan's experience on breast cancer screening. *American Journal of Public Health*, *79*(11), 1551–2.

Lane, R. (1996). Nice guys finish first. *Forbes*, 158(14), 236–42.

Langer, A. I. (2007). A historical exploration of the personalisation of politics in the print media: The British Prime Ministers (1945–1999). *Parliamentary Affairs*, *60*(3), 371–87.

— (2009). The politicization of private persona: Exceptional leaders or the new rule? The case of the United Kingdom and the Blair effect. *International Journal of Press/ Politics*, *15*(1), 60–76.

Langer, I. (1981). Television's 'personality' system. *Media, Culture & Society*, *3*(4), 351–63.

Langmeyer, L., & Shank, M. D. (1993) Celebrity endorsers and public services agencies; A balancing act. In E. Thorson (Ed.) Proceedings of the 1993 conference of the American academy of advertising (pp. 197–207). Columbia, MO: American Academy of Advertising.

Langmeyer, L., & Walker, M. (1991a). A first step to identify the meaning in celebrity endorsers. In R. R. Holman & M. R. Solomon (Eds), *Advances in consumer research* (Vol. 18, pp. 364–71). Provo, Utah: Association for Consumer Research.

— (1991b). Assessing the effects of celebrity endorsers: Preliminary findings. In R. R. Holman (Ed.), *American academy of advertising proceedings* (pp. 32–42).

Larson, R. J., Woloshin, S., Schwartz, L. M., & Welch, G. H. (2005). Celebrity endorsements of cancer screening. *Journal of the National Cancer Institute*, *97*, 693–5.

Lawrence, C. (2009). *The cult of celebrity: What our fascination with the stars reveals about us*. Guilford, CT: Globe Pequot Press.

Lee, J. G., & Thorson, E. (2008). The impact of celebrity–product incongruence on the effectiveness of product endorsement. *Journal of Advertising Research*, *48*(3), 433–49.

Leets, L., de Becker, G., & Giles, H. (1995). FANS: Exploring expressed motivations for contacting celebrities. *Journal of Language and Social Psychology*, *14*, 102–23.

Le Ferle, C., & Choi, S. M. (2005). The importance of perceived endorser credibility in South Korean advertising. *Journal of Current Issues & Research in Advertising*, *27*(2), 67–81.

Leppard, D. (2012, 18 November). Divorce judge warns of Hello! Curse. *The Sunday Times*, p. 11.

Leslie, L. Z. (2011). *Celebrity in the 21st century.* Santa Barbara, CA: ABC-Clio.

License! (2007). Celebrity brand building. *License! 19*(2), 50.

Lindenberg, S., Joly, J. F., & Stapel, D. A. (2011). The norm-activating power of celebrity: The dynamics of success and influence. *Social Psychology Quarterly*, *74*(1), 98–120.

Lines, G. (2001). Villains, fools or heroes? Sports stars as role models for young people. *Leisure Studies*, *20*, 285–303.

Litman, B. R., & Ahn, H. (1998). Predicting financial success of motion pictures. In B. R. Litman (Ed.), *The motion picture mega-industry* (pp. 172–97). Needham Heights, LA: Allyn & Bacon.

Litman, B. R., & Kohl, L. S. (1989). Predicting financial success of motion pictures: The 80s experience. *Journal of Media Economics, 2*, 35–50.

London Evening Standard (2009, 21 December). Madonna is top celebrity of the noughties. *London Evening Standard.* Available at: www.thisislondon.co.uk/showbiz/article-2386556-madonna-top-celebrity-of-the-noughties. Accessed 26 October 2013.

Louie, T. A., & Obermiller, C. (2002). Consumer response to a firm's endorser (dis)association decisions. *Journal of Advertising, 31*(4), 41–53.

Louie, T. A., Kulik, R. L., & Jacobson, R. (2001). When bad things happen to the endorsers of good products. *Marketing Letters, 12*(1), 13–23.

Lowenthal, L. (1961). *Literature, popular culture and society.* Englewood Cliffs, NJ: Prentice-Hall.

MacKenzie, R., Chapman, S., Johnson, N., McGeechan, K., & Holding, S. (2008). The newsworthiness of cancer in Australian television news. *Medical Journal of Australia, 189*(3), 155–8.

Magder, T. (2004). The end of TV 101: Reality programs, formats and the new business of television. In S. Murray & L. Ouellette (Eds), *Reality TV: Remaking television culture* (pp. 37–56). New York, NY: New York University Press.

Magee, K. (2011, 27 January). Reputation survey: Celebrity chefs – Oliver roasts his rivals. Available at: www.brandrepublic.com/features/1051435. Accessed 16 February 2013.

Makgosa, R. (2010). The influence of vicarious role models on purchase intentions of Botswana teenagers. *Young Consumers: Insight and Ideas for Responsible Marketers, 11*(4), 307–19.

Maltby, J., & Day, L. (2011). Celebrity worship and incidence of elective cosmetic surgery: Evidence of a link among young adults. *Journal of Adolescent Health, 49*(1), 483–9.

Maltby, J., Houran, M. A., & McCutcheon, L. E. (2003). A clinical interpretation of attitudes and behaviours associated with celebrity worship. *Journal of Nervous and Mental Disease, 191*, 25–9.

Maltby, J., Houran, J., Ashe, D., & McCutcheon, L. E. (2001). The self-reported psychological well-being of celebrity worshippers, *North American Journal of Psychology, 3*, 441–52.

Maltby, J., Day, L., McCutcheon, L. E., Gillett, R., Houran, J., & Ashe, D. (2004a). Celebrity worship using an adaptational-continuum model of personality and coping. *British Journal of Psychology, 95*, 411–28.

— (2004b). Personality and coping: A context for examining celebrity worship and mental health. *British Journal of Psychology, 95*, 411–28.

Maltby, J., Day, L., McCutcheon, L. E., Houran, J., & Ashe, D. (2006). Extreme celebrity worship, fantasy proneness and dissociation: Developing the measurement and understanding of celebrity worship within a clinical personality context. *Personality and Individual Differences, 40,* 273–83.

Maltby, J., Giles, D., Barber, L., & McCutcheon, L. E. (2005). Intense-personal celebrity worship and body image: Evidence of a link among female adolescents. *British Journal of Health Psychology, 10*(1), 17–32.

Maltby, J., Houran, J., Lange, R., Ashe, D., & McCutcheon, L. E. (2002). Thou shalt worship no other gods – unless they are celebrities. *Personality and Individual Differences, 32,* 1157–72.

Marketing Evaluations Inc (2011). Q Scores. Available at: www.qscores.com/web/personalities.aspx. Accessed 25th October 2013.

Marsh, D., 't Hart, P., & Tindall, K. (2010). Celebrity politics: The politics of the late modernity? *Political Studies Review, 2*(3), 322–40.

Marshall, D. W., & Cook, G. (1992). The corporate (sports) sponsor. *International Journal of Advertising, 11,* 307–24.

Marshall, D., Bonner, F., Farley, R., & Turner, G. (1999). Celebrity and the media. *Australian Journal of Communication, 27*(1), 55–70.

Marshall, P. D. (1997). *Celebrity and power fame in contemporary culture.* Minneapolis, MN: University of Minnesota Press.

Martin, C. A., & Bush, A. J. (2000a). Do role models influence teenagers' purchase intentions and behaviour? *Journal of Consumer Marketing, 17*(5), 441–53.

— (2000b). Do role models influence teenagers' purchase intentions. *Journal of Consumer Marketing, 17*(5), 441–53.

Martin, G., & Koo, L. (1997). Celebrity suicide: Did the death of Kurt Cobain influence young suicides in Australia? *Archives of Suicide Research, 3,* 187–98.

Martin, J. H. (1996). Is the athlete's sport important when picking an athlete to endorse a nonsport product? *Journal of Consumer Marketing, 13,* 28–43.

Martindale, C. (1991). *Cognitive psychology: A neural network approach.* Pacific Grove, CA: Brooks/Cole.

Maslow, A. (1954). *Motivation and personality.* New York, NY: Harper & Row.

Matheson, V. A., & Baade, R. A. (2004). 'Death effect' on collectible prices. *Applied Economics, 36,* 1151–5.

Mathur, L. K., Mathur, I., & Rangan, N. (1997). The wealth effects associated with a celebrity endorser: The Michael Jordan phenomenon. *Journal of Advertising Research, 37*(3), 67–73.

Maurstad, T. (2004, 6 February). From Hollywood to Washington: Blurring the boundaries between politics and pop culture. Available at: http://www.web.lexis-nexis.com. Accessed 17 August 2012.

McCracken, G. (1989). Who is the celebrity endorser? Cultural foundations of the endorsement process. *Journal of Consumer Research, 16*(3), 310–21.

McCutcheon, L. E., Lange, R., & Houran, J. (2002). Conceptualization and measurement of celebrity worship. *British Journal of Psychology*, 93(1), 67–87.

McCutcheon, L. E., Scott, Jr, V. B., Arugate, M. S., & Parker, J. (2006). Exploring the link between attachment and the inclination to obsess about or to stalk celebrities. *North American Journal of Psychology*, 8(2), 289–300.

McCutcheon, L. F., Ashe, D. D., Houran, L., & Maltby, J. (2003). A cognitive profile of individuals who tend to worship celebrities. *Journal of Psychology*, 137(4), 309–22.

McDonald, C. (1991). Sponsorship and the image of the sponsor. *European Journal of Marketing*, 25(11), 31–8.

McDonald, P. (2000). *The star system: Hollywood's production of popular identities*. London, UK: Wallflower.

McDonough, J. (1995). Bringing brands to life. *Advertising Age*, Special Collectors Edition, Spring, 34–5.

McGuire, W. J. (1985). Attitudes and attitude change. In G. Lindzey & E. Aronson (Eds), *Handbook of Social Psychology* (pp. 233–46). New York: Random House.

Media Vest USA (2004, 30 September). Word to presidential hopefuls: Celebrities on campaign trail to reach young voters. Available at: http://www.mediaweek.com. Accessed 17 August 2012.

Mehta, A. (1994). How advertising response modelling (ARM) can increase ad effectiveness. *Journal of Advertising Research*, 34(3), 62–74.

Meyer, D. S., & Gamson, J. (1995). The challenge of cultural elites: Celebrities and social movements. Sociological Inquiry, 65(2), 181–206.

Meyers-Levy, J. (1989). The influence of brand name association set size and word frequency on brand memory. *Journal of Consumer Research*, 16(2), 197–207.

Miciak, A. R., & Shanklin, W. L. (1994). Choosing celebrity endorsers. *Marketing Management*, 3(3), 51–9.

Miege, B. (1989). *The capitalization of cultural production*. New York: International General.

Miller, A. (2013, 10 February). Beckham's shirt sales a staggering £1 billion. *The Mail on Sunday – Sport*, p. 13.

Misra, S. (1990). Celebrity spokesperson and brand congruence: An assessment of recall and affect. *Journal of Business Research*, 21, 159–73.

Misra, S., & Beatty, S. E. (1990). Celebrity spokesperson and brand congruence: An assessment of recall and affect. *Journal of Business Research*, 21(2), 159–71.

Mistry, B. (2006). Star spotting. *Marketing*, 7 June, pp. 33–4.

Mittelstaedt, J. D., Tiesz, P. C., & Burns, W. J. (2000). Why are endorsements effective? Sorting among theories of product and endorser effects. *Journal of Current Issues and Research in Advertising*, 22(1), 55–66.

Monaco, J. (Ed.) (1978). *Celebrity: The media as image makers*. New York, NY: Dell Publishing Company.

Monbiot, G. (2005). Africa's new best friends. *The Guardian*, 5 July.

Money, R. B., Shimp, T. A., & Sakano, T. (2006). Celebrity endorsements in Japan and the United States: Is negative information all that harmful? *Journal of Advertising Research*, *46*(1), 123–30.

Mooij, de M. (2010). *Global marketing and advertising: Understanding cultural paradoxes* (3rd ed.). Thousand Oaks, CA: Sage.

Motavalli, J. (1988). Advertising blunder of the rich and famous. *Adweek*. 11 January, pp. 18–19.

Mowen, J. C., & Brown, S. W. (1981). On explaining and predicting the effectiveness of celebrity endorsers. In K. B. Monroe (Ed.), *Advances in consumer research*, 18 (pp. 437–41). Ann Arbor, MI: Association for Consumer Research.

Mukherjee, J. (2004). Celebrity, media and politics: An Indian perspective. *Parliamentary Affairs*, *57*(1), 80–92.

Murray, D., & Price, B. (2012). When sports stars go off the rails: How gender and involvement influence the negative publicity of sports endorsers. *International Journal of Business Research*, *12*(2), 84–93.

Murray, S., & Ouellette, L. (Eds) (2004). *Reality TV: Remaking television culture*. New York, NY: New York University Press.

Nash, K. (2008). Global citizenship as show business: The cultural politics of Make Poverty History. *Media, Culture & Society*, *30*(1), 167–81.

Nattinger, A. B., Hoffman, R. G., Howell-Pelz, A., & Goodwin, J. S. (1998). Effect of Nancy Reagan's mastectomy on choice of surgery for breast cancer by US women. *Journal of the American Medical Association*, *279*(10), 762–6.

Neuberg, S. L., Kendrick, D. T., & Schaller, M. (2010). Evolutionary social psychology. In S. T. Fiske, D. T. Gilbert & G. Lindzey (Eds), *Handbook of Social Psychology* (5th. ed., Vol. 2, pp. 761–96). New York, NY: John Wiley & Sons.

Noll, S. M., & Frederickson, B. L. (1998). A mediational model linking self-objectification, body shame and disordered eating. *Psychology of Women Quarterly*, *22*, 623–36.

Nownes, A. J. (2012). An experimental investigation of the effects of celebrity support for political parties in the United States. *American Politics Research*, *40*(3), 476–500.

O'Connor, B. (2012). Spaces of celebrity: National and global discourses in the reception of TV talent shows by Irish teenagers. *Television & New Media*, *13*(6), 568–83.

O'Donohue, P. (2012, 11 October). SDtar-rated therapies often useless. *The Irish Times*. Available at: http://www.irishtimes.com. Accessed 18 November 2012.

Ohanian, R. (1990). Construction and validation of a scale to measure celebrity endorsers. *Journal of Advertising*, *3*, 39–52.

— (1991). The impact of celebrity spokespersons' perceived image on consumers' intention to purchase. *Journal of Advertising Research*, *31*, 46–54.

Onkvisit, S., & Shaw, J. (1987). Self-concept and image congruence: Some research and managerial implications. *Journal of Consumer Marketing*, *4*(1), 13–23.

O'Regan, V. R. (2012, March). Celebrities and their political opinions: Who cares? Paper presented at the Annual Meeting of the Western Political Science Association, Portland, Oregon, 22–24 March.

Ostroof, R. B., & Boyd, J. H. (1987). Television and suicide. *New England Journal of Medicine*, *316*, 876–7.

Packard, V. (1957). *The hidden persuaders.* London, UK: Lowe & Brydone Ltd.

Park, A. (2008, 18 September). Celebrity worship: Good for your health? *Time Health.* Available at: http://www.time.com/time/health/article/0,8599,1841093,00. Accessed 17 August 2012.

Payne, J. G., Hanlon, J. P., & Tworney, D. P. (2007). Celebrity spectacle influence on young voters in the 2004 presidential campaign. *American Behavioral Scientist*, *50*, 1239–46.

Pease, A., & Brewer, P. R. (2008). The Oprah factor: The effects of a celebrity endorsement in a presidential primary campaign. *Harvard International Journal of Press/Politics*, *13*, 386–400.

Peck, J. (2008). *The age of Oprah: Cultural icon for the neoliberal era (media and power).* Boulder, CO: Paradigm.

Pedelty, M., & Keefe, L. (2010). Political pop, political fans? A content analysis opf music fan blogs. *Music and Politics*, *4*(1). Available at: http://www.music.ucsb.edu/ projects/musicandpolitics/archive/2010–1. Accessed on 31 October 2012.

Penfold, R. (2004). The star's image, victimization and celebrity culture. *Punishment and Society*, *6*, 289–302.

People's Daily Online (2007, 8 November). China to ban celebrities from advertising pharmaceutical drugs' effects. http://www.english.peopledaily.com. cn/90001/90776/90882/6299257/ Retrieved 25 October 2011.

Perloff, R. M. (1996). Perceptions and conceptions of political impact: The third person effect and beyond. In A. N. Crigler (Ed.), *The psychology of political communication* (pp. 177–91). Ann Arbor: University of Michigan Press.

Petroshius, S. M., & Crocker, K. E. (1989). An empirical analysis of spokesperson characteristics on advertisement and product evaluations. *Journal of the Academy of Marketing Science*, *17*, 217–26.

Petty, R. E., & Cacioppo, J. T. (1981). *Attitudes and persuasion: Classic and contemporary approaches.* Dubuque, IA: William C. Brown.

— (1983). Central and peripheral routes to persuasion: Application to advertising. In L. Percy & A. Woodside (Eds), *Advertising and consumer psychology* (pp. 3–23). Lexington, MA: Lexington.

— (1986a). *Communication and persuasion: Central and peripheral routes to attitude change.* New York: Springer-Verlag.

— (1986b). The elaboration likelihood model of persuasion. In L. Berkowitz (Ed.), *Advances in experimental social psychology* (pp. 123–205). New York: Academic Press.

Petty, R. E., Cacioppo, T., & Schuman, D. (1983). Central and peripheral routes to advertising effectiveness: The moderating role of involvement. *Journal of Consumer Research, 10*, 135–46.

Pew Research Centre (2007, 20 September). The Oprah factor and campaign 2008: Do political endorsements matter? Available at: http://www.people-press.org/report/357/the-oprah-factor-and-campaign-2008. Accessed 12 August 2012.

Phillips, D. P. (1974). The influence of suggestion on suicide. *American Sociological Review, 39*, 340–54.

Phillips, D. P., Carstensen, L. L., & Paight, D. (1989). Effects of mass media news stories on suicide with new evidence on story content. In C. Pfeiffer, (Ed.), *Suicide among youth: Perspectives on risk and prevention* (pp. 101–16). Washington, DVC: American Psychiatric Press.

Pirkis, J., & Blood, R. W. (2001a). Suicide and the media: Part I: Reportage in the non-fictional media. *Crisis, 22*, 146–54.

— (2001b). Suicide and the media: Part II: Portrayal in the non-fictional media. *Crisis, 22*, 155–62.

Platt, S. (1993). The social transmission of suicide: Is there a modelling effect? *Crisis, 14*, 23–31.

Pomerantz, D. (2012, 16 May). J. Lo's stunning career reincarnation puts her no.1 on the celebrity 100. Available at: http://www.forbes.com/celebrities. Accessed 8 November 2012.

Priester, J. R., & Petty, R. E. (2003). The influence of spokesperson trustworthiness on message elaboration, attitude strength and advertising effectiveness. *Journal of Consumer Psychology, 13*(4), 408–21.

Pringle, H. (2004). *Celebrity sells*. Chichester, UK: John Wiley & Sons.

Public Relations Society of America (2008, June). Public opinion divided about celebrity influence for causes they promote. www.prsa.com

Quigley, R. (2012, 22 October). Final humiliation for drugs cheat Lance Armstrong as he is stripped of his seven Tour de France titles and banned for life. *Mail Online*. Available at: www.dailymail.co.uk/news/article-22213346. Accessed 26 October 2013.

Rao, A. R., & Ruekert, R. W. (1994). Brand alliances as signals of product quality. *Sloan Management Review, 36*(1), 87–97.

Raphael, C. (2004). The political economic origins of reality-TV. In S. Murray & L. Ouellette (Eds), *Reality TV: Remaking Television Culture*. New York, NY: New York University Press.

Ravid, A. S. (1999). Information, blockbusters and stars: A study of the film industry. *Journal of Business, 72*, 463–92.

Raviv, A. S., Bar-Tel, D., Raviv, A., & Ben-Horin, A. (1996). Adolescent idolization of pop singers; Causes, expressions and reliance. *Journal of Youth and Adolescence, 25*, 631–50.

Raynor, G. (2012). Does celebrity involvement in public health campaigns deliver long term benefit? No. *British Medical Journal, 345*, e6364.

Redenbach, A. (1999). A multiple product endorser can be a credible source. *Cyber-Journal of Sport Marketing*. Available at: http://fultext.ausport.gov.au/fulltext/1999/cjsm/v3n1/redenbach31. Accessed 4 June 2014.

Rein, I. J., Kotler, P., & Stoller, M. (1997). *High visibility: The making and marketing of professionals into celebrities.* Chicago, IL: NTC Business Books.

Richardson, J., Owen-Smith, V., & Howe, A. (2002). The effect of 'Alm's' death on women attending for a cervical smear: A questionnaire survey. *Journal of Public Health and Medicine, 24*(4), 305–6.

Riegel, H. (1996). Soap operas and gossip. *Journal of Popular Culture, 29*(4), 201–9.

Rohrer, F. (2009). How celebrity chefs change the way we eat. BBC News. Available at: www.bbc.co.uk/1/hi/magazine/8009970. Accessed 8 January2013.

Rojek, C. (2001). *Celebrity.* London, UK: Routledge.

Roozen, I., & Claeys, C. (2010). The relative effectiveness of celebrity endorsement for print advertisement. *Review of Business and Economics, 55*(1), 76–89.

Rosen, S. (1981). The economics of superstars. *American Economic Review, 68*, 845–58.

Ross, R., Campbell, T., Wright, J. C., Huston, A. C., Rice, M. L., & Turk, P. (1984). When celebrities talk, children listen: An experimental analysis of children's responses to TV ads with celebrity endorsement. *Journal of Developmental Psychology, 5*, 185–202.

Rossiter, J. R., & Percy, L. (1987). *Advertising and promotion management.* London, UK: McGraw-Hill.

Rothschild, M. L. (1978). Political advertising: A neglected policy issue in marketing. *Journal of Marketing Research, 15*(1), 58.

Saleem, F. (2007). Effect of single celebrity and multiple celebrity endorsement on low involvement and high involvement product advertisements. *European Journal of Social Sciences, 5*(3), 125–32.

Sanbonmatsu, D. M., & Kardes, F. R. (1988). The effects of physiological arousal on information processing and persuasion. *Journal of Consumer Research, 15*(3), 379–85.

Sands, S. (2013, 27 March). Sarah Sands: Angelina Jolie and William Hague, the unlikely duo campaigning in a common cause. *London Evening Standard.* Available at: www.standard-co-ul/comment/comment/sarah-sands-angelina-jolie-william-hague-the-unlikely-due-campainging-in-a-common-cause-8551545. Accessed 6 August 2013.

Schickel, R. (1985). *Intimate strangers: The culture of celebrity.* Garden City, NY: Doubleday & Company, Inc.

Schindler, R. M., & Holbrook, M. B. (2003). Nostalgia for early experience as a determinant of consumer preferences. *Psychology and Marketing, 20*, 275–302.

Schlecht, C. (2003, 15 January). *Celebrities' Impact on Branding.* Centre on Global Brand Leadership, Columbia Business School, New York. Available at: www.worldlywriter.com/images/portfolio/Proposals/Celebrity_Branding. Accessed 23 October 2012.

Schmidtke, A., & Schaller, S. (2000). The role of mass media in suicide prevention. In K. Hawton & K. van Heeringen (Eds), *The International Handbook of Suicide and Attempted Suicide* (pp. 673–97). New York: Wiley.

Schroder, S., & Mai, L.-W. (2006). Sports celebrity endorsement in fashion marketing. Report produced by KHP Consulting, UK and the University of Westminster. Available at: www.kams.org/cyboard/cyfile.html. Accessed 18 February 2013.

Schuessler, A. A. (2000). Expressive voting. *Rationality and Society, 12*(1), 87–119.

Seno, D., & Lukas, B. A. (2007). The equity effect of product endorsement by celebrities: A conceptual framework from a co-branding perspective. *European Journal of Marketing, 41*(1/2), 121–34.

Sheridan, L., Maltby, J., & Gillett, R. (2006). Pathological public figure preoccupation: Its relationship with dissociation and absorption. *Personality and Individual Differences, 41*, 525–35.

Sheridan, L., North, A., Maltby, J., & Gillett, R. (2007). Celebrity worship, addiction and criminality. *Psychology, Crime & Law, 13*(6), 559–71.

Sherman, S. P. (1985). When you wish upon a star. *Fortune*, pp. 66–71.

Sheth, J. N., Mital, B., & Newman, B. I. (1999). *Customer behavior: Consumer behavior and beyond*. Oak Brook, Ill: US: Dryden Press.

Shimp, T. E. (1997). *Advertising, promotion and supplemental aspects of integrated marketing communication* (4th ed.). Fort Worth, TX: Dryden Press.

Siemens, J. C., Smith, S., Fisher, D., & Jensen, T. D. (2008). Product expertise versus professional expertise: Congruency between an endorser's chosen profession and the endorsed product. *Journal of Targeting, Measurement & Analysis for Marketing, 16*(3), 159–68.

Silvera, D. H., & Austad, B. (2003). Factors predicting the effectiveness of celebrity endorsement advertisements. *European Journal of Marketing, 38*(11–12), 1509–20.

— (2004). Factors predicting the effectiveness of celebrity endorsement advertisements. *European Journal of Marketing, 38*(11/12), 1509–26.

Simkin, S., Hawton, K., Whitehead, L., Fagg, J., & Eagle, M. (1995). Media influence on parasuicide: A study of the effects of the television drama portrayal of paracetamol self-poisoning. *British Journal of Psychiatry, 167*, 754–9.

Sireau, N., & Davis, A. (2007). Interest groups and mediated mobilisation: Communication in the Make Poverty History Campaign. In A. Davis (Ed.), *The mediation of power* (pp. 131–50). Abingdon, UK: Routledge.

Skeptikai (2012, 24 May). What do Japanese children want to be when they grow up? Available at: http://www.skeptikai.com/2012.05/24. Accessed 27 October 2012.

Smillie, D. (2004) Activism is entertainer's new role. *Christian Science Monitor*, 90, B1.

Smillie, I. (1998). Optical and other illusions, trends and issues in public thinking about development co-operation. In I. Smillie, H. Helmich, T. German, & J. Randel (Eds.) *Public attitudes and international development co-operation* (pp. 21–41). Paris: Organisation for Economic Co-operation and Development.

Solomon, M., Bamossy, G., & Askgaard, S. (2002). *Consumer behaviour: A European perspective*. Prentice Hall Financial Times (2nd. ed). Englewood Cliffs, NJ: Prentice Hall.

Speck, P. S., Schumann, D. W., & Thompson, C. (1988). Celebrity endorsements: Scripts, schema and roles: Theoretical framework and preliminary tests. *Advances in Consumer Research, 15*, 69–76.

Stacey, J. (1994). *Star gazing: Hollywood cinema and female spectatorship*. New York, NY: Routledge.

Stack, S. (2000). Media impacts on suicide: A quantitative review of 293 findings. *Social Science Quarterly, 81*, 957–71.

— (2003). Media coverage as a risk factor in suicide. *Journal of Epidemiology & Community Health, 57*, 238–40.

— (2005). Suicide in the media: A quantitative review of studies based on nonfictional stories. *Suicide and Life-Threatening Behavior, 35*(2), 121–33.

Stafford, M. R., Spears, N. E., & Chung-Kue, H. (2003). Celebrity images in magazine advertisements: An application of the visual rhetoric model. *Journal of Current Issues & Research in Advertising, 25*(30), 13–20.

Stanley, T. L. (2006, 22 September). Star system: Celebrities cement their influence on politics. Available at: www.adweek.com/news/advertising-branding/star-systems-celebrities. Accessed 10 October 1012.

Stanyer, J., & Wring, D. (2004). Public images, private lives: An introduction. *Parliamentary Affairs, 57*(1), 1–8.

Steele, M. F. (2009, 26 June). The psychology of celebrity worship. *US News and World Report*. Available at: http://www.health.isnews.com/health-news/faimly-health/brain-and-behavior/articles/2009. Accessed 27 August 2011.

Sternthal, B., Dholakia, R. R., & Leavitt, C. (1978). The persuasive effect of source credibility: Tests of cognitive response. *Journal of Consumer Research, 4*(3), 252–60.

Stevens, J. A., Lathrop, A. H., & Bradish, C. L. (2003). Who is your hero? Implications for athletic endorsement strategies. *Sport Marketing Quarterly, 12*, 103–10.

Stever, G. S. (1991). The celebrity appeal questionnaire. *Psychological Reports, 68*, 859–66.

Street, J. (2002). Bob, Bono, and Tony B: The popular artist as politician. *Media, Culture & Society, 23*, 433–41.

— (2004). Celebrity politicians: Popular culture and political representation. *British Journal of Politics and International Relations, 6*(4), 435–52.

— (2005). Politics lost, politics transformed, politics colonised? Theories of the impact of the mass media. *Political Studies Review, 3*(1), 17–33.

Stuart, J. (2007). Heroes in sport: Assessing celebrity endorsers' effectiveness. *International Journal of Sports Marketing & Sponsorship, 8*(2), 126–40.

Swami, Chamorro-Premuzic, T., Mastor, K., Hazwari, S., Fatin, S., Mohammed, M. M., Jaafar, J., Sinniah, D., & Pillai, S. K. (2011). Celebrity worship among university students in Malaysia: A methodological contribution to the Celebrity Attitude Scale. *European Psychologist, 16*(4), 334–42.

Tannen, D. (1991). *You just don't understand: Women and men in conversation*. London, UK: Virago.

Taylor Herring (2009, 6 October). Revealed – The top career choices then and now. Available at: http://www.taylorherring.com/blog/index.php/tag/traditional-careers. Accessed 27 October 2012.

Telegraph Media Group Limited (2009, 1 October). Children would rather become popstars than teachers or lawyers. Available at: http://www.telegraph.co.uk/education/educationnews/6250626. Accessed 27 October 2012.

Temperley, J., & Tangen, D. (2006). The Pinocchio factor in consumer attitudes towards celebrity endorsement: Celebrity endorsement, the Reebok brand and an example of a recent campaign. *Special Edition on Consumer Satisfaction – Global Perspective, Innovative Marketing, 2*(3), 97–108.

Temple, M. (2006). Dumbing down is good for you. *British Politics, 1*, 257–73.

't Hart, P., & Tindall, K. (2009). Leadership by the famous: Celebrity as political capital. In J. Kane, H. Patapas, & P. 't Hart (Eds), *Dispersed leadership in democracies*. Oxford, UK: Oxford University Press.

The Electronic Intifada (2005, 5 January). Free and fair Palestinian elections not possible under military occupation. Available at: www.electronicintifada.net/content/free-and-fair-palestinian-elections-not-possible-under-military-occupation.

The Front Runner (2004, 26 October). Poll indicates public has unfavourable view of celebrity endorsements. The Front Runner, Washington News. Available at: http://www.web.lexis-nexis.com. Accessed 4 October 2012.

The Marketing Arm (2012). Celebrity DBI. Available at: http://www.dbicelebrityindex.com. Accessed 2 November 2012.

The Smoking Gun (2003). Ben Affleck, Hollywood hypocrite. The Smoking Gun. Available at: http://www.thesmokinggun.com/archive/affleck_doc.html. Accessed 4 October 2012.

Thompson, J. R. (1978). Celebrities strike it big as endorsers. *Industrial Marketing*, January, p. 85.

Thompson, S. (1990). Thank the ladies for the plates: The incorporation of women in sport. *Leisure Studies, 9*, 135–42.

Thrall, T., Lollio-Fakreddine, J., Berent, J., Donnelly, L., Herrin, W., Paquette, Z., . . . Wyatt, A. (2008). Star power, celebrity advocacy and the evolution of the public sphere. *The International Journal of Press/Politics, 13*(4), 362–84.

Till, B. D. (1998). Using celebrity endorsers effectively: Lessons from associative learning. *Journal of Product & Brand Management, 7*(5), 400–9.

Till, B. D., & Busler, M. (1998). Matching products with endorsers: Attractiveness versus expertise. *Journal of Consumer Marketing, 15*(6), 576–86.

Till, B. D., & Shimp, T. A. (1998). Endorsers in advertising: The case of negative celebrity information. *Journal of Advertising, 27*(1), 67–75.

Till, B. D., Haas, S., & Priluck, R. (2006). Understanding celebrity endorsement: A classical conditioning approach. *American Marketing Association*, Conference Proceedings, Chicago, Vol. 17, p. 241.

Till, B. D., Stanley, S. M., & Priluck, R. (2008). Classical conditioning and celebrity endorsers: An examination of belongingness and resistance to extinction. *Psychology & Marketing, 25*(2), 179–96.

Time (2012, 27 September). Should celebrities endorse health causes? A gallery of winners and losers. Available at: http://www.healthland.time.com/2012/09/27/. Accessed 29 October 2012.

Toltz, M., & O'Donnell, J. (1994). I hate myself and I want to die. *Juice, 16,* 38–45.

Tom, G., Clark, R., Elmer, L., Grech, E., Masetti, Jr, J., & Sandhar, H. (1992). The use of created versus celebrity spokespersons in advertisements. *Journal of Consumer Marketing, 9*(4), 45–51.

Tozer, J., & Horne, M. (2011, 26 February). Cocktail parties in stretch limos, catwalk shows and fake tattoos – the disturbing sexualisation of little girls revealed. *Daily Mail*, pp. 40–1.

Treme, J. (2010). Effects of celebrity media exposure on box-office performance. *Journal of Media Economics, 23*(1), 5–16.

Tripp, C., Jensen, T. D., & Carlson, L. (1994). The effect of multiple product endorsement by celebrities on consumers' attitudes and intentions. *Journal of Consumer Research, 20*(4), 535–47.

Tucker, N. (2012, 26 September). Are celebrity endorsements a gift or a curse for public health campaigns? *Medical Daily*. Available at: http://www.medicaldaily.com/articles/12357/20120926/. Accessed on 29 October 2012.

Turner, G. (2004). *Understanding celebrity*. Thousand Oaks, CA: Sage.

— (2006). The mass production of celebrity. *International Journal of Cultural Studies, 9,* 153–65.

Twenge, J. (2007). *Generation me: Why today's young Americans are more confident, assertive, entitled – and more miserable than ever before*. New York, NY: Free Press.

Twenge, J., & Campbell, W. C. (2010). *The Narcissism epidemic*. New York, NY: Free Press.

Twine, C., Barthelmes, L., & Gateley, C. A. (2006). Kylie Minogue's breast cancer: Effects on referrals to a rapid access breast clinic in the UK. *Breast, 15,* 667–9.

Um, N. H. (2008). Exploring the effects of single vs multiple product and multiple celebrity endorsements. *Journal of Management & Social Sciences, 4*(2), 104–14.

Urwin, R. (2013, 15 January). Pippa's got a brand new bag. *Evening Standard*, p. 23.

Usry, K., & Cobb, M. D. (2010). Seeing stars: Are young voters influenced by celebrity endorsements of candidates? Paper presented at the 2010 Annual Meeting of the Midwest Political Science Association, Chicago, Illinois, 22–25 April.

Van der Waldt, D. L. R., Schleritzko, N. E. A., & Van Zyl, K. (2007). Paid versus unpaid celebrity endorsement in advertising: An exploration. *African Journal of Business Management, 197,* 185–91.

Van Zoonen, L. (2006). The person, the political and the popular: A woman's guide to celebrity politics. *European Journal of Cultural Studies, 9*(3), 287–301.

— (2007). Audience reactions to Hollywood politics. *Media, Culture & Society, 4,* 531–47.

Veer, E., Becirovic, I., & Martin, B. (2010). if Kate voted Conservative would you? The role of celebrity endorsements in political party advertising. *European Journal of Marketing, 44*(3/4), 436–50.

Verma, T., Adams, J., & White M. (2007). Portrayal of health-related behaviours in popular UK soap operas. *Journal of Epemiology and Community Health, 61*(7), 575–77.

Vincent, J., Hill, J. S., & Lee, J. W. (2009). The multiple brand personalities of David Beckham: a case study of the Beckham brand. *Sport Marketing Quarterly*, September, pp. 173–80.

Walker, M., Langmeyer, L. & Langmeyer, D. (1992). Celebrity endorsers: Do you get what you pay for? *Journal of Consumer Marketing, 9*(2), 69–76.

Wallace, T., Seigerman, A., & Holbrook, M. B. (1993). The role of actors and actresses in the success of films: How much is a movie star worth? *Journal of Cultural Economics, 17*(1), 1–27.

Wansink, B., & Ray, M. L. (1996). Advertising strategies to increase usage frequency. *Journal of Marketing, 60*(1), 31–46.

Warren, J. R., & Halpern-Manners, A. (2007). Is the glass emptying or filling up? Reconciling divergent trends in high school completion and dropout. *Educational Researcher, 36*(6), 335–43.

Washburn, J. H., Till, B. D., & Priluck, R. (2004). Brand alliance and customer-based-equity effects. *Psychology and Marketing, 21*(7), 487–508.

Weiskel, T. (2005). From sidekick to sideshow: Celebrity, entertainment and the politics of distraction. Why Americans are 'sleep walking towards the end of the earth'. *American Behavioural Scientist, 49*(3), 393–403.

Wells, W., Burnett, J., & Moriarty, S. (1989). *Advertising principles and practice.* Englewood Cliffs, NJ: Prentice-Hall.

West, D. (2003, 3 October). Arnold Schwarzenegger and celebrity politics. *InsidePolitics. org.* http://insidepolitics.org/heard/westreport903.html

West, D., & Orman, J. (2003). *Celebrity politics.* Englewood Cliffs, NJ: Prentice-Hall.

West, D. M. (2008). Angelina, Mia, and Bono: Celebrities and international development. In L. Brainard & D. Chollet (Eds), *Global Development 2.0: Can philanthropists, the Public and the Poor Make Poverty History?* (pp. 75–84). Washington, DC: Washington Brookings.

White, E. (2004). Found in translation. *Wall Street Journal*, 20th September, 244(56), B1–B6.

Wildschut, T., Sedeikes, C., Arndt, J., & Routledge, C. (2006). Nostalgia and consumption preferences: Some emerging patterns of consumer tastes. *Journal of Consumer Research, 20*(2), 975–93.

Williamson, J. M. L., Jones, I. H., & Hocken, D. B. (2010). How does the media impact of cancer compare with prevalence? *Annals of the Royal College of Surgeons of England, 93*, 9–12.

Willigan, G. E. (1992). High-performance marketing: An interview with Nikes' Phil Knight. *Harvard Business Review*, July–August, pp. 91–101.

Wonderlich, A. L., Ackard, D. M., & Henderson, J. B. (2005). Childhood beauty pageant contestants: Associations with adult disordered eating and mental health. *Eating Disorders*, *13*(3), 291–301.

Wood, J. V., & Taylor, K. L. (1991). Serving self-relevant goals through social comparison. In J. Suis & T. A. Wills (Eds), *Social comparison: Contemporary theory and research* (pp. 23–50). Hillsdale, NJ: Lawrence Erlbaum Associates.

Wood, N. T., & Herbst, K. C. (2007). Political star power and political parties: Does celebrity endorsement win first-time voters? *Journal of Political Marketing*, *6*(2/3), 141–58.

Ybarra, O., & Stephan, W. G. (1996). Misanthropic person memory. *Journal of Personality and Social Psychology*, *45*, 961–77.

Yip, P. S. F., Fu, K. W., Yang, K. C. T. et al. (2006). The effects of a celebrity suicide on suicide rates in Hong Kong. *Journal of Affective Disorders*, *93*(1–3) 245–52.

Young, S. M., & Pinsky, D. (2006). Narcissism and celebrity. *Journal of Research in Personality*, *46*, 463–71.

Yue, X., & Cheung, C. (2000). Selection of favourite idols and models among Chinese young people: A comparative study in Hong Kong and Nanjing. *International Journal of Behavioural Development*, *24*, 91–8.

Zahaf, M., & Anderson, J. (2008). Causality effects between celebrity endorsement and the intentions to buy. *Innovative Marketing*, *4*(4), 57–65.

Zhou, N., & Belk, R. W. (2004). Chinese consumer readings of global and local advertising appeals. *Journal of Advertising*, *33*, 63–76.

Zona, M. A., Sharma, K. K., & Lane, J. (1993). A comparative study of erotomanic and obsessional subjects in a forensic sample. *Journal of Forensic Sciences*, *38*, 894–903.

Zukier, H. (1982). The dilution effect: The role of the correlation and the dispersion of predictor variables in the use of nondiagnostic information. *Journal of Personality and Social Psychology*, *43*, 1163–74.

Index